LOSING
the PEACE

LOSING
the PEACE

FAILED SETTLEMENTS AND
THE ROAD TO WAR

Matthew Hughes & Matthew S. Seligmann

First published in 2002
This edition published in 2009
Reprinted 2020

The History Press
97 St George's Place, Cheltenham,
Gloucestershire, GL50 3QB
www.thehistorypress.co.uk

British Library Cataloguing in Publication Data.
A catalogue record for this book is available from the British Library.

ISBN 978 0 7524 5238 8

Typesetting and origination by The History Press
Printed in Great Britain by TJ International Ltd, Padstow, Cornwall.

Contents

Acknowledgements

For help in the production of this book, the authors would like to express their gratitude to: the British Academy Elie Kedourie Award fund; the European Studies Research Institute, University of Salford; the Moshe Dayan Center, Tel Aviv University; the American University in Cairo; the US Marine Corps University Foundation and the gift of Mr and Mrs Thomas A. Saunders; and the Widener Library, Harvard University. For permission to examine and reproduce papers and documents in their possession, we are indebted to: the trustees of the British Library Board; the fellows and scholars of Churchill College, Cambridge; the Houghton Library, Harvard University; the clerk of the House of Lords Record Office; the trustees of the Imperial War Museum; and the trustees of the Liddell Hart Centre for Military Archives, King's College London. Crown copyright material in the National Archives (formerly the Public Record Office) is reproduced by permission of the Controller of Her Majesty's Stationery Office. Having made these acknowledgements, the authors would like to state that they alone are responsible for the opinions expressed in this book. They also take responsibility for any errors of fact that should be found in this work.

Introduction
Does Peace Lead to War?

'War and Peace are ideas that in their foundations can have no gradations'

Carl von Clausewitz[1]

'The first object of a treaty of peace,' so wrote Lord Salisbury in 1870, 'should be to make future war improbable.'[2] Yet, all too often such treaties, to cite the words of the English philosopher Henry Sidgwick in 1891, have only resulted in a 'temporary suspension of hostilities, terminable at any time by the wronged state'.[3] Why should this be? After all, a recipe for preserving peace has existed since biblical times. Conflicts will end, so wrote the Hebrew poet, when 'mercy and truth are met together; righteousness and peace have kissed each other.'[4] Yet, the clarity and commonsense of this vision notwithstanding, it has consistently proved difficult to realize this ideal. To paraphrase St Augustine, men have asked God to grant them peace, but as with chastity, not quite yet.

As Sir Michael Howard has observed, the result of this unwillingness to engage with peace is that, sadly, too much of our history has consisted of long periods of conflict, only occasionally tempered with shorter moments of peace. As one study has shown, there have only been 268 years free of war in the last 3,421 years.[5] Such universal bellicosity led theorists to the belief that war rather than peace was the norm. So much so that, in Thomas Hobbes' world view, peace was not a state in its own right, but merely the absence of war. Count Leo Tolstoy propounded a similarly fatalistic view in the concluding chapters of his epic novel *War and Peace* (1868–9). For Tolstoy, war was an act of God over which man has little or no control.⁶ It is only recently that this nihilistic perception has changed. It is in the modern era, according to Howard, that peace first became highly valued, and strenuous efforts were then made to create and promote this 'invented' concept of a naturally pacific state system and impose it on a recalcitrant world. This strategy has, however, met with little success.⁷ The paradox of the twentieth century illustrates the dialectic of war and peace, for it has witnessed the most brutal wars of all times, alongside the most concerted efforts to institutionalize peace through international organizations, conventions limiting or, even, outlawing war, arbitration agreements, war crimes trials and, finally, detailed and comprehensive peace treaties. Standing testament to this hope for peace are, *inter alia*, the Hague Conferences of 1899 and 1907; the creation of the League of Nations in 1919; the signing of the Kellogg-Briand pact of 1928; the Nuremberg, Tokyo and, more recently, Hague and Arusha (Tanzania) war crimes trials; the United Nations Organization; the International Criminal Court established in 2002 and based in The Hague; and the Geneva Protocol and Convention. But, standing testament to the failure of the efforts to promote peace are the two World Wars, the Cold War, and the numerous post-1945 conflicts that have scarred and seriously retarded the development of the 'Third World'.

Why, if peace is so universally desired in the modern era, has it been so difficult to attain? Many scholars have attempted to furnish an answer to this question. Eminent historians such as Sir Michael Howard, A.J.P Taylor, Jeremy Black and Erik Goldstein have all looked for the underlying causes and have suggested that there are, indeed, generic factors leading to war.⁸ In addition to these holistic analyses, there are also works that explore the genesis of particular wars. The First World War is a case in point of a conflict that has attracted such scrutiny. A long list of monographs and more general studies could be cited, but illustrative of the intense interest in why war broke out in 1914 is the Macmillan series looking at each of the major protagonists and their part in the outbreak of this conflict.⁹

There has been a similar level of interest in the foundations of the Second World War and the Cold War. In addition to those series that focus exclusively on one war, there are also collections such as the Longman 'Origins of Modern Wars' series that provide, in a common format, an explanatory framework for the outbreak of a number of wars over the span of the contemporary period. Between them, these diverse studies by a range of authors go a long way to helping us understand how and why modern wars happen.

For all their merits, none of the above works takes as a specific theme the idea of how peace settlements lead to war. And yet, as the opening quotations by Salisbury and Sidgwick illustrate, it has been assumed for many years that there is, indeed, a direct relationship between the peace that ends one war and the outbreak of the next conflagration. If one accepts the premise that the peace settlement reached after a war is invariably decisive in determining whether peace breaks out or another war erupts, then the fact that this has not been examined as a central theme is a significant gap in the historiography on the origins of wars. Existing studies too often either look at the general question of why wars happen or why particular wars have started without exploring the specific linkage provided by the common theme of peace settlements and their significance in leading to war.

With this in mind, this book will complement the extensive and formidable set of existing studies on the origins of war by taking as its starting point the idea that peace settlements are a neglected thematic strand linking up modern wars. Peace settlements, it will be maintained, not only end wars, they also cause them; indeed, the way in which a war ends will determine if there will be another conflict.

Examples of the importance of peace settlements abound throughout history. Certain settlements achieved the goal of a lasting peace. For instance, in 146 BC, at the end of the Punic Wars, Rome imposed such a harsh peace settlement on its enemy, Carthage, that the latter disappeared as an empire and never re-emerged as a power to threaten the Roman Empire. There were no more Punic Wars. In 1815, as Henry Kissinger outlined in *A World Restored*, following the French Revolutionary and Napoleonic Wars, the Congress of Vienna imposed on France a conciliatory settlement that restored the balance of power in Europe.[10] As a consequence, there was to be no recurrence of general war in Europe for a hundred years. By contrast, there are numerous examples of peace settlements that have not only failed to restore stability and order, but, by the nature of their terms, have actually made a resumption of hostilities highly likely, if not inevitable. The peace treaties at Dresden and Aix-la-Chapelle that ended the War of the Austrian Succession, for instance, led inexorably into the Seven Years' War in 1756. This in turn was ended by a peace – the Treaty of Paris in 1763 – that left a resentful France eager for revenge and willing to support the American settlers in their fight against Britain after 1776. Thus, despite a series of peace settlements, the European powers engaged in a near continuous bout of fighting from 1740 to 1783.

If, as these examples show, peace settlements are a core determinant engendering war, then the reason for studying their impact becomes evident. The eight chapters in this work do just that. Taking modern industrialized warfare as the basis of its timeframe, this book examines the years from 1870 to 1975. This period covers some of the bloodiest and most intractable conflicts in history, starting with the Franco-Prussian War, including two 'total wars', and culminating with the Cold War fought out in the jungles of Vietnam. All of these wars, as will be shown, emerged out of the ruins of previous peace settlements. As the question of what constitutes a peace settlement is not always straightforward, the definition that will be used in this work will encompass formal conventions and treaties, but also, where applicable, the informal *de facto* settlements that, even if not officially codified, represented the effective termination of hostilities.

The structure of the book emerges out of the aforementioned periodization and definition of what constitutes a peace settlement. To provide added cohesion, and allow for ready comparison, the essays in this book are grouped geographically into regional sub-sections. The first of these concentrates on Europe and examines the origins of the First and Second World Wars, along with the

Cold War. The three chapters in this section unpack how the Treaty of Frankfurt in 1871 helped lead to war in 1914; how the Treaty of Versailles in 1919 resulted in war in 1939; and how the Treaty of Brest-Litovsk in 1918 and the settlements at Yalta and Potsdam in 1945 caused the Cold War in the late 1940s. The second part to the book focuses on the Near East. Firstly, there is an examination of the negotiations surrounding the Treaty of Sèvres with Turkey in 1920 and the role of this peace in causing the Graeco-Turkish War. This is followed by an essay that examines the failed peace talks following the first Arab-Israeli War of 1948–9 and the vexed question of how this contributed to later conflicts in the Levant region. The final section moves the focus to East Asia with three interrelated chapters looking at the period from 1945 to 1975. The first essay explores the Yalta Far Eastern Accords of February 1945 and the way in which these agreements shaped the fighting between the communist and nationalist forces, propelling them into the Third Revolutionary Civil War. Thereafter, the settlement for Korea, also decided in 1945, that divided the peninsula comes under scrutiny and it is shown how the mismanagement of the partition settlement led to the Korean War in 1950. Finally, as will be shown, it was the failure of the Geneva settlement that ended the First Indochina War in 1954 that led ineluctably to the Second Indochina War that lasted until 1975.

The wars that were fought as a result of the peace settlements discussed in this volume played a major part in shaping the landscape of the modern world. This illustrates the significance of the central theme of this volume: that peace, if not properly managed, leads to war. One major lesson can be learnt from this. Diplomats, politicians and generals cannot afford to assume that the settlements that they negotiate will automatically endure. Rather, as will be shown, the forging of a settlement is but the first step of a much longer journey towards peace. It can prevent the outbreak of future wars, but will not do so without careful diplomacy and a fortunate conjunction of circumstances. In other situations it becomes the first step on the road to another war, which in turn leads to a vicious cycle of violence and counter-violence.

skills make this happen; it is a bottom-up movement and one that will make a viable peace. In some measure the wars that exhausted Yugoslavia in the 1990s had the same end point. The same cannot be said for the Middle East.

Introduction to updated edition

The conclusion from the first (2002) edition of this book, namely that poorly managed peace settlements can spark further wars and cycles of violence, not only remains valid but is further starkly illustrated by the recent turmoil in Iraq and the on-going civil war in Syria. The admittedly tendentious claim made by Islamic State as it overran swathes of Iraq and Syria that it was deliberately overturning the peace settlement of the First World War that carved up the Middle East between Britain and France, is a case in point. By sweeping away what it viewed as the 'artificially created' states of Syria and Iraq established after 1918 by the Western Powers, Islamic State sought to recreate a largely mythic pan-Arab and pan-Islamic unity. This was an explicit rejection of the settlement that Britain's Mark Sykes and France's François Georges-Picot had prefigured when in late 1916 they drew lines on the map of the Middle East considering possible conquest of the region and so created Syria, Iraq, Lebanon, Jordan and Palestine from the ashes of the Ottoman Empire. Islamic State's 'blessed advance' would not stop until it had 'hit the last nail in the coffin of the Sykes-Picot conspiracy.'[11]

The Great War borders have been contested ever since and Islamic State is only the latest in a long line of players seeking to undo, refashion and redraw what European powers had made real after the peace of 1918: Arab nationalists, Kemalist Turkey, the Kurds, the Armenians, Ibn Saud, Zionist pioneers and Israel after 1948, Gamal Abdul Nasser's union of Egypt and Syria, the Muslim Brotherhood, Baathists, Saddam Hussein, and Iran's theocracy. None has yet smashed the borders of the Middle East decided after the Great War, but this has not stopped them trying, decade after decade for over one hundred years. Both the borders and the settlement endure, but peace does not. Successful peace settlements are in considerable measure the function of thoughtful statecraft by clever diplomats. But the long-lasting ramifications of the various peace deals that forged the modern Middle East make us think about popular acceptance of any arrangements made and how subsequent history may well ruin a workable settlement.

PART ONE

Europe

ONE

The Treaty of Frankfurt and the Origins of the Franco-German Antagonism, 1870–1914

'I hear talk of the ideas of revenge you French are supposed to be entertaining. . . . You would not be good patriots . . . if you did not cling to the thought that the day would come when you would regain possession of your lost provinces; but between this very natural sentiment and the idea of launching some sort of a provocation with a view to realizing it, . . . there is a great distance. . . .'

Tsar Alexander III, December 1893[1]

In July 1870, in what can only be described, in retrospect, as an act of suicidal folly, France declared war on the kingdom of Prussia. Amazingly, most people at the time expected the conflict to end in a resounding French victory. For reasons that are mysterious to the modern observer, the decadent and decaying empire of Napoleon III – who was more famous for his 'campaigns in the boudoir'[2] than for those on the battlefield – was credited with being the leading military power in Europe, while Prussia, whose armies were led by that genius of military organization, Helmuth von Moltke the elder, was not held in the same high esteem.[3]

Yet, if Prussia began the conflict as the underdog, this image would not last beyond the opening engagements. As soon as battle was joined, Napoleon III's Second Empire suffered a series of ignominious defeats, culminating on 2 September with the capitulation of the Emperor himself at Sedan. In the face of such an overwhelming humiliation, the regime quickly collapsed. However, contrary to popular hopes, the fall of the Second Empire was not the prelude to immediate peace, but to even more bitter fighting. For, although the Government of National Defence of the new Third

3

Republic was anxious to settle the conflict, it soon became apparent that the Prussian Minister-President, Otto von Bismarck, soon also to be Chancellor of the newly proclaimed German Empire, intended to exact a high price for coming to terms. In addition to a large war indemnity, he proposed a rectification of the Franco-German frontier, involving the annexation by Germany of the entire province of Alsace and parts of the province of Lorraine.

In a move that is indicative of how the peace settlement would later be regarded, the French delegates initially refused to negotiate on the basis of such punitive terms. Instead, the republic's new government attempted to continue the war. 'There can be no answer to such insolent demands', so ran the official communiqué, 'but *guerre à outrance.*'[4] Echoing such sentiments, *La guerre illustrée*, a popular Parisian periodical, called on the public to rise up against the 'barbaric and devastating enemies [that] have invaded our land'.[5] This was a futile endeavour by this stage. With her offensive power already smashed, France had, in the end, little choice other than to comply. By the Treaty of Frankfurt of 10 May 1871, Alsace-Lorraine was ceded to the German Empire, into which it was incorporated as a *Reichsland*.

INITIAL REACTIONS TO THE SETTLEMENT: AN UNJUST PEACE AND CAUSE OF FUTURE WAR?

While the annexation of Alsace-Lorraine was greeted with near universal euphoria in Germany, there were some serious misgivings raised among international observers about this territorial transaction. So strongly felt were these doubts that their holders began to express their concerns from the very moment that the first information about Bismarck's terms became known, that is well before the actual treaty was even negotiated, signed or ratified. Among the earliest critics of the proffered peace settlement were two British statesmen – William Ewart Gladstone, then Prime Minister and leader of the Liberal Party, and Lord Salisbury, a future Conservative Foreign Secretary and Prime Minister.

Gladstone's objections to the terms were both moral and practical; he believed that what Bismarck sought to do would both commit a wrong to the people of Alsace-Lorraine and, even more importantly, would endanger the future peace of Europe. As he explained the matter in a memorandum that he later put to his Cabinet colleagues:

> The thing that is demanded is that a country with its inhabitants shall be transferred from France to Germany. More than a million and a quarter of men who, with their ancestors for several generations, have known France for their country, are henceforth to be severed from France, and to take Germany for their country in its stead.
>
> The Transfer of the allegiance of citizenship . . . from one sovereignty to another, without any reference to their own consent, has been a great reproach to some former transactions in Europe; has led to many wars and disturbances; is hard to reconcile with considerations of equality; and is repulsive to the sense of modern civilization.[6]

This argument, whatever its ethical merits, did not appeal to a British Cabinet that saw in the execution of a policy based upon such principles the makings of an unwelcome confrontation with the Prussian government. Accordingly, they declined to endorse it. Undeterred, Gladstone decided to put his views directly before the public. Writing anonymously in the *Edinburgh Review*, he elaborated upon those exact same themes that had been at the heart of his memorandum to the Cabinet. 'Wrenching a million and a quarter people from the country to which they have belonged for years', he wrote, '. . . will lead us from bad to worse, and be the beginning of a new series of European complications.'[7]

In expressing this sentiment, Gladstone found himself in the unusual position of being in complete agreement with the Conservative politician Lord Salisbury. Writing in the October edition of the *Quarterly Review*, Salisbury also propounded the view that the transfer of Alsace-Lorraine would bring additional tensions to Europe. As he pictured the new diplomatic environment,

We have been wont to talk of the burden of an armed peace; but the peace with which we are threatened will resemble the quiet of an ambuscade. Europe will look on while France is watching Prussia with affected amity but with unsleeping hatred, waiting till her enemy makes some false step or falls into trouble from war, or revolution, or misgovernment; sacrificing all other objects of policy to the one hope of retaliating in some moment of weakness upon the conqueror who has despoiled her. Is there no neutral that will make one effort to rescue Europe from such a future of chronic war?[8]

Such was the judgement of two of Britain's most perceptive politicians; a peace settlement of this kind contained the seeds not of tranquillity but of renewed conflict.

THE VIEW FROM THE 1920s: ALSACE-LORRAINE AND COMING OF WAR

In articulating the notion that, by taking an unwilling Alsace-Lorraine away from France, the Treaty of Frankfurt was a dangerous peace settlement that would engender future wars, Gladstone and Salisbury were – unbeknown to them – taking the first steps on to what would later become a well-trodden analytical path. After 1918, countless other individuals would make the very same assertion. The reason for their doing so was, of course, the outbreak of the First World War. Here, or so it seemed to these observers, was the brutal bloodbath that demonstrated the malicious effects of the peace settlement of 1871 and proved that, just as Gladstone and Salisbury had so presciently claimed, the Treaty of Frankfurt was, indeed, a source of war. Yet, were these events really linked?

Many commentators from the 1920s were convinced that they were. In Germany, for example, the semi-official publicist Max Montgelas made prodigious efforts to advance this perspective. Writing in his book *The Case for the Central Powers*, he asserted as the very first of his seventeen conclusions about the causes of war in 1914 that 'France aimed at recovering Alsace Lorraine . . . knowing well that . . . [this] could not be achieved without a European war'.[9] In a similar vein, the America revisionist historian Harry Elmer Barnes included in his book, *The Genesis of the World War*, an entire section entitled 'The War of 1870 and the World War'.[10] In it, he maintained that

> The Franco-Prussian War has a direct bearing upon the causes of the World War chiefly because at its close Bismarck . . . annexed a part of . . . Alsace-Lorraine to Germany. . . . [This] proved the most disastrous act in the history of contemporary European diplomacy. From 1871 onwards there was a strong group in France which was determined never to rest until a victorious war over Germany should have restored the 'Lost Provinces'.[11]

Fellow American historian Sidney Bradshaw Fay drew a similar conclusion. 'France,' he wrote,

> including the annexed districts of Alsace and Lorraine, had become one body, powerfully conscious of its unity and nationality; if one of its members suffered, all suffered together. Bismarck had mutilated a living body and the wound would not heal; it was to remain an awful open sore, threatening the peace of Europe for fifty years. . . . [This] was to be one of the main underlying causes of the World War. . . .[12]

As we can see, during the 1920s there was no shortage of commentators who sought to establish that there was a direct link between the peace of 1871 and the war of 1914 to 1918. Moreover, the proponents of this view, just like Gladstone and Salisbury before them, unanimously focused upon the issue of Alsace-Lorraine. France, it was maintained, was never able to reconcile herself to the loss of these provinces. Despite the passage of time and the best endeavours of the German government and people to foster amicable mutual relations between the two countries, French irredentist ambitions never wavered. Instead, France consistently pursued a policy, the ultimate aim of which was a *guerre de revanche* (war of revenge) against Germany to restore her lost honour and reclaim her lost territory. The First World War, so the argument goes, was the bitter fruit of these unwavering French sentiments.

EVIDENCE OF REVANCHISM

Is there any evidence for this perspective? That the so-called *'provinces perdues'* ('lost provinces') of Alsace-Lorraine became a potent symbol of French patriotism is undeniable. For four and a half decades the statue of Strasbourg in the Place de la Concorde in Paris was always shrouded in mourning. Wreaths were laid there daily to symbolize France's sorrow and to keep the memory alive that the nation had been robbed of its rightful frontier on the Rhine by Germany's territorial amputation of France's eastern lands. With constant reminders such as this, it is true that France did not quickly forget the humiliation of 1871.

It is also true that for French citizens of all descriptions, including some important figures in the nation's public life, dissatisfaction with the new border along the Vosges mountains was a major motivating force. Raymond Poincaré, a leading politician who was to become both Premier and Foreign Minister in 1912 and then President in 1913, was one such individual. As he explained to an audience of university students in 1920, the question of Alsace-Lorraine had heavily influenced his life's work. 'In my years at school', he informed them,

> my thought, bowed before the spectre of defeat, dwelt ceaselessly upon the frontier which the Treaty of Frankfurt had imposed upon us, and when I descended from my metaphysical clouds I could discover no reason why my generation should go on living except for the hope of recovering the lost provinces. Could life present any more satisfactory spectacle than to witness the reunion in Strasbourg of the youth of Alsace and the rest of France?[13]

Poincaré was not alone in these views. Théophile Delcassé, French Foreign Minister from 1898 to 1905, was so devoted to the lost provinces, so his daughter later recalled, that when she was growing up 'the word "Alsace-Lorraine" was never mentioned either by my brother or myself; we had the confused feeling that it was too sensitive a subject to be spoken of'.[14] In a similar manner, Marshal Ferdinand Foch, who was to play such a major role in the Allied victory over Germany in 1918, also felt strongly on this issue. As he explained to the *New York Times*, 'From the age of 17, I dreamed of revenge, after having seen Germans at Metz.'[15] As we can see, many of the leading figures of the Third Republic did, indeed, harbour strong irredentist sentiments.

Importantly, these feelings were not confined to the elite alone. On the contrary, they were shared in full by some highly vocal elements of the French population, including France's many patriotic pressure groups. Prominent among these was the *Ligue des Patriotes*. Founded in 1882 by the poet-soldier Paul Déroulède, the organization's sole *raison d'être* was to keep alive the issue of Alsace-Lorraine. As one member explained their activities:

> [Since our establishment] we have continually appealed to those who were tempted to forget; don't you hear yonder your brothers of Alsace-Lorraine who are weeping! And, like the surgeon who would cauterize a wound in order to heal it, we have turned and turned the hot iron in the wound from which France is bleeding, renewed the pain, but reminding the sufferer of the debts she owes and the duties which she must fulfil.[16]

And remind the sufferers they did. As the members of the *Ligue des Patriotes* would demonstrate by their activities during the Boulanger crisis, they were more than capable of undertaking a noisy and effective nationalist agitation. Indeed, so successful were they in promoting the idea that Minister of War Georges Boulanger was '*Général Revanche*' – the man who would restore France's military strength and lead the nation to a glorious victory – that they even managed to alarm Bismarck. He paid them the ultimate unintended compliment of seeing in their activities 'the stirring of flames by an active minority' and took precautions against them.[17] In this way, the *Ligue* and its associates helped create one of the most serious crises of the Third Republic. They also demonstrated that after nearly two decades the spirit of *revanche* in France had by no means been quelled.

Finally, it should also be mentioned that just as the French public could be motivated by the question of Alsace-Lorraine, there was also a strong revanchist streak in the army. In part this was due to the strongly nationalist message that permeated all aspects of army life, and which was designed to keep the Franco-German antagonism firmly in the thoughts of the French armed forces. Thus, for example, it was the case that French military cadets learned their trade from textbooks – the *Exercices et problèms* – that deliberately focused the minds of their readers on the challenges incumbent in a future war with Germany.[18] Once commissioned, French officers continued to be exposed to such sentiments, for army periodicals, including the prominent *La France Militaire*, were filled with such revanchist observations as '"Alsace", "Lorraine", these two words cry out what the policy of France ought to be'.[19] That such indoctrination was not entirely without effect might be judged by an account of a farewell dinner held on the retirement of Colonel Goepp, a French officer of the 26th Infantry Regiment. Speaking to the assembled guests, he declared that his main regret as he approached the end of his military career was that his retirement should occur even though 'the war of revenge which we are expecting every day has not taken place'. General Bailloud, who was responsible for the valedictory oration, responded sympathetically to this point. 'This war will take place,' he told his audience, 'Let us hope that the 26th . . . will contribute to return to us the lost provinces.'[20]

Taken together, evidence such as that detailed above has been advanced to show the magnitude of French resentment over the loss of Alsace-Lorraine. Germany's seizure of these districts, it has been said, left the country traumatized, with French citizens considering their nation to have been cruelly dismembered. Accordingly, the cry of '*la patrie mutilée*' became a rallying call for those who advocated *revanche* against Germany. The fact that the list of those irreconcilable to the separation of the 'lost provinces' included leading members of the government, opinion formers, propagandists and army officers, and that many of these people were in positions of power in 1914, has been deemed especially significant. These were the people who, when the moment came – as it did in 1914 – were entrusted with deciding whether to fight or not. It is hardly surprising, so the argument goes, that, given their attitudes, they chose war.

ALTERNATIVE PERSPECTIVE: THE LIMITS OF REVANCHE

Is this a judgement that has withstood the test of time? In 1999, the Canadian author Edward E. McCullough, in a sterile attempt to prove the Entente powers culpable for the outbreak of the First World War, revived the old charge that in 1914 France had '. . . aimed at objectives which could only be accomplished by war'. She fought, he declared, to 'reconquer Alsace-Lorraine . . .'.[21] Had McCullough been writing in the 1920s he would have been in good company when making this claim. Then, as we have already seen, historians such as Montgelas, Barnes and Fay were very active in promoting the view that the desire for *revanche* that emerged in France as a result of the Treaty of Frankfurt had been a major reason for the war that began forty-three years later. However, in 1999, McCullough's was something of a lone voice. By then almost all serious analyses of the Third Republic rejected the idea that plans for *revanche* played a significant part in the formulation of French policy. France, it was now maintained, was an inherently peaceful nation in 1914, an assessment that was based upon two major changes of emphasis in the historical literature.

The first of these concerns the connection that used to be made between the French aspiration to reclaim Alsace-Lorraine and the nation's decision for war in 1914. According to the likes of Montgelas, France wanted to regain Alsace-Lorraine, knew that this could only be brought about by war, and so deliberately provoked hostilities for this purpose. Now, even presupposing that strong irredentist sentiments existed in France – and, as we shall see below, the magnitude of these emotions is strongly challenged by many historians – that does not, in itself, mean that the French government was looking to start a war over this issue. After all, it is possible to desire something without wishing to resort to warfare in order to achieve it. And it is just such an absence of desire to go to war with Germany that most scholars working on this question today see as the hallmark of French foreign policy in the run up to 1914.

Their reason for this view is that the goals of France's leaders – and, most especially, of Raymond Poincaré – have undergone a significant re-evaluation. In the 1920s, Harry Elmer Barnes described Poincaré as the 'leader of the revenge and military group in France' and the man who worked consistently 'to advance . . . a European war which would accomplish the . . . result of returning Alsace-Lorraine to France . . .'.[22] By contrast, current assessments by those historians who, unlike Barnes, have had the opportunity to study his diaries and papers are altogether more favourable. M.B. Hayne is indicative of the new perspective. 'Poincaré', he states, 'was no *revanchiste*. . . . The idea of employing bellicosity for domestic or even foreign purposes was consonant with neither his legalism nor his idealism.'[23] In a similar fashion, John Keiger, Poincaré's most recent biographer, has judged that, far from being anti-German, 'the desire to have a working relationship with Germany would characterize [Poincaré's] foreign policy . . .'.[24] He cites the opinion of leading French diplomat, Jules Cambon, that Poincaré had, in fact, 'flung the motors of an anti-German policy into reverse'.[25]

On the basis of evidence such as this, the current perception among scholars differs markedly from that of the 1920s. As the American historian Stephen Rock observes, in a paragraph that provides a solid summary of today's opinion on the matter, 'Germany, in the final analysis, had little to fear from France, her traditional adversary. Despite enduring bitterness over Alsace and Lorraine, the French evinced little interest in the notion of *revanche*, owing mainly to their inferior military capabilities.'[26] Significantly, this view is more than borne out by the opinions expressed by contemporary commentators. One acute observer, who visited France, Germany and Alsace-Lorraine in the summer of 1913, was David Starr Jordan, the prolific author, renowned natural historian and President of Stanford University. As he saw the matter, 'France has lost faith in revenge by force of arms. Serious men doubted first the possibility, then the wisdom and at last the righteousness of the "War of Revenge".'[27] Fellow American, Colonel Edward House, who was sent to Europe in early 1914 by President Woodrow Wilson to promote the new administration's agenda for international peace, concurred in this judgement. He noted that 'French statesmen had given up all idea of revenge and the recovery of Alsace-Lorraine . . . they would be content with the position of France as it is now. . . .'[28] In a similar vein, no less a person than Germany's Kaiser Wilhelm II endorsed this view. As he told the British Military Attaché, Lieutenant-Colonel the Hon. Alexander Russell, 'France will not try to regain Alsace-Lorraine; if they did attempt such a thing, they would get a worse beating than they ever dreamed of.'[29] In saying this, Wilhelm was echoing a view shared by many important German diplomats. Graf Münster, for example, the German Ambassador in Paris, reported in 1900 that 'the hope of being able to reconquer Alsace-Lorraine is diminishing year by year and only a few think seriously of a war to this end'.[30] His successor, Wilhelm von Schoen, felt likewise. 'The wound of 1871', he reported in February 1914, 'burns in every French heart; but nobody is inclined to risk his bones or those of his sons for Alsace-Lorraine. . . .'[31] In short, from all quarters, it was readily acknowledged that France would not start a war over Alsace-Lorraine.

The second change of emphasis in the historical literature concerns the extent to which historians believe that feelings of *revanche* motivated the French government and people. As we have already seen, Montgelas, Barnes and Fay thought that it played a significant part in determining French policy. However, more recent research has demonstrated that, while the memory of Alsace-Lorraine continued to be a highly sensitive issue for French citizens right up to 1914, it was nevertheless also the case that the passage of time was eroding its emotive power, especially as a prospective appeal to arms. Part of the reason for this can be explained by developments in Alsace-Lorraine itself. In 1871, when the provinces had been annexed by Germany, the parliamentary deputies from the region had issued an emphatic statement that 'Alsace and Lorraine are opposed to alienation. . . . With one accord . . . [they proclaim] to Germany and to the world, the unalterable determination . . . to remain French.'[32] That this had been no mere rhetorical flourish but a genuine expression of patriotic feeling can be demonstrated by the movement of people that followed in its wake. Given the choice between staying in Alsace-Lorraine or emigrating to France, tens of thousands, maybe even hundreds of thousands, of citizens from these provinces uprooted and crossed the border in order to remain in the country, if not the district, of their birth. Naturally, the devotion of these *optants* (those who opted to stay French) made a significant impression upon other French citizens, who were, accordingly, drawn all the more strongly to the irredentist cause.

However, a few decades later, little of the patriotic ardour that had inspired the *optants* of 1871 seemed to have survived in Alsace-Lorraine. Instead, there were many indications that the people there had become acclimatized to their new status as German citizens. In 1898, for example, twelve of the fifteen parliamentary deputies from the region declared their loyalty to the German Reich. Others demonstrated their acceptance of the *status quo* by marrying Germans (by 1909, 16.4 per cent of all marriages in the provinces were mixed), speaking German or Alsatian dialect rather than French, or by campaigning for autonomy for the *Reichsland* rather than a return to France.[33] It is significant in this latter respect that the main piece of political doggerel heard in Alsace in 1913 was an expression of regional particularism rather than of French patriotism. As the cry went:

> *Français ne peux,*   (Frenchman I can't be,
> *Prussien ne veux,*   Prussian I won't be,
> *Alsacien suis.*   Alsatian I am.)[34]

The signal this sent out about attitudes in the two provinces was unmistakable. As one of the leading historians of Alsace-Lorraine's development under German rule has concluded, 'there was at least an even chance that Alsace-Lorraine might be integrated successfully into imperial Germany. . . . By 1914, most Alsace-Lorrainers were willing to become German citizens in the full sense of the word.'[35] Naturally, this process did not go unnoticed in France, where it had a significant effect on popular sentiments. As one leading scholar has observed, 'because Alsace and Lorraine were dissociating themselves from France so French opinion's interest in the provinces was diminishing'.[36]

The cooling of passions in France over the question of Alsace-Lorraine was not, however, merely a reciprocation of the diminished interest in the issue exhibited by the people of the provinces themselves, it also reflected a major shift in attitudes among the French populace. The reason for this was demographic change. As was always inevitable, the generation that had experienced the humiliation of 1871 first hand was growing older and fewer in number, while a new generation for whom the topic was a matter of much less urgency was gaining greater weight as a proportion of the French population. The result was a growing, if begrudging, resignation in France to the idea that it might be necessary to accept the settlement of 1871 as a *fait accompli*. Certainly there was no enthusiasm for recovering the provinces by waging an aggressive war against a powerful Germany, especially given that the likely consequences of such a struggle were all too predictable. The French economist, Paul Leroy-Beaulieu, epitomized this perspective when he wrote in the journal *Économiste Française* in May 1881 that 'we must dispel the illusions which would lead us into new catastrophes. In the presence of a Germany of 45 millions, which will have 60 [millions] in twenty years, and 80 [millions] in fifty years, the hope of revenge is chimerical.'[37] Naturally, the widespread realization of the validity of this argument would have a significant effect on the French public. As an article in the *Revue des Deux Mondes*, also from 1881, recognized, there had been a major change in attitude in France since the signing of the Treaty of Frankfurt:

'One would say that a century has elapsed since 1871! Today people try to avoid thinking of the past, to throw a veil over unhappy memories. It is the style to be indifferent to old wounds and to believe in all sorts of good fortune.'[38] And the passage of time only solidified this sentiment. As the ultra-nationalist paper *Patrie* commented on 24 May 1908, 'the dismemberment is an event as distant as the Seven Years' War for the new generations'.[39] Nothing had changed by 1914. The monumental research on French public opinion conducted by Jean-Jacques Becker has conclusively proven that, on the eve of war, a peaceful outlook pervaded the French nation. Such cries of *revanche* as could be found were restricted to nationalist organizations and certain sections of the Parisian bourgeoisie, and such people were far from typical of France as a whole.[40]

In short, the picture of France that has emerged in recent years differs markedly from the view presented by Montgelas, Barnes, Fay and McCullough. Contrary to their belief in a *revanchiste* republic always ready to provoke a conflict in order to restore the lost provinces, the evidence available today suggests that French nationalism had developed a much more rational quality. Most French citizens – extreme patriots excluded – were coming to accept that Alsace-Lorraine was unlikely to be recovered by France. To be sure, this was not a decision that they made willingly, but the alternative of war against Germany held little appeal outside of the most chauvinistic circles. As Becker observes, by 1914, 'war was not going to be declared in a climate of revenge . . . [as] . . . the refusal to make war for the lost provinces was a general one. . . .'[41] Thus, if the Treaty of Frankfurt is to be held in any way responsible for the outbreak of hostilities in 1914, all the evidence suggests that this cannot be on the grounds that it inspired France to commit an act of *revanche* against her eastern neighbour. No undertaking of this kind was ever seriously proposed or, more tellingly, ever occurred.

ALSACE-LORRAINE AND THE INTERNATIONAL SYSTEM

However, dismissing the idea that the First World War began as an act of *revanche* on the part of France does not, in itself, mean that there is no longer a basis for arguing that a link exists between the provisions of the Treaty of Frankfurt and the outbreak of conflict in 1914. For, irrespective of the question of *revanche*, it is still the case that the German annexation of Alsace-Lorraine had a considerable impact on the pattern of interactions within the European state system. Briefly put, the transfer of these provinces created a situation in which France and Germany, despite the restoration of 'correct' diplomatic relations between them, were never, thereafter, willing to engage in close collaboration on the international stage. It is true that cordial relations between these two powers was certainly a realizable – albeit rarely achieved – possibility, but any form of meaningful Franco-German *rapprochement* was quite simply out of the question. This would be demonstrated time and time again.

For example, following the British occupation of Egypt in 1882 – a unilateral action to which the French government strongly objected – an opportunity seemed to exist for France and Germany to cooperate together in the realm of colonial affairs. What made the situation seem especially promising was that Bismarck and French Premier Jules Ferry both saw the merits of joint action against Britain. This was not to be. In no small part, this was because key sections of the French public saw no virtue in colonial advancement if the price was intimacy with Germany. The newspaper *La Républic Française* summarized their opinion on this matter clearly: 'Egypt? What is Egypt? We take 1870 for our starting point and the only question of foreign policy that concerns us is that of the eastern frontier.'[42] In the face of such sentiments, it is not altogether surprising that Franco-German cooperation at the Berlin Africa Conference of 1883/4 failed to develop into real friendship.

Moreover, this would be no isolated incident, for the passage of time would not make it any easier for France and Germany to cooperate over colonial affairs. In 1895/6, for example, British behaviour in Africa once again seemed to offer an opportunity for joint Franco-German action. This time the occasion was provided by the Jameson Raid, an opportunistic attempt by British South Africa Company officials to take over the Boer republic of the Transvaal by force of arms. In response, the German government sounded out the

French authorities with a view to making common cause. The result was anything but favourable. As the State Secretary at the German Foreign Office reported, the French government reacted negatively; so, too, did the French media:

> Not only the independent, but also the official French press, in particular the mouthpiece of the French Foreign Ministry, *Le Temps*, after a few days of observation took up the task of pointing out that the Transvaal was not sufficient to turn the attention of France from Alsace-Lorraine. The headline of *Le Temps*, which was taken up by the rest of the press, was 'no unnatural alliances'.[43]

Needless to say, such sentiments provided no basis for Franco-German collaboration over the question of South Africa. Accordingly, the idea of making common cause in this instance, as in so many others, was allowed to wither away.

Yet it was not only France that made Alsace-Lorraine into a barrier for common Franco-German undertakings. After the outbreak of the Boer War in 1899, it was France's turn – in conjunction with Russia – to recommend to Germany some form of joint intervention to protest against British behaviour in South Africa. The German reply, in March 1900, was to suggest that before such an act, the powers involved 'should guarantee each other their territorial possession in Europe for many years ahead'.[44] In effect, the Germans were demanding a French renunciation of Alsace-Lorraine as the price of cooperation. Not surprisingly, this was refused, for France, as was well known, would not willingly 'approve the treaty of Frankfurt all over again'.[45]

As the above examples illustrate, even when considering the future of parts of the globe as distant from the Rhine as the south-eastern Mediterranean littoral and the South African subcontinent, the question of Alsace-Lorraine remained a decisive barrier to Franco-German cooperation. Why was this? Contrary to traditional explanations based upon the notion that France was dominated by feelings of *revanche*, the reason had nothing to do with hatred or revenge; rather, it was the question of national security that was the paramount consideration.

In essence, the French felt threatened by Germany. This was readily understandable. The Franco-Prussian War had, after all, unambiguously demonstrated that the nearest and most dangerous hazard to France was, indeed, Germany. Moreover, with their seizure of Alsace-Lorraine, the Germans had provided a vivid demonstration both of France's vulnerability to German power, as well as of the severe consequences that derived from such a state. Given that Germany's military might was unlikely to diminish in the foreseeable future – if anything, Germany's growing population and ever-increasing industrial strength pointed the other way – it naturally became the priority of successive French governments to guard against a renewed assault by their eastern neighbour. In this context, Bismarck's wish that France would 'pardon Sedan as [she had] pardoned Waterloo' utterly failed to strike a chord in France, where the chancellor's request was perceived less as a gesture of reconciliation than as a means of putting the French off their guard before ensnaring them once again. Those in power were determined not to fall for this. 'Listen [to Bismarck],' warned the French diplomat, the Baron de Courcel, and 'perhaps one day one of his successors would say to our descendants, "I want you to pardon a new defeat and a new dismemberment as your fathers pardoned Sedan."' It was for this reason the Baron concluded that 'in the matter of dismemberment a nation, unless it is prepared to meet with indifference the fate of Poland, ought never to pardon and never forget'.[46] Many other French decision-makers felt likewise, with the result that a guarded attitude towards Germany became the basis of French policy.

Thus, the German annexation of Alsace-Lorraine, far from engendering a French desire to launch a war of revenge against Germany, actually provided the French with good reason to consider that their country needed protection from their powerful neighbour. Given this belief, the French declined any form of *rapprochement* with their former foe lest such cooperative action should lull the nation into a false sense of security and, thereby, provide the Germans with a further opportunity to dominate France. In this way, the Treaty of Frankfurt precluded the re-emergence of real Franco-German friendship.

This chill in relations between France and Germany would prove to be more than just an impediment to colonial diplomacy; it also created a major fault line running through the heart of Europe. This would have serious consequences. Slowly but surely, this Franco-German fissure would crystallize into a binary alliance system that bifurcated the continent into mutually suspicious blocks. As the eminent historian George Peabody Gooch describes the process: 'The story of Franco-German relations since 1871 is the record of France's endeavour to regain her lost territories and of Germany's attempts to retain them. . . . Each of the protagonists sought and found allies, until almost the whole of Europe was involved in their implacable vendetta.'[47] Writing as he was in the early 1920s – that is to say, in the immediate aftermath of all the bloodletting pursuant to the First World War – Gooch undoubtedly overemphasizes the degree of hostility between the two continental powers. Nevertheless, he is surely correct in suggesting that it was no coincidence that France and Germany found themselves at the heart of two opposing international politico-military groupings, and that the issue of Alsace-Lorraine was at the root of their mutual mistrust. In any case, events bear out his analysis.

From 1871 through to 1914 it was clear that the French, although not actually contemplating launching an aggressive war for this purpose, were nevertheless unwilling to renounce their claim to Alsace-Lorraine. However unlikely it might seem (especially to the French themselves), they hoped someday to effect the recovery of these provinces. Moreover, while they were maintaining this aspiration, French power and influence increased considerably both as a result of France's own military development programme, which saw the size and power of her armies increase enormously, and also through her ability to forge closer ties with other European great powers. This latter phenomenon, which began with the signing of an alliance with Russia in 1894 and culminated in 1904 with the formation of the Entente Cordiale with Britain, was particularly significant. Although neither Russia nor Britain would ever contemplate going to war with Germany to further France's aspiration for a frontier on the Rhine, their friendship did, at least, end once and for all French vulnerability to German pressure. French diplomats in the *Quai d'Orsay* could thenceforth adopt a more vigorous stance in their dealings with their German counterparts. In effect, therefore, the German dominance of the European continent that had been established by Bismarck gave way under his successors to a more balanced continental system: France with her ties to Russia and Britain could hope to hold her own against Germany and her allies.

But this was not how the matter was seen in Berlin. From the perspective of the diplomats in the *Wilhelmstraße* – whose paranoia was legendary – the friendship of France, Russia and Britain looked like an attempt to encircle Germany. Under these conditions, which it should not be forgotten were largely of her own making, Germany never felt secure. And it was this insecurity that would ultimately have such profound consequences for the peace first in Europe and then the world. As recent research has demonstrated, the First World War began because leading figures in the German leadership – especially, but not exclusively, in the military – believed that the long-term balance of power was moving against them. Accordingly, they sought to strike out against this 'encirclement' while there was still the chance of their doing so successfully.[48] 'War, the sooner the better' was the phrase used by Chief of the Great General Staff, Helmuth von Moltke the younger, in December 1912. Eighteen months later his wish would be granted. When it was, it came as no surprise to Moltke, or for that matter anybody else, that France and Germany found themselves ranged on opposing sides.

CONCLUSION

The French desire to regain Alsace-Lorraine has been categorized by many writers as the principal cause of the First World War. France, it was said, started the conflict as a war of *revanche*. There is some evidence to support the view that the French had strong feelings

21

about the lost provinces. Also, there were French citizens, such as General Boulanger, who saw it as France's duty to regain these territories. However, the argument is overstated. Contemporaries realized that with the passage of time, French ardour over Alsace-Lorraine had diminished. Neither the French government nor the French people would be willing to start a bloodbath for such a purpose. That said, the French were never reconciled to the loss either. French diplomacy was predicated thereafter on the notion that Germany was the main threat to France's security, that France needed allies against Germany and that, should a European war start, Alsace-Lorraine should be one of France's goals. This brought instability to Europe, as relations between France and Germany never rose beyond the level of *détente*. In 1914, the war was begun by German aggression, but the pattern of the alliance blocs that fought it was determined in part by the Treaty of Frankfurt.

TWO

The Treaty of Versailles and the Origins of the Second World War

'We have indeed lost the Peace'

Lord Grey of Fallodon[1]

On 28 June 1919, in the imposing setting of the *Galerie des Glaces* ('Hall of Mirrors') in the palace of Versailles, the treaty was signed that brought to a close the war that had begun in August 1914 between Germany and what would later become known as the Allied and Associated Powers. For the citizens of Europe the ending of this conflict was a momentous event. The war, which had originally seemed to many to be a great adventure, had quickly proven itself to be a more massive undertaking than most people had previously considered possible. Yet, therein lay its significance. Causing untold suffering and destruction and acting as the Moloch for millions of men, women and children, its very magnitude demanded that it should have been fought for some greater and nobler purpose than mere victory in a Clausewitzian trial of strength between nations resolving their quarrels 'by other means'. And so it was that the First World War acquired the rationale of 'the war to end all wars' and the peace treaty that followed it became laden with the expectation that it should be the instrument to fulfil this worthy goal.

With such hopes pinned upon it, it was probably inevitable that the Treaty of Versailles would, with the passage of time, prove to be a disappointment. No one political agreement between nations

23

could, after all, really hope to abolish war – humankind's second oldest pastime – at a single stroke. Yet, even by such standards, surprisingly little time was required for the Versailles agreement to fail the test of popular expectation. Even before the ink on the document had dried, numerous commentators, informed and otherwise, were expressing first their doubts and then their misgivings about the treaty's capacity to bring peace and stability to Europe. 'This is not peace. It is an armistice for twenty years',[2] decried no less a figure than Marshal Ferdinand Foch, the French general who had overseen the Allied victory. Others agreed. Jan Christiaan Smuts, the South African statesman, lambasted the treaty in a letter to his wife. 'It is a terrible document,' he complained to her, 'not a peace treaty but a war treaty. . . .'[3] Moreover, as he informed the British Prime Minister, David Lloyd George, its enactment was likely to have dire consequences. 'This Treaty breathes a poisonous spirit of revenge,' he wrote, 'which may yet scorch the fair face – not of a corner of France, but of Europe.'[4] Similar sentiments were expressed by the British Colonial Secretary, Alfred Lord Milner, who excoriated the treaty as 'the peace to end peace'.[5]

If that was how the prospect of the treaty looked to victorious Allied statesmen closeted in the comfortable surroundings of Paris in 1919, examined in retrospect by commentators who possessed the knowledge that, within twenty years of its signing, Europe was to be racked by the even greater carnage and destruction of the Second World War, it appeared an even worse disaster. Not only had the treaty demonstrably failed to prevent further conflict, some now considered that the worst prophecies about it had, in fact, been underestimates of its baleful effects. All the ills and sorrows of the interwar years were now laid at the treaty's door, from Germany's hyperinflation of 1923,[6] to the Wall Street crash and the global depression of 1929,[7] to the rise to power of Hitler and the Nazis in 1933[8] – all were said to be products of Versailles. Most significantly of all, a corpus of opinion emerged that Versailles' deadliest legacy was the outbreak of the Second World War in 1939. This conflict, which according to the renowned historian A.J.P. Taylor might better be called 'the war between the three western powers over the settlement of Versailles', 'had been implicit,' he explained, 'since the moment when the first war ended'.[9] He was not alone in this view. 'During the 1930s,' so wrote Professor R.J. Schmidt in his revealingly titled book *Versailles and the Ruhr: Seedbed of World War II*, 'the younger generation of Germans refused to bear the stigma of sole war guilt and turned eagerly to listen to the diatribes of the Nazi Führer against the Versailles Treaty. Seeds planted during the fateful era from 1919 to 1925 were finally producing bitter fruit.'[10]

Do these charges stand up to scrutiny? With respect to the first three – the German hyperinflation, the Wall Street crash and the rise of the Nazis – this is clearly not the case. The German hyperinflation of 1923, for example, derived less from any burdens that Versailles imposed upon the Reich (i.e. reparations), than from the German government's refusal to levy extra taxes in order to meet its financial obligations – a large proportion of which was made up of war debts that had been accrued during four years of fighting. Instead, the state started an inflationary cycle, first by borrowing money and then, when this proved inadequate, by printing paper currency in enormous quantities. Very soon, Germany was engulfed in an inflationary torrent of its own making.[11] Yet, while this was disastrous for the German middle class, who saw their savings wiped out overnight, it was of enormous value to the state and to many industries, whose debts were effectively eliminated by the inflationary surge.

In a similar fashion, there is little to connect the Wall Street crash with Versailles. Far from being caused by any financial uncertainty prompted by the treaty, the plunge in the American stockmarket can be explained as the inevitable price correction that follows any period of runaway speculation. While certainly more severe, it was, like the South Sea Bubble of the 1720s or the dot.com boom and bust of the year 2000, a 'bear market' that occurs when speculators rush en masse to withdraw their money before prices fall – an act that, of course, ensures the very phenomenon least desired, namely a fall in prices.

Likewise, short shrift can be made of the accusation that Versailles propelled the Nazis to power. This is not to deny that attacks on the alleged iniquities of the treaty formed an important part of Hitler's propaganda for winning the hearts and minds of the German people. However, constant reference to such matters failed to bring electoral dividends throughout the 1920s. Only once the German economy combusted in the early 1930s did the Nazis experience any major gains in voter support. Yet, even then, it took the stupidity of the German conservatives, who believed that Hitler could be controlled and who persuaded the reluctant German President, Paul von Hindenburg, of this notion, to bring Hitler to office. Of course, once Hitler was in power, he never relinquished it, with consequences that are well known. Nevertheless, this cannot realistically be blamed on the Versailles treaty, which should not be made to serve as the scapegoat for the failure of democracy in Weimar Germany. Yet if these three accusations can easily be countered, what of the charge that the Treaty of Versailles sowed the seeds of the Second World War? Can this, too, be dispatched so readily?

THE THEORY OF 'THE CARTHAGINIAN PEACE'

The argument most commonly made to explain how and why the Treaty of Versailles caused the Second World War is normally summed up by three words – 'the Carthaginian peace'. This classical allusion to the Third Punic War, in which Rome utterly destroyed her old enemy Carthage, after accusing the latter of breaching the impossible treaty terms that the Romans had imposed upon her after the Second Punic War, was first used as an analogy for Versailles by the scholar-statesman Jan Christiaan Smuts. The treaty, he fulminated, is 'the most reactionary [peace] since Scipio Africanus dealt with Carthage'.[12]

Like all good phrases, the term 'the Carthaginian peace' promptly gained a widespread circulation and such was its explanatory power that its message soon became common currency. These three words conveyed the notion that the Treaty of Versailles offered not a peace of reconciliation but one of revenge. It encapsulated the idea that the settlement was so punitive that it must in the end fail. Either the Germans must attempt to evade its terms – because to implement them would be to sign away their national existence – or the Allies must eventually choose to revise them – for to insist upon them would be deliberately to bring about Germany's destruction, an act that was surely unthinkable once the passions of the war had faded. Yet, whichever way the treaty's severity finally led it to be undermined, one fact remained constant in this analysis: Germany would emerge from the process bitter, resentful and desirous of challenging the new order. And what firmer foundations could exist for a new war? Such was Smuts' opinion in 1919. 'Under this Treaty,' he proclaimed, 'Europe will know no peace.'[13] Today, this view still enjoys scholarly support. In 1996, for example, seventy-seven years after Smuts made his fatal prophecy, Jay Winter, the eminent historian of the First World War, pronounced, albeit retrospectively, in a similar vein. 'The Peace Conference which ended the Great War', he wrote,

> was more about punishment than about peace. Perhaps inevitably, anger and retribution followed four years of bloodshed, ensuring the instability and ultimate collapse of the accords signed in the Hall of Mirrors at Versailles on 28 June 1919. The road to World War II started here.[14]

THE REALITY OF 'THE CARTHAGINIAN PEACE'

Yet, if the theory of 'the Carthaginian peace' has proven an enduring one, it is, nevertheless, also a misleading one. For this proposition hinges on one key (and demonstrably false) tenet: namely, that the treaty terms were fundamentally unjust and punitive. However, all the complaints about the settlement's severity notwithstanding, there are few, if any, grounds for believing that the Versailles settlement was 'the slave treaty' that its opponents labelled it. Unlike the Carthaginian state, which was destroyed by its dealings with the Romans, Germany was manifestly *not* destroyed by the Treaty of Versailles. Nor did her citizens become 'slaves and Helots'[15] as the new German Chancellor, Philipp Scheidemann, erroneously maintained. On the contrary, as we shall see, in almost every respect Germany remained essentially undiminished as a result of the peace process.

In territorial terms, for example, Germany emerged from the Paris peace conference largely unscathed. Under the treaty, the new republic had to forego Bismarck's conquests of 1866 and 1871 and yield seven peripheral border adjustments to her neighbours that removed the country's long-suffering French, Danish and Polish minorities from German control. Yet, even after these cessions, Germany remained 87 per cent intact. She lost just 13 per cent of her pre-war landmass, a figure that, as Niall Ferguson has observed in a rather ingenious analogy, compares favourably with the 22 per cent of national territory lost by the United Kingdom on the creation of the Irish Free State, an event that, no less than Versailles, was a product of the First World War.[16]

It also compares favourably with the fate of Germany's allies in the Central Alliance, the Austro-Hungarian and Ottoman empires.[17] Austria, for example, once the heart of a great multinational empire, was turned after defeat into a small landlocked state of 6 million people, 2 million of whom lived in the fading glory of the now overlarge capital, Vienna. At the same time, Hungary lost 70 per cent of its pre-war territory and likewise became a small landlocked state. Similarly, the Ottoman empire was reduced to its Turkish-Anatolian heartland, with all its territories in the Levant and Middle East passing to mandates and successor states. Among the Central Powers, therefore, it was these countries and not Germany that paid the territorial price of defeat.

The 13 per cent of national territory lost by Germany compares more favourably still with the peace treaties that Germany imposed or would have imposed upon her enemies. Given the opportunity of victory, Germany was punitive in the extreme. For example, in the Treaty of Brest-Litovsk, which Germany forced upon her defeated eastern neighbour in March 1918, Russia had been deprived of Poland, the Baltic provinces, Finland, the Ukraine and much of the

Caucasus. In effect, she lost a quarter of her population, arable land and railway network, a third of her manufacturing industry and three-quarters of her iron reserves and coal fields.[18]

Wartime documents reveal that France, had she too been defeated by Germany, would have fared no better. Nor would Belgium. As Reich Chancellor Theobald von Bethmann Hollweg put it in his now infamous statement of German war aims, the 'September Programme' of 1914, 'Belgium, even if allowed to continue to exist as a state, must be reduced to a vassal state'. Liège, Veviers and possibly Antwerp were earmarked for annexation.[19] What, one might ask, were the so-called deprivations of Versailles compared to this?

In short, while it could not be said that Germany was dismembered territorially by the Treaty of Versailles, it might well be observed that, in comparison either to the Reich's allies or to those opponents that she managed to defeat herself, Germany received uncommonly generous treatment. The result of this was that, despite all the claims that have been made to the contrary, Germany's powerful political position in Europe – just like her territorial position – was also *not* destroyed by the Treaty of Versailles.

As the historian Sally Marks has observed, the effect of the war and the peace treaty 'was the effective enhancement of Germany's relative strength in Europe, particularly in regard to her immediate neighbours'.[20] The reason for this was straightforward. Prior to 1914, German power had been limited by the presence of strong states on her borders. There was the massive Tsarist empire to the east, a resurgent and confident France to the west, and, to the south, the Habsburg monarchy – a fading empire to be sure, but still one of Europe's great powers, and very far from being a *quantité negligeable*. Yet, come 1919, none of these conditions still applied. Russia, for example, was broken, defeated in battle, thrown into disorder by revolution, and on the verge of civil war. Similarly, France, though victorious, lay in ruins: her most prosperous industrial regions had been laid waste by four years of war and her 1½ million fatalities had left her demoralized and demographically weak. Finally, Austria-Hungary was no more. In her place was a group of successor states, small, weak, insecure, impoverished and, as H.A.L. Fisher has laconically noted, 'of questionable stability'.[21] None of them was a power of the first rank.

This combination of circumstances worked entirely in Germany's favour. France was too exhausted to stand up to Germany for long. Russia had no interest in so doing, indeed, Russia was a potential ally of Germany's in challenging the new borders in eastern Europe, many of which had been established at her expense. And the dissolution of the Habsburg empire created a power vacuum in central Europe which, of all nations, Germany was best equipped to fill. Clearly, therefore, Germany's great power potential was not destroyed by the peace settlement. On the contrary, it created a situation in which there was no longer any counterweight to German power. As a result, in Anthony Lentin's judgement – a judgement with which this author concurs – Germany emerged from Versailles 'not only the dominant continental power, but potentially more preponderant than in 1914'.[22] This was very far from being a Carthaginian outcome.

In a similar fashion, just as the Treaty of Versailles failed to undermine Germany territorially or politically, so, too, did it fail to destroy Germany's military potential. The German army was, in theory, limited by the settlement to 100,000 men with no tanks or heavy artillery. A military control commission was set up to ensure compliance. This commission was, from the outset, inadequate to supervise the German army in Germany, let alone to follow its activities in the Soviet Union, the arena in which the testing of forbidden weapons actually took place. In any event, its mission was deeply flawed. Germany complied with the 100,000-man limit in the 1920s when it could not afford a larger force, but nurtured it with a view to later expansion. In the 1930s, these 100,000 long-term professional servicemen supplied the fighting elite that was to provide the bedrock for a new army, one that would prove more than capable of overrunning western and central Europe in 1940 and 1941. It is for this reason that, when looking back at the treaty terms, the eminent military historian Brian Bond has concluded that 'the victors unwittingly did Germany a favour by obliging her to concentrate on high-quality personnel and training, modern weapons and equipment, and mobility in theory and practice'.[23] After all, it was this more than anything that gave the German army another opportunity to conquer Europe. Clearly, therefore, even if the military terms were Carthaginian in intent, they were anything but that in terms of their outcome, a reality clearly encapsulated in Margaret MacMillan's observation that 'the clearest demonstration that the peacemakers did not emasculate Germany came after 1939'.[24]

Finally, it is necessary to consider whether or not the Treaty of Versailles was punitive in respect to its financial stipulations. Ever since the British economist John Maynard Keynes published his denunciation of the treaty's reparations clauses in the bestselling book *The Economic Consequences of the Peace* (1919), the idea that the settlement imposed an insuperable monetary burden on Germany has been widely accepted.[25] But is it really true that the treaty crippled Germany economically and consigned the German people to abject poverty?

The answer is, of course, a resounding 'no'. In 1919, Germany, unlike France, Belgium and Russia, had not been a battleground. As a result, with the very minor exception of some air-raid damage, Germany's industrial infrastructure was undamaged by the fighting. Accordingly, her economy was in a relatively advantageous position to benefit from the restoration of peacetime conditions. Reparations did nothing to alter this fact. To begin with, the figure set, while designed to appear high, was in reality not excessive. The headline figure for reparations was set at the sum of 132 billion gold marks (£6.6 billion). However, this figure was purely notional. In reality, the debt was divided into three segments. Germany would have to pay interest and amortization on two bond series (A and B bonds) totalling 50 billion marks (£2.5 billion) – an amount that corresponded closely with what the Germans maintained they could pay. In theory, the Reich also remained liable for an additional 82 billion marks worth of C bonds. However, it was never expected or intended that these should be issued and, thus, no interest or amortization was due on them. They were, as Belgian Premier Georges Theunis noted, quite worthless. One could, he dryly commented, 'stick them in a drawer without bothering to lock up, for no thief would be tempted to steal them'.[26] Their sole purpose was to inflate the reparations figure for public consumption so that Allied leaders – especially in Britain, where the government had promised to squeeze Germany 'until the pips squeak'[27] – could tell their public that they had made Germany pay.

The reality, however, was somewhat different. It is one of the paradoxes of modern warfare, and particularly wars fought by western democracies, that the victors are more likely to pay the full costs of the conflict than the losers. In part, this is due to regime continuity. Victorious governmental systems tend to survive the test of war. Come peacetime, therefore, they are faced with debts of their own making. These they need to meet if only because to do otherwise would be to destroy their reputation for financial probity and undermine the loyalty of their citizens who have lent them money. By contrast, losing regimes are often swept away in a revolutionary tide and their successors have no incentive to inherit their predecessor's financial obligations. Accordingly, they default at the earliest opportunity. Added to this, it has also proved the case that victorious democracies have tended to see benefits in the economic reconstruction of their defeated adversaries. Impoverished nations, after all, make poor trading partners and undermine global stability. As a result, nations defeated by democracies often find that they are advanced money by their former enemies.

Both of these phenomena would apply to the Versailles treaty. The new German republic, for example, saw no reason to pay reparations for damages caused by its imperial predecessor. As a result, it continually attempted to default on its obligations. Ultimately, it was successful. The London schedule of payments issued in 1921 was first reduced under the Dawes plan of 1924, then reduced further by the Young plan of 1929, and finally eliminated altogether by the Lausanne Convention of 1932. Reparations, planned to be spread over fifty years, barely survived a decade. In addition, such money as the Germans did pay, in the brief period in which such transfers were made, was not their own. Throughout the 1920s, large loans were advanced to Germany by the Americans.

A small proportion of these funds (the majority of the money was used to enhance German industry) was grudgingly handed to the western Allies as reparations payments. It is for this reason that the economic historian Stephen A. Schuker writes about 'American reparations to Germany'. As he sees it, 'the flow of capital from the United States and certain European countries to Weimar Germany in the 1920s gave rise to one of the greatest proportional transfers of real wealth in modern history'.[28] In short, Germany made a profit out of reparations!

How then is one to evaluate Keynes' claim that, in respect to its financial provisions, the Treaty of Versailles was a Carthaginian peace? First of all, it is necessary to dispute Keynes' assessment of the consequences of reparations. They were neither a burden that was impossible to meet, nor did they 'sign the death warrant of many millions of German men, women and children' as Keynes professed to believe. As A.J.P. Taylor has remarked in respect to this latter point,

> Keynes, I am told, was a very good economist, but there can be few examples in history of a judgement that went more astray. . . . Not a single man, woman or child died in Germany as a result of the peace of Versailles. Indeed, the children whom it was supposed to sentence to death were the Nazi soldiers of 1940, about the toughest fighting men the world has ever known.[29]

However, perhaps the clearest proof that reparations were not the Carthaginian exactions that has been claimed of them comes from the sight of what a truly punitive financial settlement really looks like. Under Hitler's occupation of Europe enormous sums of money were seized from the occupied territories. France alone surrendered annually between 25 per cent and 50 per cent of her national income to her Nazi conquerors. By comparison, the 5.37 per cent of domestic products demanded of Germany at Versailles – a total that the Germans claimed was unpayable – looks like small change.

All in all, it seems clear that, whatever else it might have been, the Treaty of Versailles was not a Carthaginian peace. It neither dismembered Germany nor ruined her economically, nor did it remove her political power or military potential. Unlike Carthage, Germany was not destroyed. This being so, the theory that the inherent severity of the treaty was a cause of future war cannot be allowed to stand. The Second World War did not have its origins in the punitive exactions of the politicians who gathered in Paris in 1919 for the very simple reason that the terms imposed on Germany were not punitive.

Yet, the fact that the Carthaginian peace theory does not stand up to scrutiny does not mean that there is no connection between the Treaty of Versailles and the outbreak of the Second World War. For the peace settlement, even if it was not 'Carthaginian', did have failings that were to facilitate future conflict.

THE SURVIVAL OF GERMAN MILITARISM

The first of these shortcomings was that the Versailles settlement utterly failed to achieve one of the Allies' principal goals, namely the discrediting in Germany of 'militarism' – that is to say, popular respect for military institutions and the general belief that such institutions were the best means of enhancing German power and prestige abroad. That the eradication of the German military mentality had long been one of the Allies' major objectives had been clear since the earliest days of the war. In December 1914, for instance, the American Ambassador in London, Walter Hines Page – an astute, if not entirely neutral observer – had composed a long letter dealing exclusively with this point: 'If England wins decisively,' he had remarked at the time,

> the English hope that somehow the military party will be overthrown in Germany and that the Germans, under peaceful leadership, will go about their business – industrial, political, educational, etc. [–] and quit dreaming of and planning for universal empire and quit maintaining a great war machine, which at some time for some reason must attack somebody to justify its existence. . . . To patch up a peace leaving the German war party in power, they think, would be only to invite another war.[30]

34

Yet, that is precisely what occurred. At the war's end the German military authorities, while certainly subdued, were by no means repentant or discredited. Why was this so?

In 1918, Germany was heavily defeated in battle. Exhausted by the failure of the deeply flawed Ludendorff offensives of the spring, Germany had no reserves with which to resist the Allied counter-offensives that began that summer. Moreover, the German army found itself unable to devise a proper defence against the Allies' now perfected combined arms tactics. A series of shattering reverses pushed back the German line and made the army's ultimate collapse certain.

In this context, the German High Command – aware that the impending military débâcle would destroy its standing among the German people – decided to end the war while its forces were still intact and while the presence of its soldiers on foreign soil hid the magnitude of its failure. Naturally, however, it did not wish to do anything so revealing as to ask the Allies for terms itself. Accordingly, at the generals' insistence, the old autocratic regime was swept away and a new government of democratically elected party politicians installed in its place. It was these unfortunate men, later branded as the 'November criminals', who the generals selected to make the necessary overture to the Allies and, thus, relieve them of the odium of defeat. From this set of circumstances the 'stab in the back' myth was born. Germany, it was said, did not lose the war. Rather, her armies were victorious and her soldiers were heroes, but they were let down – 'stabbed in the back' – by Jews, socialists and revolutionaries at home. By fostering and perpetuating this devious and malicious calumny, Germany's generals escaped censure and the reputation of the military in Germany was allowed to survive intact to fight another day. As one astute German commentator noted in 1921, 'In other European countries the people hold their military and political leaders responsible for defeat. In Germany, the generals have succeeded in organizing the vilification and accusation of their own nation.'[31]

The peace settlement facilitated this deception, for in its symbolism it did not dispute the claims of the German generals that their armies were undefeated. The end of the fighting, for example, was the product not of Germany's surrender, but of an armistice, one moreover that had been signed on the Reich's behalf by a civilian politician, Matthias Erzberger, whose delegation contained not a single member of the High Command. By the terms of this agreement, the German soldiers were allowed to march home from the front in good order and bearing arms. This concession, granted by Marshal Foch on the grounds that as 'they fought well, let them keep their weapons',[32] while certainly a noble gesture, did little to suggest to the German people that their forces had been defeated in battle. Equally, the fact that Allied soldiers entered the Rhineland but left the rest of Germany unoccupied represented a missed opportunity to bring the reality of defeat home to most Germans. Likewise, the placing of the Allied-German Supervisory Commission in the sleepy backwater of Spa rather than in a highly visible location like Berlin also seemed designed to play down the notion that the Reich had been defeated. Finally, and in many ways most glaringly, it was German rather than Allied soldiers who marched through Berlin in a victory parade. Hailed at the Brandenburg Gate by the new Chancellor (soon to be President), Friedrich Ebert, they were given one simple message: 'As you return unconquered from the field of battle, I salute you!'[33]

Some Allied leaders realized that, by not making the magnitude of their defeat manifestly clear to the entire German population, they were making a fatal error. 'I am of the opinion', exclaimed American general John J. Pershing with admirable foresight, 'that we shall not be able in case of an armistice to reap the benefits of a decided victory which has not yet altogether been accomplished.'[34] Unfortunately, his was largely a lone voice. Typical of the majority opinion was a report sent to Washington by the normally perceptive American diplomat Ellis Loring Dresel.[35] 'No question exists in my mind', he wrote,

> but that the Germans are thoroughly 'down and out' for generations to come, and that another war on a big scale is not even a remote possibility. The officer and Junker classes have retired completely into the background, and I cannot see any

danger of reaction. I believe that the moderate parties under the leadership of the majority socialists will end by working out an orderly and stable government, without the slightest tinge of militarism. . . .[36]

If all of the above turned out to be a gross misjudgement, at least the next six words of the paragraph have survived the test of time, for Dresel concluded his exposition on the death of German militarism with the remark, 'However, I may be an optimist'.[37] Sadly, in respect to this particular subject, that was undoubtedly so.

THE PROBLEM OF ENFORCEMENT

An even more serious defect in the peace settlement related to the question of its enforcement. For the Treaty of Versailles to be successfully implemented, one of two things had to happen. Either the German government had to comply voluntarily with its provisions or the Allied powers had to force them to do so.

The very idea that the Germans might chose of their own volition to honour the Versailles settlement can only be viewed in hindsight as a preposterous proposition. From the very moment when the treaty's terms were made known, both the German government and, perhaps more importantly, the people made it clear that they regarded the settlement as being entirely devoid of any moral legitimacy. 'The peace of Versailles', so spoke German politician Gustav Stresemann in a passage typical of popular sentiment, 'is based on a violation of international law.'[38]

With only one example to the contrary, successive German governments based their policy towards the treaty on this premise. The exception was the Cabinet of Dr Joseph Wirth, whose Foreign Minister, the industrialist Walther Rathenau, articulated a policy of 'fulfilment' based upon that rarely followed notion, *dictum meum pactum*. As he explained it to the Reichstag,

We Germans are obligated by our signature, by the honour of our name that we have placed under the treaties. We will fulfil and we will go to the limit of our ability in order to preserve the honour of our name, which stands affixed to the treaties, and we recognize their binding character even though they do not express our wishes.[39]

Rathenau was assassinated for his pains. And the policy of fulfilment, poorly received even in its author's lifetime, was never revived thereafter. All subsequent governments worked instead on the premise that the treaty needed to be subverted.

Yet, the idea that the Germans would willingly comply with the treaty was a central assumption of the document's framers. As Marc Trachtenberg has observed of the British delegates, although the description would do just as well for the plenipotentiaries of most of the other nations, 'Lloyd George evidently supposed that the German people would share his conception of justice, that they would feel "in their hearts" Germany's guilt and their consequent obligation to pay . . . .'[40] Belief in this fallacious assumption ensured that the treaty contained few hard sanctions to guarantee German compliance. On the contrary, most of the treaty was based on the expectation that Germany would cooperate. Thus, Germany was required to disarm to agreed levels, but the implementation of this was put in German hands; Germany was required to pay reparations, but German officials had to collect the money and transfer it to the Allies; and Germany was required to surrender war crimes suspects for trial, but it was the German police and judiciary who had to carry out the arrests.[41] The question that remained unanswered was what would happen if they did not discharge these obligations?

In theory, institutions existed to deal with this problem. The Allies had established various control commissions to oversee the execution of the peace terms. In respect to their attempts to monitor German compliance, these bodies were, on the whole, successful: they observed the consistent German efforts to default and generally recognized them for the deliberate abuses of the treaty that they were. The problem was that they proved largely powerless to do anything about it. This was not because the remedy was not perfectly obvious. In August 1919, Hugh Gibson, the newly appointed American Minister to Poland, was monitoring the situation in Upper Silesia, an area where a plebiscite was scheduled to take place to determine whether the territory's future lay with Germany or Poland. This was a process that the Germans were determined, if it were at all possible, to frustrate. 'There is not a day goes by', Gibson wrote, 'without some flagrant violation by the Germans, not only of the terms of the Treaty but acts of war. . . .' Yet, as he went on to record:

> I am convinced that at any time we could, by perfectly plain warning to the Germans and perhaps the adoption of threatening military measures, have brought about an orderly situation in these territories.[42]

Here, however, was the heart of the matter: German compliance depended upon Allied coercion. But, unwittingly though it may have been, the Allies had severely restricted their room for manoeuvre in this respect by the terms of the peace settlement. A comparison between the Treaty of Frankfurt and the Treaty of Versailles illustrates the nature of the difficulties that the Allies created for themselves. By the terms of the former treaty, the Germans had stationed a large army in northern France, which they would only remove if and when the French complied with their demands. If the French defaulted, German soldiers, already on French soil in large numbers, would remain there. By contrast, at Versailles, the Allies decided to place a small garrison in the Rhineland but promised in advance to undertake a progressive withdrawal over fifteen years. Admittedly, they reserved the right to prolong their stay if the Germans defaulted on their obligations, but this placed the onus for taking positive action on the Allies. Thus, if the Germans dragged their feet, there were no automatic consequences, rather the Allies had to galvanize themselves to take costly measures. As Niall Ferguson observes, 'this was psychologically misconceived, as it encouraged the Germans to gamble that . . . [the Allies] were bluffing'.[43] But, were they? Sadly, circumstances after 1919 suggested to the Germans that this was, indeed, the case.

THE BREAKDOWN OF ALLIED SUPPORT FOR THE TREATY

In April 1917, when the United States entered the war against Germany, most observers would have assumed that, come the eventual Allied victory, the peace settlement that was created would have behind it the backing of four major powers: Russia, America, Great Britain and France. Had this been so, then it is most unlikely that Germany would have been able to evade the consequences of defeat. Yet, when the time came, it was not this grouping of states upon which the enforcement and preservation of the Treaty of Versailles came to depend, but another combination – one much reduced both in terms of the number of its adherents and in respect to their power and influence.

The collapse of Allied unity was a gradual affair. The first country to break ranks was Russia. Following the October Revolution (November in the new calendar) and the Bolshevik seizure of power, Russia left the war, a situation that received formal ratification with the signing of the Treaty of Brest-Litovsk in March 1918. While this hardly endeared the new regime to the remaining Allied combatants, this was nothing compared to the western powers' revulsion at the ideological stance of Lenin's government. Given its adherence to the Marxist doctrine of revolutionary class warfare, many Allied statesmen wanted to 'strangle Bolshevism at birth'. If that were not possible, then they at least hoped to isolate the new regime. Accordingly, communist Russia became a pariah state and was excluded from the negotiations over the Versailles settlement. This was of the greatest significance. Russia had no reason to be a party in the enforcement of the treaty if it was not involved in its formation. As a result, the one great power in the east – indeed, the only one there capable of facing up to Germany – was not to be used to ensure German compliance with its international obligations.

Even more significantly nor was America. The tale of Woodrow Wilson's role in the conference and his subsequent failure to persuade the American people of the value of his endeavours has often been told.[44] Yet, the implications of this disaster cannot be stressed too strongly. America's failure to ratify the treaty removed its strongest support. It is true that some American diplomats hoped that this would be but a temporary setback and that active engagement in world affairs was still possible. In December 1921, for example, Ellis Dresel, by this time American *Chargé d'Affaires* in Berlin, wrote to fellow diplomat Christian Herter to express the

> hope that our representatives on the Reparation Commission and elsewhere will be authorized to take as active a part as possible in whatever future negotiations take place. We simply cannot afford to cut loose altogether from this immensely difficult problem and say that it is no concern of ours.[45]

Unfortunately, all too few Americans felt likewise and their country retreated into isolationism. As William Phillips, Assistant Secretary of State, recorded in his memoirs:

> The Senate refused to approve the treaty and the United States turned its back on the great edifice which Wilson had erected to preserve peace, leaving other nations to do the best they could without the support or even encouragement of the most powerful nation in the world.[46]

Those other nations were Britain and France. Whether or not these two nations were strong enough to enforce the treaty on their own is a matter about which historians have long speculated. However, we will never know the answer, for the tragedy is that, when it came to the test, only one of these countries proved committed to the peace settlement.

Charitably inclined Anglophile historians have generally ascribed Britain's attempts to wriggle out of enforcing the treaty – to which as a signatory the country was honour bound to stand firm – to the nation's indefatigable liberal sentiment. There is some truth to this. Many figures in British public life were deeply unhappy with the treaty and hoped to revise it. Moreover, the British public, who had been so rabidly anti-German at the time of the 'coupon' election, quickly moderated their feelings. In this they were aided by the publication of an epoch-changing book by John Maynard Keynes, who had been a British Treasury delegate at the peace conference. Entitled *The Economic Consequences of the Peace*, this work was a devastating indictment on the Versailles treaty. Blasting it as neither practical nor wise, this bitter critique convinced numerous people in Britain that the treaty was unfair and unworkable. Rather than enforce it, they hoped instead to change it, possibly even to get rid of it. Thus, we are told, the British – unlike the hard-hearted French, who were unaffected by Keynes' message – came to abandon their role as enforcers of the peace settlement.

Without disputing the validity of any of the above explanations, it remains the case that this is only part of the story. The other factor that needs to be recognized is that Britain had less reason than France to want to enforce the treaty. Separated from Europe by the English Channel, Britain was not preoccupied by German power in the same way as France, who, after all, shared a common border with the Reich – a border, moreover, that German armies had crossed twice in fifty years. Consequently, facts that had an immediate significance to the French, such as Germany's population of 70 million, did not seem so pressing to the British.

And then there was the question of what would be gained from enforcing the treaty. Britain was fortunate in that what she wanted from the peace – the elimination of Germany as an imperial and naval rival – had been achieved even before the treaty was signed. Germany's colonies, for example, had been conquered during the war and there was not the slightest possibility of their being returned. The German navy, which had loomed so large in British anxieties prior to 1914, was by 1919 sitting peacefully on the sea-bed at Scapa Flow. Germany, who had become Britain's adversary in the years when she practised *Weltpolitik*, had in effect been forcibly returned to the status of a 'mere' European power. Britain did not have to do anything more to achieve this.

By contrast, everything that the French wanted from the peace settlement required constant vigilance and effort. Firstly, the French wanted reparations payments from Germany in order to restore their shattered northern region. Yet, if France did not press for these funds, Germany certainly would not deliver them up of her own volition. Secondly, France wanted security from future German invasion. But, once again, if France did not act to ensure it, Germany would not voluntarily refrain from testing forbidden weapons, or desist from surreptitiously building up her armed forces, or abstain from keeping them out of the Rhineland. In other words, for France – unlike Britain – the key elements of the settlement were not self-enforcing. Unfortunately, this meant that, whereas the French had something to gain from applying pressure on Germany, all Britain gained from sending in the troops was a new source of expense.

The result of these differences in national sentiment and of national interest was that Britain and France did not maintain a common front in enforcing the treaty. While the French wanted to stand firm behind their treaty rights, the British wanted to negotiate away perceived German grievances. Needless to say, none of this escaped the notice of the Germans themselves, who saw in this disunity endless opportunities to advance their cause. 'One of the annoying features of the situation', wrote American diplomat Ellis Loring Dresel,

> is the Germans are, of course, making all the capital they can out of the discords between the Allies. . . . They are redoubling their efforts to drive a wedge between the Entente and it is necessary to be constantly on one's guard in talking to them, as they seize upon any incautious word of condemnation of the French with the utmost avidity.[47]

Yet the fact remains that, in the end, the Germans were successful. When it came to the crunch, Britain did not provide full backing to the French. On the contrary, one might even argue that during the Ruhr crisis, Britain actually opposed her supposed ally. This is certainly the view of Sally Marks. 'Britain', she writes, 'was increasingly opposed to all French claims, however well-grounded, particularly if Germany was likely to refuse.' Thus, when the

French most needed support, they 'faced [instead] an adamant Anglo-American-German front opposing application of the peace treaty . . .'.[48] The impact of this development was enormous. Abandoned as she was by her allies, even France was forced to give up on enforcement. Thus, by 1924, the once promising combination of powers who would uphold the peace settlement had been whittled away until none were left. What would that mean for the future?

THE ROAD TO WAR

In February 1919, Colonel Edward House, Woodrow Wilson's closest friend and confidant, wrote in his diary, 'If . . . we are so stupid as to let Germany train and arm a large army and again become a menace to the world, we would deserve the fate which such folly would bring upon us.'[49] This, of course, was the problem that the Treaty of Versailles had been designed to forestall. Yet, it failed to do so. Within less than twenty years large, highly trained and well-equipped German armies were once again marching through Europe, menacing the world. Traditional explanations account for this by means of the 'Carthaginian peace' theory – German resentment at their unjust treatment made a reaction inevitable. But Germany was not treated with all that much severity at Versailles. To begin with the terms were not, as we have seen, punitive. But, even if they had been, this would have been mitigated by the fact that they were not enforced. Almost from the very outset, the structure of limitations that were imposed on Germany were allowed progressively to unwind. Here was the treaty's key defect. 'The weakness of Versailles', as Walter McDougall has observed, 'was not that it displeased the Germans but that it also displeased the Allies. The Americans defected, the British turned pro-German. . . .'[50] And the Germans took full advantage of this fact to evade the treaty and rebuild their military strength.

Need it have been this way? On this point, it is hard to argue with the judgement of American historian William Keylor. The Treaty of Versailles, he observes, proved to be a failure less because of the inherent defects it contained than because it was never put into effect. It is impossible to imagine a Germany that had been compelled to fulfil its treaty obligations in their entirety endangering the peace of Europe.[51]

But a Germany that managed to persuade itself that it had not been defeated and which was allowed to evade its obligations was altogether another matter. It was just such a Germany that would invade Poland on 1 September 1939 and against whom Britain and France would then find themselves at war two days later.

THREE

From the Treaty of Brest-Litovsk to the Potsdam Conference: the Origins of the Cold War

'A World divided against itself cannot stand. . . . We do not expect the world to fall; but we do expect it will cease to be divided. It will become all one thing, or all the other'

Abraham Lincoln[1]

From the very moment of its outbreak, countless attempts have been made to explain the origins of the Cold War. Historians, political commentators and security analysts of all philosophical and ideological persuasions have cast their eyes back upon the unfolding international hostility with a view to finding the explanatory framework that best reveals how it came to pass. It is something of an irony, therefore, that the two works that shed the greatest light upon the origins of this conflict were not composed as part of this process of retrospective analysis, but were actually written prior to 1947, the 'watershed year' that many conventional accounts of the Cold War regard as its starting point.

The more famous of these two works was George F. Kennan's 'Long Telegram'. In 1946, Kennan, formerly head of the Russian desk at the State Department, but at that point *Chargé d'Affaires* at the American Embassy in Moscow, was called upon to compose a memorandum explaining the deterioration in Soviet–American relations that had followed the conclusion of the war against Nazi Germany. Kennan set about his task with a passion.[2] The root of the problem, he explained, was the different ideological perspectives of the two countries and their governments. While America and the western democracies, with their long traditions of compromise, might emphasize political pluralism and the toleration of alternative ideological viewpoints, this was anathema to Russia's Marxist government. Soviet dogma, Kennan explained, asserted that only communism was a valid political belief system and only communism could produce a reasonable form of government. All alternatives were, at a practical level, flawed and, at a moral level, evil. From this assumption, Kennan elaborated, there logically flowed a belief in an innate antagonism between communism and capitalism. This provided Soviet leaders with grounds for believing that the western democracies were irrevocably hostile to them. Further, it endowed the Soviet government with a political mission to undermine capitalist democratic governments and to replace them with Marxist regimes. As Kennan put it, it was from their communist ideology that Soviet leaders 'found justification for their instinctive fear of the outside world' and it was from the self-same ideology that they felt cause 'to seek security only in patient but deadly struggle for total destruction of rival power . . .'.[3] Such was Kennan's explanation for the problems which were bedevilling Soviet–American relations in 1946, and which he believed would continue to poison them in the years thereafter.

Less famous, but no less influential than Kennan's 'Long Telegram', was Sir Halford Mackinder's *Democratic Ideals and Reality*. Published in 1919 as an updated and expanded version of ideas that had first been aired in his ground-breaking 1904 article, 'The Geographic Pivot of History', this book postulated that much of mankind's story consisted of a struggle for global power. Such had been the pattern of the past and such would continue to be the pattern in the future. What made this less-than-original concept so important was Mackinder's prediction about the form that this contest would take in the coming era. He forecast that the key participants in this forthcoming struggle would be Germany and Russia and that the crucial battleground for their rivalry would be eastern Europe. Were either Germany or Russia to master eastern Europe and use it as a springboard to overrun the other, then,

Mackinder warned, that nation would be in a position to dominate the globe. This prophecy that a future German–Russian war, fought in and through eastern Europe, might leave one power controlling the other and ready to exert a hegemonic influence on the world, filled Mackinder with dread. Such an outcome, he warned, must be prevented by the other great nations combining in opposition. To many observers in later years, Operation Barbarossa in 1941 and the subsequent Soviet advance to the Elbe river in 1945 seemed to bear out Mackinder's prophecy. It also lent credence to his suggested countermeasures and explained why it was that Russia and the western powers found themselves in opposition following the defeat of Nazi Germany.[4]

Kennan's 'Long Telegram' and Mackinder's *Democratic Ideals and Reality* would be remarkable texts in almost any light. However, in the context of an examination of the origins of the Cold War, they acquire an extra prominence. Each of them encapsulates with astonishing clarity a particular theory as to how this conflict came into being. Kennan, with his emphasis on the different political belief systems of Soviet Russia and the democratic western states, provides the most cogent articulation of the view that rivalry between the Soviet Union and the west was, by definition, an ideological conflict.[5] Mackinder, by contrast, in suggesting that, for geographical and political reasons (the two staples of *realpolitik*) Russia was bound to attempt a push through eastern Europe into Germany as a platform for global power, presents the Cold War, in essence, as a geopolitical conflict. It was a Russian drive for power-political hegemony that met an inevitable counterreaction.

As the above examples illustrate, even before the Cold War was properly under way, explanations, both ideological and geopolitical, for a conflict between Russia and the west over the future of both eastern and central Europe had already been devised and refined. What is significant in the context of this study is that both theories, although purposely constructed by their respective authors in broad terms – the grand sweeps being ideology and geography – can, nevertheless, be used as the basis for much narrower analyses that have at their heart a discussion of the impact of different peace settlements. Kennan's view of the Cold War as an ideological conflict, for example, inevitably poses the question, how did a doctrinaire Marxist polity, able to challenge the democratic west, come into being in the first place? And no answer to this question can easily ignore the role of the Treaty of Brest-Litovsk in the formation of the Soviet Union. Equally, the use of Mackinder's geopolitical discourse as a basis for explaining the Cold War legitimizes detailed consideration of any international political agreements that put the Soviet Union in a position to exert its power over eastern Europe and certain portions of Germany. This, of course, leads directly to consideration of the wartime conferences between the Allied powers – especially those at Yalta and Potsdam – at which the future of Europe was discussed and decided.

Thus, in respect to both the ideological and the geopolitical explanations of the origins of the Cold War, it is apparent that these theories can be traced back to particular peace settlements. Consequently, it is to these settlements that this chapter will now turn.

THE TREATY OF BREST-LITOVSK AND THE IDEOLOGICAL ORIGINS OF THE COLD WAR

As the Seven Years' War or the Crimean War amply illustrates, over the centuries, Russia has regularly found herself involved in military and political disputes with its neighbours. Yet, these conflicts have rarely, if ever, been labelled as ideological in origin. Rather, they are normally perceived as 'Cabinet wars', fought, as was traditionally the case in the era of Clausewitzian great power rivalry, for dynastic, territorial or power-political reasons. Yet, as we have seen, the Cold War, like the French Revolutionary wars before it, is regarded as different in this respect. In this instance, a school of thought exists that holds the conflict to have been ideologically driven. What makes this interpretation possible, is the existence of the Soviet Union as a state dedicated to one particular political doctrine. As a result of its communist antecedents, the USSR was committed to a Marxist political system at home and to the advancement of the communist ideology abroad. As no other country shared this political position, this was a posture that put Soviet Russia into direct opposition to the world's other nations. Quite naturally, they felt threatened by the presence of a neighbouring state that advocated their overthrow by revolutionary means. Equally, the Soviet Union felt insecure in the knowledge that it was a solitary bastion of communist ideology in a hostile world. These feelings of threat and insecurity, it has been suggested, were at the heart of the Cold War.

The implications of this theory for a proper understanding of the origins of the Cold War are profound. If, as is posited, a direct relationship exists between the ideological position of the Soviet government and its political conflict with the west, then it naturally follows from this that the process by which the Russian state acquired its unique ideological character is central to the origins of the Cold War. So, how did Russia emerge as a messianic Marxist state? At one level, it might be assumed that the key determinants of this were the two revolutions of February and October 1917 (March and November 1917 in the new calendar). The first of these, after all, was responsible for the overthrow of the Tsarist regime; the second put the government into the hands of the Bolsheviks. Yet, while a case can certainly be made for the centrality of the Russian revolutions of 1917, several eminent historians believe that it was the Treaty of Brest-Litovsk rather than the revolutions that laid the definitive foundations of the Soviet regime. Prominent among such historians is the Harvard scholar Adam Ulam. 'Nothing in the history of Communism', he has asserted,

> . . . was of equal importance [to the Treaty of Brest-Litovsk]. October 25, 1917, was the day of the Bolshevik Revolution; March 3, 1918, when the agreement (if such it can be called), was signed in that dingy provincial town, was the real day of founding the Bolshevik-Communist state.[6]

The reasoning behind this statement, and others like it, is straightforward. As a result of the October Revolution, the Bolshevik forces had seized no more than the most tenuous control over a few of the key metropolitan centres in Russia, principally Petrograd and Moscow. This toehold gave them the opportunity to assert that they were the new sovereign authority in Russia on the basis that they occupied the main government buildings and dominated the capital, but it did not, in any sense, put this claim beyond contention. Large parts – indeed, the majority – of the country were still outside Bolshevik control, there were several rival centres of power, and many people saw no reason to recognize the legitimacy of the new regime and, in fact, had every intention of challenging it vigorously and at the earliest opportunity. In short, the Bolsheviks' grip on the reins of power was still anything but firm. As Richard Pipes observes in a view typical of much historical opinion, 'On October 26, 1917, the Bolsheviks did not so much seize power over Russia as stake a claim to it.'[7] Few contemporary observers believed that this assertion of authority would stand the test of time.

That the Bolsheviks were able to turn their uncertain claim to power into hard reality can be attributed in large measure to the Treaty of Brest-Litovsk. This is ironic given just how unpopular the peace settlement actually was among both the party leadership and the rank and file of the workers' movement. Nikolai Bukharin, the leading figure on the Left of the party, was only voicing the opinion of many senior Bolsheviks,[8] for example, when he maintained that accepting the harsh German terms was tantamount to 'turning the Party into a dungheap'.[9] 'No conscious revolutionary', he later added, 'would agree to such dishonour.'[10] Popular opinion was no less outraged than Bukharin. The *Petrogradskoe Ekho*, a moderate evening newspaper, was far from alone in damning the agreement as 'treasonous, . . . destructive to the international proletarian movement, and deeply harmful to the interests of Russian workers, the revolution, and the Russian economy in general'.[11] Nevertheless, the Bolshevik leader, Vladimir Illyich Lenin, insisted that the new government sign the treaty and he did so for the simple reason that, so far as he was concerned, the survival of the new regime was totally dependent upon it. This is a judgement with which many historians would readily concur. As a recent study has put it, utterly unacceptable though it may have been, the treaty was 'the price Lenin had to pay to acquire and retain power'.[12] This relationship between the Bolsheviks' future as a government and the signing of the treaty reflected what Lenin called 'the facts and the potentialities of the situation', that is to say the hard reality of circumstances in Russia at the time.

Foremost among these 'realities' was the unpalatable truth that the country that the Bolsheviks had seized was a nation breaking down under the strain of war. So disastrous was the military situation that, as Lenin was acutely conscious, without an immediate peace settlement, the Bolshevik government was in danger of being rapidly swept away by the Germans, whose armies were but a short distance from the capital.

In part, this situation was an inherited one. It reflected the fact that Russia had been at war for three years and had, to all intents and purposes, been defeated. The Russian army, after three years in the field, was experiencing the inevitable demoralization and lack of cohesion that came from poor leadership, inadequate supplies, mounting casualties and constant retreats. As the *Stavka*, the Russian High Command, readily acknowledged, these privations had reduced the army to 'a huge, weary, shabby, and ill-fed mob of angry men united by their common thirst for peace and by common disappointment'.[13]

However, this was not the only reason that the Russian military was in tatters by the end of 1917. A further factor in the army's sorry condition was of the Bolsheviks' own making and stemmed from their seizure of power and the methods that had been used to achieve this. In order to ensure that their *coup d'état* would be successful, the Bolsheviks had done everything possible to undermine the military potential of the previous regime, the 'Provisional Government' of Alexander Kerensky. Accordingly, they had spent the months prior to the October Revolution spreading dissent and causing disaffection among the already weary Russian soldiery. While this had ensured that Kerensky's supporters had been unable to mount an effective opposition to the Bolshevik *fronde*, and was, at one level, responsible for the Bolsheviks being in government in the first place, it also meant that the new regime inherited weakened armed forces that lacked the will, let alone the ability, to stem a future German assault.[14] Consequently, unless the fighting was ended – and soon – there was little to prevent the German military, should they so choose, from sweeping away the new regime. But, unless the Bolsheviks were willing to sign a peace settlement, what incentive had the Germans to restrain their military might?

This was the argument that Lenin presented to the party leadership. 'At present Russian armies are powerless to stop a German advance', he informed them. As a result, he continued,

> if Russia persisted in its refusal to accept current German peace terms, it would eventually have to accept even more onerous ones: but this would be done not by the Bolsheviks but by their successors, because in the meantime the Bolsheviks would have been toppled from power.[15]

When this point of view was questioned – Josef Stalin, for one, asked, 'Maybe we don't have to sign the treaty?' – Lenin was forthright. 'If you don't, you're signing the death warrant for the Soviet regime within three weeks. I haven't the slightest hesitation.'[16] By contrast, as Lenin never ceased to point out, signing the treaty, notwithstanding its admittedly humiliating terms, 'did not affect Soviet authority'.[17] For Lenin this was the cardinal point: everything and anything could legitimately be sacrificed in order to stay in power. Since the Germans had the means to end the revolution and destroy the Soviet state, but would refrain from doing so if appeased, their terms had to be met. Such is what transpired and, thus, did the Treaty of Brest-Litovsk preserve Bolshevik power from its most immediate threat – the Prusso-German war-machine.

It was not only against the danger of external threats that the Treaty of Brest-Litovsk served to preserve Bolshevik power; the treaty also acted to enhance the party's chances of survival *vis-à-vis* the many difficult internal challenges that had to be faced within Russia.

One of the key problems facing the new regime was that it lacked a broad domestic powerbase. As elections to the Constituent Assembly would clearly demonstrate, the Bolsheviks, despite their pretensions to govern in the name of the masses, were decidedly a minority grouping. That they had come to power at all was due partly to their ability to concentrate their forces in the key urban centres of Petrograd and Moscow – this had obviously paid major dividends during the October Revolution – and was partly due to their skill at gaining, through effective propaganda, the tacit acceptance of large numbers of people from outside their core supporters' network. In this latter context, it must be recognized that among their most memorable and successful slogans was the rallying cry of 'Peace, Bread and Land'. The significance of this slogan starting with the word 'peace' cannot be stressed too much – in war-weary Russia this was the most compelling concept imaginable. Many of the people who were willing to tolerate the Bolshevik seizure of power, and a fair proportion of those who actively supported it, did so in the belief that what differentiated the Bolsheviks from their rivals was this unambiguous promise to end the war. Lenin was conscious of this. Unless the new regime quickly brought the fighting to a close, he maintained, 'the peasant army, unbearably exhausted by the war, . . . will overthrow the socialist workers' government'.[18] Most contemporary historians would concur with Lenin's judgement on this issue, as a passage from Adam Ulam illustrates. 'The Bolsheviks', he observes, 'had promised peace. If peace were not forthcoming, if the soldier could not go home, no excuses would prevent Lenin from sharing the fate of Nicholas Romanov and Kerensky.'[19] The Treaty of Brest-Litovsk as the vehicle for bringing this promise of peace to fruition was, therefore, a prerequisite for the regime's long-term existence.

This was not the only aspect of the domestic situation that made peace essential. Equally salient was the fact that the Bolsheviks had numerous internal enemies. Although some of them had been temporarily silenced by the October Revolution, it was clear that in the long term the new regime would have to fight for its very existence. But herein lay a problem: at this stage, the

Bolsheviks lacked the military muscle to withstand a concerted attack from their numerous opponents. As Lenin all too readily admitted, 'The formation of a Socialist army, with the Red Guard as its nucleus, has only just begun. . . . It will take months and months to create an army imbued with socialist principles.'[20] Accordingly, a *peredyshka*, or breathing space in which to prepare for this struggle, was vital to the survival of the new regime. No one was more conscious of this fact than Lenin. 'To make a success of Socialism in Russia,' he informed his fellow Bolsheviks in his now-famous *Twenty-One Theses for Peace*, 'a certain time, some months at least is necessary, during which the Socialist Government can have a free hand. . . .'[21] The reason for this was straightforward. 'The bourgeoisie', he explained with customary bluntness, 'has to be throttled and for that we need both hands free.'[22] It was just this function of freeing the Bolsheviks of their external difficulties so that they could concentrate on their domestic problems that he intended the Treaty of Brest-Litovsk to fulfil. In achieving this, as John Wheeler-Bennett has noted, 'The Peace of Brest-Litovsk preserved Bolshevism. Its conclusion provided Lenin with the essential "breathing-space" for consolidating the Russian Revolution against the attempts to overthrow it from within.'[23]

If the transformation of Russia into a revolutionary Marxist state was the essential precondition for the Cold War, then it can be seen that the Treaty of Brest-Litovsk played an essential part in the origins of this conflict. True, it was as a result of the October Revolution rather than the treaty that the Bolsheviks found themselves ensconced inside Russia's government buildings, able to make the claim that they were now the legitimate political authority in the country. However, it cannot be denied that the foundations of their power remained anything but solidly grounded at this time. Not only were they required to stage another coup in January 1918 to retain control (the action in question was the dispersing of the Constituent Assembly)[24] but, in addition, they still faced the very real possibility of being overthrown either by their foreign or by their domestic enemies. It was against these dangers that the Treaty of Brest-Litovsk offered meaningful solutions. It was, for example, the Treaty of Brest-Litovsk that neutralized the danger of German military power by removing the incentive for the Germans to continue their operations in the eastern theatre. Similarly, it was the Treaty of Brest-Litovsk that provided the new regime with the opportunity to prepare for the inevitable civil war against the Bolsheviks' internal enemies. Of course, the Treaty of Brest-Litovsk did not, in itself, alleviate the need for the Bolsheviks (by then known as the Communists) to fight the Russian Civil War – and, during the course of this struggle, the Soviet state could still have fallen – but the Treaty of Brest-Litovsk did give Lenin and his party the time necessary to make themselves ready for this conflict. In effect, therefore, the breathing space of Brest-Litovsk meant the difference between the Communists winning and losing the civil war; as such, it meant the difference between the establishment and the overthrow of the Soviet state; and, for this reason and on this basis, it meant the difference between the creation and the early demise of the one essential prerequisite for the Cold War: an ideologically based Marxist revolutionary regime ready to challenge the existing order. No wonder, therefore, that a recent television documentary series on the Cold War has concluded that 'it was after the First World War, in a clash of ideologies . . . that the Cold War had its origins'.[25]

THE POTSDAM CONFERENCE AND THE GEOPOLITICAL ORIGINS OF THE COLD WAR

If, as we have just seen, there is one school of thought that regards the Cold War as an ideological conflict born out of the dying days of the First World War, then it must be acknowledged that this is by no means an uncontested point of view. Another perspective exists that, while perceiving the Cold War to have emerged out of the embers of an earlier conflict and its subsequent peace settlement, also holds that the war in question was not the First World War, but the Second and that the peace settlement at issue was not the Treaty of Brest-Litovsk but the arrangement of European affairs implemented by the Allies in the wake of the German surrender on 8 May 1945. This latter interpretation regards the Cold War less as a clash of ideologies than as a geopolitical struggle that had as its roots a conflict over how the future of Germany should be determined. Typifying this viewpoint is the statement by British historian David Reynolds that 'the struggle for mastery of Germany lay at the heart of the grand alliance and also of the Cold War'.[26]

That a vigorous debate should have taken place in the mid-1940s over the destiny of Germany was the inevitable product of that nation's recent history. On two occasions in the first half of the twentieth century, the German Reich had launched premeditated wars of aggression that had devastated her continental neighbours and plunged the globe head first into the horrors of total war. The Second World War, the most recent example of this phenomenon, had been especially horrific. Not only had tens of millions of service personnel died on the battlefield but an even larger number of non-combatants had also been viciously slaughtered in the most dreadful of circumstances. In part, this was because of improvements in weapons technology that made the comprehensive aerial bombardment of cities both possible and commonplace. More particularly, however, it reflected the fact that Nazi Germany's initial campaign successes had given this most brutal of regimes the opportunity to export its barbaric and inhuman ideological programme to numerous occupied countries. The bestial treatment accorded to those people unfortunate enough to fall under the Nazi yoke – including the cruel and systematic murder of millions of innocent civilians condemned on the sole grounds of their ethnic origin, sexual orientation or political affiliations – naturally left a lasting impression on global opinion and served to underscore the point that German behaviour had been beyond the pale. The inevitable consequence of this was that by the early 1940s all of the other great powers regarded Germany as the principal threat both to their own security and to the peace of the world. It naturally followed that solving the so-called 'German problem' in a manner that guarded against a repetition of the recent catastrophes was the major issue on the minds of the world's leaders. However, as events were soon to show, identifying that this was the central problem in global affairs and actually finding a solution to it were two very different matters. At the heart of the difficulties that were to be faced in this respect was the inadequate framework for peace that had been laid down in 1945.

In spite of all the thought that went into it, the settlement imposed upon Germany immediately after the Second World War was a most haphazard affair. As the ever-erudite Arthur M. Schlesinger Jr put it, 'Peacemaking after the Second World War was not so much a tapestry as it was a hopelessly raveled and knotted mess of yarn'.[27] This situation was not for want of prior discussion. The main Allies in the anti-Hitler coalition – at this stage, Great Britain, America and the Soviet Union – had gathered to deliberate upon the arrangements for the postwar settlement of the German question on numerous occasions, of which the 'Big Three' meetings at Teheran in November 1943, at Yalta in February 1945, and Potsdam in July and August of the same year were only the most famous.[28] Yet, despite the high profile nature of these conferences, no final or conclusive decisions on future policy were ever reached. Instead of the outlines of a peace settlement that might have been ratified in the form of an international treaty, the Allies arrived only at interim arrangements for the administration of their defeated foe pending the conclusion of the still elusive final settlement.

These interim arrangements were nothing if not paradoxical: they were at once both clear and at the same time contradictory; they were simultaneously comprehensive and yet incomplete. Nothing illustrates this better than the stipulations on German unity.[29] On the one hand, the Allies seemed to have possessed a common conception that Germany should be kept together as a unified nation state.[30] Therefore, while the government of the Third Reich, which was equally repugnant to all the Allies, was dissolved and its leadership arrested, in its place was established an Allied Control Council, which, in theory at least, exercised supreme authority over the entire country. Moreover, special emphasis was placed on the fact that the German economy was to be run as a common entity, the management of which was to be undertaken jointly by the Allies. As the protocol of the Potsdam conference put it, 'During the period of occupation Germany shall be treated as a single economic unit. To this end common policies shall be established. . . .' These, the protocol went on to observe, were to be formed in such key areas as 'mining and industrial production . . .; agriculture, forestry and fishing; wages, prices and rationing; import and export programmes . . .; currency . . .; reparation . . . [and] transport and communications'.[31]

These pronouncements about a comprehensive quadripartite regime for Germany would have been quite unremarkable were it not for the fact that all the practical measures taken to give force to these principles vitiated (according to American historian Marc Trachtenberg this was deliberate)[32] against their successful implementation. To begin with, it was decided that all the decisions taken by the Allied Control Council would have to be unanimous; the Allies – now four in number with the addition of France – would act together in German affairs or not at all. It soon became evident that this rule, far from demonstrating a common Allied front to the world, actually stopped nearly all common action dead in its tracks. For, while the Allies could all accept that Germany should be subject to denazification, demilitarization, decartelization and democratization, the aptly named 'four ds', they soon discovered that they could agree on precious little else. Thus, few measures of an all-German character were ever implemented by the council.

This proved problematic because of another decision that had been taken at Yalta and Potsdam, namely that each of the four Allies should be assigned an occupation zone within Germany, the administration of which would be entrusted to the occupying power. The natural consequence of this arrangement was that executive authority in Germany was divided among the different Allies, each of which was able to run a section of Germany according to its own distinct policy preference agenda. In the best of circumstances this was hardly a recipe for German unity. In the situation that actually prevailed, with the four Allies quite unable to agree upon joint decisions for Germany as a whole, it inevitably led to the various powers going their own way in their respective occupation zones. It soon became common practice that contentious policies that could not command unanimity among the Allies were introduced by one or more of the powers on a zonal rather than on an all-German basis. In this manner, there was created a *de facto* division of Germany along the administrative lines instituted at Yalta and Potsdam that ran contrary to the *de jure* pronouncements about German unity that had been issued simultaneously at the very same conferences.

The implications of this situation for the future conduct of international relations were to prove profound. As a result of the different interpretations placed upon the Yalta and Potsdam accords, two contradictory potential settlements of the German question were created at the same time. On the one hand, it was proposed that a united but peaceful Germany should be the end result of the Allied deliberations; on the other hand, a divided Germany, the different parts of which were tied to different global powers, was emerging as a distinct practical possibility. That these outcomes were incompatible and that this miscegenation could only be resolved by some kind of agreement among the victorious powers was always apparent. Unfortunately, the question of which of these alternative arrangements would be brought into effect and on what basis, far from producing concurrence among the Allies, quickly became a major source of dissonance among them, putting them at loggerheads and, thus, in effect, engendering the Cold War.

That there should have been disputes among the powers over any ambiguities in regard to the future of Germany was, as we have seen, a natural reflection of the country's potential to influence the direction of global affairs. This was, after all, the nation that had launched two devastating world wars. It was also a country that many people believed was aggressive by nature and which might, under certain circumstances, embark upon a third attempt at global conquest. Not surprisingly, preventing this was the paramount consideration of the victors, who looked to the forthcoming peace treaty to ensure their security against a resurgence of German power. But which of the two possible settlements now available best offered protection against this eventuality?

In theory, as the various Potsdam declarations on German unity make clear, the preferred solution of the major powers – in their public pronouncements at least – was to create a unified German state, the peaceable nature of which would be ensured by viable international guarantees. However, there were problems of interpretation in implementing such a settlement. What, after all, constituted acceptable international guarantees?

Individual countries had difficulties establishing a position on this point. The initial British proposals on achieving 'Security against the possibility of future German aggression', for example, concentrated on disarmament and 'eliminating the basis of Germany's industrial war potential'. As a Cabinet memorandum on this matter recorded, 'Germany would be prohibited for an indefinite period from maintaining armed forces, possessing arms and munitions or maintaining plant for their manufacture'. Furthermore, Germany would be occupied 'for a sufficiently long period . . . to allow the changes in her industrial structure . . . to have a chance of becoming permanently established'.[33] Yet, as policymakers in London were all too well aware, this proposal looked very much like the formula that had been tried after the First World War and which had so conspicuously failed. If introduced a second time, might it not merely fail once again? This possibility was raised by British officials in the annexed discussion papers. One leading anxiety, forcefully expressed by an anonymous civil servant, was that any Allied 'action taken during the occupation can in the course of time be reversed by the Germans . . .'. Yet, if draconian measures were taken to prevent such a reversal, this merely exposed the countervailing danger that a 'system of industrial security . . . so oppressive . . . would only give an opportunity to another dictator to seize power on a programme of national revenge'.[34] In other words, under the British scheme, one was damned whatever one did and there seemed no way out of this conundrum that would avoid a repetition of the 1920s and 1930s. As the American historian Marc Trachtenberg has shown, this sense that a policy of guarantees might duplicate the perceived failings of the Versailles settlement of 1919 and lead inexorably to the same unwelcome results, quite naturally, tended to discredit it as a solution.[35] But, where, then, did this leave British policy?

If the policymakers of individual Allied countries had difficulties in ascertaining the best method of ensuring the future good behaviour of a united Germany when discussing it privately among themselves, this was nothing compared to the problems that arose when the various Allied leaders began to consider this point collectively on a quadripartite basis. For, it quickly transpired that each of the Allied nations had its own ideas as to what a future united German state might look like and was quite unwilling to entertain alternative suggestions. Inter-Allied meetings called to deliberate about such matters tended, in the words of Sir William Strang, the chief political adviser to the British occupation authorities, to be 'unusually unfruitful'. Not only did the contradictory positions advanced by the various delegations act as a 'red rag' to the other parties to the discussion, but they invariably led to 'some display of bad temper'. His description of one such meeting from early October 1945 is illustrative of the mood of such events:

> The broad position, therefore, is that the French, by their reservations on Central German Administrations, are bringing almost all important business to a stand-still; that the Russians oppose any proposal that is likely to open a window into their zone; that this attitude on the part of these two delegations exasperates the U.S. delegation and almost brings them to say that if it cannot soon be decided to govern Germany as a whole through Central German Administrations, it will hardly be worth while maintaining the Quadripartite Organisations at all.[36]

What made it so difficult to agree a common programme for Germany? The root of the problem was security. All the Allies, with the major exception of France, believed that a reformed and united country was the best solution to the German problem, but – and this was the significant proviso – only if the new Germany was created in such a manner that it could never again pose any kind of threat to them. To achieve this, each of the Allies believed that the new Germany had to be put together in a particular way.

In practice, this meant that everyone wanted to solve the German problem but only on their own terms. For example, politicians in the United States hoped to see a Germany emerge that was organized on the western political model and which was orientated towards the democratic world in global affairs. This, however, was totally unacceptable to the leaders of the Soviet Union who were worried that a united Germany tied to the west might one day be used against them politically or even militarily. After the experience of the two world wars, this was not a possibility, however remote it might have been, that could be countenanced. Yet, their alternative programme of a Soviet-sponsored unitary Germany, diplomatically orientated towards Russia, was no less intolerable to the western powers, who were not in any sense prepared for the entirety of Germany's military and industrial potential to fall into Stalin's grasp. After all, if Russia dominated Germany, it had in its hands a sufficient concentration of raw economic power and political influence to dominate the rest of Europe, if not the globe. And none of the western powers, to cite Paul Kennedy's telling phrase, 'wanted to see the Wehrmacht's domination of Europe merely replaced by the Red Army's'.[37]

With no version of a unified Germany acceptable to all of the powers, deadlock in the negotiations was almost inevitable. This would not have mattered if the alternative option of a divided Germany had been something that the Allies were willing to endorse instead. But this was not a direction – again, France excluded – that they wanted to take.

For the Russians, a divided Germany, where they controlled only the east of the country, had the major disadvantage of putting Germany's industrial heartland, that is to say the Ruhr valley, outside their reach. In the short term this was problematic because the Soviet Union, having been systematically despoiled and looted during the recent conflict with the *Wehrmacht*, hoped to receive significant reparations payments from Germany to help rebuild the shattered Russian economy. Yet the prospect of their receiving a large transfer of resources diminished considerably if Germany were not treated as a single economic unit and if, as a consequence, they could only obtain production or capital from the eastern zone. Because the eastern zone was more rural than the western zones, it did not contain the plant or output that the Soviets needed in the quantities that they wanted.

In the long term such an outcome was also problematic because there were major military and strategic implications to the division of Germany if, as would inevitably be the case, it led to the creation of a west German state, formed out of the American, British and French zones, that incorporated the Ruhr valley. Such a polity, by virtue of containing the major component of Germany's industrial strength, would certainly have considerable military potential. Furthermore, if it were tied to the western powers, and therefore outside Soviet control, how would this military potential be used? It was naturally feared by the authorities in the Kremlin that such a state would lay claim to the Soviet zone of Germany or, even worse, attempt to gain control of those lands east of the Oder–Neisse line that had been forcibly transferred from Germany to Poland and Russia in 1945. Given that such a policy of territorial irredentism could only be carried out militarily, the Soviets' major nightmare of a revived and actively hostile Germany was implicit in a policy of division carried out by the western powers.

If the Russians had such grounds for opposing the partition of Germany, the British and Americans also had reasons for being sceptical about the desirability of a divided Germany. For one thing, given the historic strength of German nationalism, there was perceived to be a danger that the process of division could alienate the Germans from those held to be the destroyers of their national unity. If this were so then to accept publicly the inevitability of division was tantamount to surrendering any possibility of possessing long-term influence over the German people. Consequently, partition was only acceptable, so noted a senior British official, if it were possible to 'make the Russians appear to the German public as the saboteurs of German unity'.[38] Until such time, however, it would hardly be pragmatic to adopt it as western policy.

In addition to this, there was also the matter of public perception in their own countries. Given that a four-power solution to

Germany had been the professed intention of the Potsdam agreement and that mechanisms like the Allied Control Council, however feeble they might have been, had been created to ensure it, there was a real danger that, were the British and Americans seen to be going back on this, it would be perceived at best as an act of weakness, or at worst as a retreat tantamount to a severe diplomatic defeat. Some might also ask: was it desirable to give up on this outcome and hand millions of Germans over to a harsh future of Soviet rule? This was not a public relations challenge that western leaders approached with any relish.

Clearly, therefore, just as in the case of establishing a unitary German state, there were complexities to advocating a policy of Germany's partition. It seemed that whichever way the victorious powers turned in their efforts to interpret the principles enshrined in the Potsdam accords, major obstacles were encountered. This, of course, made the practical application of the Potsdam agreement next to impossible and this, in turn, made disagreements about the future of Germany almost inevitable. Yet, given that the solution to this question was universally acknowledged to be vital to the security of all the powers; that none of these powers could, therefore, afford to back down over this issue; and that, by virtue of them all possessing an occupation zone within Germany, and, thus, a direct military presence there, none of them could be compelled to give way either, the potential clearly existed for bitter diplomatic and political conflicts to emerge and escalate.

In any case this was what transpired. Discussions over Germany, being essential, were held with regularity but consistently ended in deadlock. For the reasons already outlined, no agreement could be reached on a unitary solution but equally the powers refused to compromise and settle on a scheme of division. Partition, when it did come, was less an indication of a new spirit of cooperation than a sign that relations between the victorious powers had reached such a nadir that the *status quo* had been institutionalized for want of an acceptable alternative. Naturally, a pattern of political conflict emerged to reflect this new situation. Ensconced in their own zones, the former Allies resorted to developing them separately, maintaining vociferously all the while that they still sought an all-German solution, that it was the other powers that were responsible for blocking this outcome, and that the actions of their opponents in this respect were illegitimate. In effect, a geopolitical struggle over Germany's future had begun. This conflict was to be called the 'Cold War'.

CONCLUSION

As we have seen, first in 1918 and again in the years from 1943 to 1945, peace settlements were arranged that had considerable bearing on the future pattern of conflict in Europe and, indeed, the wider world. At Brest-Litovsk in 1918, German and Bolshevik negotiators hammered out a treaty that, in preserving the Russian powerbase of Lenin's messianic revolutionary government, made possible a later ideological conflict between the capitalist west and the communist east. During the Second World War two-and-a-half decades later, at several inter-Allied conferences held at various times and locations, the essential basis for a future confrontation over the political destiny of Germany was methodically, if accidentally, put into place. In this paradoxically amicable way the foundations for a 45-year geopolitical conflict between America and the Soviet Union were laid.

Which of these interpretations better explains the genesis of the Cold War? Any process of evaluating these theories should acknowledge that both of them have well-grounded analytical roots that hark back to old-established philosophical traditions. The notion that Russia would one day be at the centre of an international ideological rivalry, for example, is an idea that has had a considerable pedigree in western political thinking. As early as 1851, the French historian Jules Michelet observed with some prescience the Russian tendency to position ideology in the vanguard of its progress into world affairs. As he put it, 'Yesterday Russia told us, "I am Christianity"; tomorrow she will tell us, "I am Socialism".'[39] In recasting this idea to fit the circumstances of 1946, George Kennan and the other advocates of 'containment', were, therefore, merely adapting themselves to a venerable epistemological tradition of seeing ideology as the core of Russia's international behaviour.

Explaining the Cold War as a geopolitical rivalry, however, can likewise be rooted in early theoretical precedents. Alexis de Tocqueville, to cite a famous example, had predicted as early as 1835 in his ground-breaking analysis *De la Démocratie en Amérique* that Russia and the United States were the globe's incipient superpowers. As he put it, these were the only nations

> still in the act of growth . . . these alone are proceeding with ease and celerity along a path to which no limit can be perceived. . . . Their starting-point is different and their courses are not the same; yet each of them seems marked out by the will of Heaven to sway the destinies of half the globe.[40]

Thus, even before Mackinder, whose views we have already looked at, provided his analysis of the geopolitical potential for an east-west antagonism, the future status and collision of Russia and America had been foreseen. It was, in other words, already a venerable leitmotiv of western political thinking.

Given the deep antecedents and thorough development of both the ideological and geopolitical explanations for the origins of the Cold War, it is perhaps not altogether surprising that many current analyses of the genesis of this rivalry are unwilling to choose between them. Instead most commentators are apt to suggest that in explaining the outbreak of this conflict one is presented not so much with an either/or as with a both/and scenario: neither theory has a monopoly on the truth, it is said, both have some validity and explanatory power. Illustrative of such thinking is the opinion of Imanuel Geiss that 'the Cold War combined a contest between two global ideological systems with power-political rivalry between two superpowers'.[41] In the context of this study of the role of peace settlements in engendering renewed conflict, this is a framework that fits perfectly. As we have seen, the ideological preconditions for the Cold War were forged by the Treaty of Brest-Litovsk; the actual occasion for the blossoming of this rivalry was provided by the failure of Russia and America to agree on the meaning of the inter-Allied pronouncements over Germany that had been concluded during the Second World War. Both circumstances were necessary for the Cold War to come into being, and both were the by-products, intended or otherwise, of complex but flawed peace negotiations.

PART TWO

The Near East

FOUR

The First World War and the Turkish Peace Settlement: from Mudros to Sèvres to Lausanne, 1918–23

In his Whig history of England, G.M. Trevelyan observed that in the 'successful conduct of a world war there are two distinct operations both very difficult – the winning of the victory in arms, and afterwards the making of a stable peace'.[1] While the First World War ended in an Entente victory, the peace settlements decided at the Paris Peace Conference did not stand the test of time. Nowhere is this more apparent than with the peace settlement with Turkey. Following an armistice at Mudros in October 1918, Turkey and the Entente powers signed a peace treaty for the Middle East at Sèvres in August 1920.[2] Never ratified by the government in Istanbul, the Turkish element of the Sèvres settlement neither created nor restored stability; instead, it led to a war between Greece and Turkey as Turkish nationalists fought to overturn the terms of Sèvres.[3] They succeeded. Victorious over the Greeks in 1922, Turkey was able, within the space of three years, to reverse the peace settlement and negotiate as an equal for a new, durable peace treaty at Lausanne in 1923.[4] Sèvres ranks as one of the biggest failures of the Paris Peace Conference, to be compared with the much-maligned Versailles settlement with Germany. So how did the victorious Entente powers after the First World War turn the peace into another war that consumed and laid waste western Asia Minor from 1919 to 1922?

A JUST PEACE?

Firstly, the proposed Turkish settlement was not a 'just' peace but one dictated by Britain and designed to meet a key foreign policy objective of securing imperial communications across the eastern Mediterranean and Middle East so as to link up the British empire. As Harry N. Howard observed, the settlement sidelined France, Italy and America, and was effectively 'the English terms of peace'.[5] The American diplomat Joseph C. Grew described it as 'one of the most primitive peace arrangements and one of the most daring and deliberate divisions of war spoils in modern history'.[6] The terms imposed were harsh: while the Sultan remained as a titular figurehead, the Ottoman empire ceased to exist and it lost all its territory in the Arab Middle East. What would become Turkey was reduced to an Anatolian rump, plus a small strip of European Turkey up to the Chatalja lines 20 miles west of Istanbul. Sèvres added parts of eastern Anatolia to a new republic of Armenia, gave substantial parts of Thrace to Greece and raised the possibility of an autonomous Kurdistan. In addition, the settlement gave the administration of the town of Smyrna (Izmir) and its hinterland to Greece, Turkey's long-standing rival, with the promise of a plebiscite for the local population after five years of Greek occupation. Finally, Sèvres allowed for international control of Istanbul and the surrounding Straits zone.[7]

Greek control of Smyrna ran counter to the notion of self-determination embodied in the Fourteen Points of America's President Woodrow Wilson. While Eleutherios Venizelos, the articulate Greek leader, based his claim to expand Greek territory around Smyrna on the principle of self-determination, his population statistics for western Anatolia are contestable and open to the charge of manipulation.[8] Venizelos established a marginal Greek majority for Smyrna by using pre-war statistics, and by including the Greek population on neighbouring Aegean islands. However, the population changes of the war years meant that the pre-war census figures failed to match the demographic position of 1919.[9] The Greeks' misuse of statistics had little impact on the pro-Greek British leader, David Lloyd George, who recorded in his memoirs how the Turks rather than the Greeks were working 'incessantly and with a barbaric guile to improve their statistical position'.[10] In April 1919, the 'big four' of Britain, France, Italy and America unilaterally agreed that Turkey would not be consulted on new boundaries, and that the limit of Greek-run Smyrna could 'be extended beyond strictly ethnographic lines, in such a way as to give the ports on the western coast some breathing space'.[11]

Why did the Allies impose such a harsh peace on a marginal central alliance power? The answer can be found in the marriage of the foreign policy objectives of the two great victors in the 'spoils' of Sèvres: Britain and Greece.[12] The Turkish settlement was the opportunity for Lloyd George to solve the perennial problem of the 'eastern question' by establishing Greece as Britain's ally in the region; for Greece, the peace was an opportunity to stake its irredentist claim, with British assistance, to large swathes of Asia Minor. As Lloyd George wrote in his account of the peace conference, a strong Greece, with the coast of Asia Minor and allied to Britain, would prevent the Mediterranean from becoming an 'Italian lake'.[13] Lloyd George envisaged Greece as Britain's 'future agent', able to exert control over the eastern Mediterranean.[14] Lloyd George even conceived of a 'greater' Greece that would have done away with Turkey altogether.[15] When, in 1920, pro-Turkish British MPs lobbied Lloyd George, his reaction was to 'wait and see' before tearing up treaties 'based on vital British interests'.[16] In his sympathetic biography of the Turkish nationalist leader Mustafa Kemal, Patrick Balfour (Lord) Kinross argued that Lloyd George viewed Turkey as a 'convenient repository from which other powers might be compensated and other concessions obtained in return'.[17] Kinross was right. The Greeks could serve Britain by replacing the Ottoman empire as the guardian of imperial communications to India. Frances Stevenson, Lloyd George's secretary (and mistress), noted in her diary that Lloyd George 'says that if the Greeks succeed . . . Turkish rule is at an end. A new Greek empire will be founded, friendly to Britain, & it will help all our interests in the East. He is perfectly convinced he is right over this, & is willing to stake everything on it.'[18] With this in mind, Lloyd George gave his full support to Venizelos, stating that it was British policy 'to assist and support Greece and especially M. Venizelos as a close and friendly ally'.[19]

By using Greece as the proxy to pursue his strategy, Lloyd George opened a Pandora's box of contending nationalisms. In the nineteenth century there had emerged in Greece a *'megali idhea'* ('great idea') to restore all 'historic' Greek lands in the Balkans, Aegean and Asia Minor.[20] The 1864 constitution gave King George I the title 'King of the Hellenes', rather than 'King of Greece'. The nineteenth-century Greek nationalist John Kolettis was not alone when he claimed Constantinople as the 'great capital' for Hellenism.[21] After victory in the Balkan wars of 1912–13, Greece emerged as a regional power and, under Venizelos's leadership, the 'great idea' moved, as Richard Clogg observed, beyond the 'romantic nationalist to the realms of possibility'.[22] The defeat of the Ottoman empire in 1918 boosted Greek territorial claims and opened the eyes of Greek nationalists to the vision of a restored Byzantium with, once again, Constantinople as its capital. In November 1918, Earl Granville, Britain's Minister in Athens, wrote home to A.J. Balfour, the Foreign Secretary, detailing the extensive Greek nationalist claims across the region:

> I have addressed to you a series of despatches recording the views expressed in the Greek press, with ever-increasing strength and even violence, regarding the right of Greece in the final settlement after the war. At first the claims were moderate, or were, at all events, put moderately, but now it may, I think, be said that there is not a single paper . . . which does not claim for Greece Northern Epirus, the Dodecanese, Cyprus, Thrace, and the western coast of Asia Minor, while many also claim Constantinople and the northern coast of Asia Minor.[23]

Venizelos's debating skills and charm facilitated the strategic union of Britain and Greece. After Venizelos paid a visit to the

Foreign Office, Lord Curzon wrote to Granville how he 'contented himself with admiring the formidable argumentative arsenal which the Greek statesman had provided himself'.[24] When presenting his case at the Paris Peace Conference, Venizelos 'flattered Lloyd George with a reference to his Welsh speaking, complimented Wilson on the virtues of American teachers in northern Epirus, and put the council in a good mood by showing them photographs of sponge fishing in the Dodecanese'.[25] The press baron Lord Beaverbrook recalled how Venizelos was Lloyd George's 'intimate friend', while Grew, the American diplomat, remembered how 'Venizelos's personality is so attractive and his manner so forceful and convincing that one is always impressed when he talks.'[26] While military figures such as General Henry Wilson, the British Chief of the Imperial General Staff (CIGS), were less impressed by Venizelos, his determination was very apparent: 'Amongst the "Frocks" he [Venizelos] holds a very strong position because, alone of all the "Frocks", he knows exactly what he wants.'[27]

Venizelos was also fortunate in that he was putting his case to a receptive Turkophobe audience. In November 1912, at a dinner held at 11 Downing Street for the Greek Consul General in London, John Stavridi, following Turkish defeats in the first Balkan War, Lloyd George proposed a toast: '"I drink to the Allies, the representatives of one of whom we have here tonight, and may the Turk be turned out of Europe and sent to . . . where he came from".' Stavridi noted in his diary that Lloyd George also wanted to evict the Turks from Constantinople.[28] Later, in May 1919, the month that Greek troops landed at Smyrna, Lloyd George told President Wilson and Georges Clemenceau, the French leader, that he had no 'scruples' regarding the Turks. In his view, the Turks had 'no rights over a country which they were only able to turn into a desert. . . . The Turk, when he has the slightest degree of power, is a brute. Whatever the difficulties we may encounter from the Mohammedans of India, we must put an end to the Turkish regime.'[29] Beaverbrook recalled how Lloyd George was a 'great partisan of Greek imperial pretensions. He believed the Greeks were a strong people, prolific, and capable of establishing and maintaining a domination of the Eastern Mediterranean.'[30] Harold Nicolson, with the British delegation in Paris, echoed the sentiments of many brought up on stories of Turkish atrocities, writing that he had 'no sympathy whatsoever' for the Turks, and how behind 'his mask of indolence, the Turk conceals impulses of the most brutal savagery'. Unlike the Greeks, the Turks had 'contributed nothing whatsoever to the progress of humanity: they are a race of Anatolian marauders: I desired only that in the Peace Treaty they should be relegated to Anatolia'.[31] As Michael Dockrill and J. Douglas Goold observed, most leading British statesmen, including Lloyd George, Balfour and Curzon, 'thought that nothing was too bad for the cruel, despicable and downright evil Turks'.[32]

The Turkish settlement lacked any sense of proportion or justice and, more than the relatively benign Treaty of Versailles, merits the epithet 'Carthaginian peace'. Fuelled by personal prejudices and racial stereotypes about the Turks, it was a peace designed to fulfil avaricious Greek and British foreign policy objectives. These prejudices led Britain into supporting Greece's invasion of Turkey. However, if the peace were not just, it might at least have had some merit if it could be enforced, order restored and a new balance of power created. Was the peace enforceable?

AN ENFORCEABLE PEACE?

The two years between the armistice agreed at Mudros on 31 October 1918 and the signing of the Treaty of Sèvres on 10 August 1920 proved fatal for the peace settlement. In April 1919, Curzon vainly pointed to the advantages accruing to the Turks because of the delay over the peace settlement:

Can it be wondered that he counts every moment of delay as so much gain, and watches with increased satisfaction how the failure to reach any settlement in Paris, and the growing jealousies and dissensions of the Allies, are placing him every day in a better position to resist the conditions to be imposed on him, and may even enable him in the end to take his revenge?[33]

However, with the pressures of the European settlements with Germany and Austria-Hungary, it seemed to many that Turkey was at the 'disposal' of the Allies and could be dealt with at a later date.[34] This was not the case. The breathing space afforded the Turks by the decision-makers in Paris allowed Mustafa Kemal in the Anatolian interior to build up a fighting opposition to the impending peace settlement. As France's President Raymond Poincaré observed, the vacillation over Turkey 'gave renewed vigour to our worst enemies . . . and favoured their resistance to the Peace Conference'.[35] The Kemalist renaissance upset the Sèvres settlement, defeated the Greeks and, finally, confronted British forces at the town of Chanak in 1922. Because of the long delay in implementation, the decision-makers in Paris were responding to, rather than controlling, events on the ground in Asia Minor. In the end, the politicians lost control of the decision-making process and, instead of a planned peace settlement, the two sides turned to war and a military rather than a diplomatic solution. As Winston Churchill wryly observed following the signing of Sèvres: 'At last peace with Turkey: and to ratify it, war with Turkey.'[36]

The British commanders on the spot witnessed first hand the effects of the delayed settlement. Admiral J.M. De Robeck, commander of the Mediterranean fleet, reported in November 1919 how, at the time of the Mudros armistice, 'Turkey was so cowed that she would have accepted almost any terms; but between then and now the Turks have had time to pull themselves together'.[37] Lieutenant-Colonel Alfred Rawlinson, a British officer in the Anatolian interior tasked with verifying Turkish demobilization, instead witnessed the Turks' rearmament. The effects of the delay were apparent to Rawlinson: 'the Turks were becoming more and more restive in the face of the inexplicable delay of the Allies in reaching any definite decision with regard to the future'.[38] After a Turkish mob attacked him, Rawlinson was subsequently arrested and imprisoned by Kemalist forces. Rawlinson's account of his time in Turkey gives a good sense of the harsh terrain of the Anatolian interior and the psychological and physical distance of the Kemalist base at Ankara from Constantinople. This gave those opposed to Sèvres a safe haven from which to organize resistance. As the Sultan's regime in Constantinople – already tarnished by its association with British occupation of the city – was expected to sign a treaty that would have effectively done away with Turkey, many Turks looked to the Kemalist movement as an 'effective separate government' that offered a means of making a new state.[39]

The delay outlined above was a crucial factor in the failure of the peace settlement. Curzon had put forward a moderate settlement for Turkey in January 1919. This had the merit that it could have been enforced as, in early 1919, the Turks had not recovered their strength and the Greeks had not yet landed at Smyrna. As Dockrill and Douglas Goold noted, a settlement in early 1919 could have been imposed and enforced.[40] What upset the negotiated settlement was the landing of Greek troops at Smyrna in May 1919, almost a year before the peace terms were agreed at San Remo in April 1920, and over a year prior to the signing of Sèvres in August 1920. This suggests a serious mismatch between what the politicians were planning in Paris and London, and what the generals were doing in western Anatolia. There were, in effect, two parallel processes at work, one political and one military, that failed to connect and create a cohesive strategy for an effective peace settlement.

The Smyrna landings and Greek advance inland from the town were undertaken with the knowledge and sanction of the Allied powers in Paris. 'Greatly alarmed' by an Italian landing at Adalia in March 1919, Lloyd George wanted to forestall any Italian landing at Smyrna that would have scuppered his exclusionary diplomacy.[41] The decision to land Greeks at Smyrna was made suddenly, in great secrecy and with Venizelos's encouragement. If the objective of the landings was to keep the peace at Smyrna, then the occupation should have been genuinely and not nominally inter-allied. As it was, the landing was an exclusively Greek affair. Moreover, once landed, the Greek troops were involved, as Curzon wrote to Balfour, in 'discreditable and unprovoked' atrocities.[42] The Greek officers accompanying the troops landing at Smyrna made, as Paul C. Helmreich noted, little effort to prevent outrages against Turkish soldiers and civilians.[43] Reports soon reached Constantinople concerning the misbehaviour and cruelty of elements of the Greek army. The Greeks were, as one report stated, in the same class of 'semi-barbarity' as the Turks.[44] From his ship in Smyrna harbour, a British naval officer saw a Greek woman urinate into the mouth of a wounded Turkish soldier who was crying out for water. It was not long before the bodies of dead Turks were floating in the harbour. Greek officers looked on with disinterest as Greek civilians and soldiers continued to commit atrocities.[45] The captain of HMS *Adventure*, also in Smyrna harbour when the Greeks landed, witnessed a Turkish officer with his hands up, and part of a column of Turkish POWs being marched away by Greek troops, 'veer out of line. A Greek soldier struck him on the head with his rifle butt. When the Turk rose, he was struck again and then bayoneted. Finally, the top of his head was blown off.'[46]

The Allies were aware of the Greek atrocities but, having sanctioned the landings, were unable, or unwilling, to restrain the Greeks. Having spoken to Clemenceau, Balfour informed London that the main purpose of an inquiry into the atrocities at Smyrna was to 'reassure the Turks in view of the excesses which the Greek troops had undoubtedly committed'.[47] As the Greeks pushed inland, credible reports of atrocities increased.[48] The inquiry set up to examine the reports of atrocities in Smyrna presented its findings in October 1919, confirmed the accounts of atrocities and concluded that the initial disorder had been 'due to the actions of the Greek High Command'.[49] Genuine efforts by the Greeks to punish those responsible did little to assuage Turkish fear and anger at the initial outrages. Arnold Toynbee, covering the Graeco-Turkish War for the *Manchester Guardian*, observed that 'the Greeks have shown the same unfitness as the Turks for governing a mixed population'. Toynbee concluded that the commission of inquiry into the atrocities of May 1919 proved that abuses were 'not the peculiar practice of one denomination or nationality'.[50]

At this stage it was not too late to stop the Greek advance inland, or even order the Greeks to withdraw. However, Lloyd George had no intention of terminating his policy of sponsoring the Greek invasion. Maurice Hankey, the Cabinet secretary, spent a sleepless night 'obsessed by the decision to support Venizelos's plan to send Greek troops to Smyrna'. Hankey wrote a note expressing his concerns that once the Greeks had landed it would be very hard to withdraw. He personally took the note to Lloyd George. Having read it, Lloyd George simply passed it on to Venizelos who ignored Hankey's prescient advice.[51]

The Greek landing at Smyrna had the effect of galvanizing Turkish opposition to the peace settlement. The landing of Greek troops provided a common cause around which the Turks could unite. As H.W.V. Temperley observed in his history of the Paris peace talks, the Turks did not regard the Greeks as their equals and they were 'mortally afraid' of any Greek foothold in Anatolia. At the same time, the Turks were quite willing to meet Greek forces in battle. The Turks saw the Smyrna landings as a deliberate violation of the armistice by the Allies and a foretaste of future aggression. The landings polarized the two sides, offered the diplomats little chance of effecting a peaceful solution and greatly increased the chance of a full-scale war.[52] While the Turks were already organizing to fight Armenian claims in eastern Anatolia, the Greek landing of 1919, condoned by Britain, gave a massive boost to the nationalist movement under Mustafa Kemal that would eventually force the British and Greeks to leave Asia Minor.

For the Turks, the landing of Greek troops at Smyrna was the 'supreme indignity'.[53] The British Control Officer at Ankara reported how the Greek landings not only angered the Turks but stiffened their resolve to resist: 'The news regarding the occupation of Smyrna town by Greek troops has been the talk of the day. . . . The burning point is that it is Greek troops who have occupied the town. . . . About 5 days ago the Kaimakan Bala [lieutenant or deputy-governor] of Bala [south-east of Ankara] rang up the Vali [governor] . . . and in connection with the Smyrna affair said "the inhabitants here are all ready and are awaiting orders".'[54] The Greek invasion also had the effect of ending any moves towards Turkish demobilization. General G.F. Milne, commander of British forces in Constantinople, reported that the landing at Smyrna brought the progress of

Turkish demobilization and arms decommissioning 'to an abrupt conclusion'. Milne's report shows just how fatal and short-sighted was the decision to allow the Greeks to land at Smyrna:

> The surrender of armament by the various [Turkish] commanders
> . . . was an indication that up to the month of May [1919], no
> plans for further resistance had been contemplated. Even the
> present Nationalist leaders, MUSTAFA KEMAL and DJEMAL PASHA,
> sent in large consignments from their respective commands. By
> the commencement of June the surrender of armament from
> central and eastern ANATOLIA entirely ceased and the Nationalist
> movement had begun.[55]

Similarly, De Robeck, in charge of the Mediterranean fleet, reported how the Greek occupation of Smyrna had 'stimulated a Turkish patriotism probably more real than any which the war was able to evoke. That patriotism has enabled Mustafa Kemal to raise a force which, if he decides to resist the peace terms, might cause the Allies considerable embarrassment.'[56] The Chanak crisis three years later, which helped bring down Lloyd George's administration, would prove the correctness of De Robeck's assessment. As De Robeck observed, by supporting the Smyrna landings, the British were destroying their 'honesty of purpose very considerably in Turkish circles potentially friendly to us'.[57] As the French discovered in the 1950s and 1960s in the independence war in Algeria, without any moderating *interlocuteurs valables* able to liaise between the two sides, a bloody denouement was likely.[58]

If the peace terms were to be enforced on the Turks, Britain and Greece needed to present a united front. With the emergence of Kemalist military opposition, they would also need to wield sufficient military strength to be able to beat the Kemalist forces on the field of battle. Britain, however, was far from united on the policy of supporting the Greek invasion. In particular, military planners questioned the wisdom of alienating the Turks, much preferring to appease the Kemalists while concentrating limited British resources on containment of the emerging Soviet threat.

Therefore, Lloyd George set out on the road to war against the advice of his military and political experts, many of whom had little sympathy for the Greek cause. For example, Wilson, the CIGS, wrote to General Charles 'Tim' Harington, the British commander in Istanbul, 'As regards your funny old Turks and Greeks, I wish the Turk would hurry up and throw the Greek into the Mediterranean at Smyrna, and then perhaps at the last moment, under the most disadvantageous circumstances imaginable, our Government will be forced to treat with the Turks.'[59] Wilson wrote to Charles Sackville-West in September 1919 how he was 'all in favour of making friends with the Turks and I cannot understand our Foreign Office view of backing perfectly rotten people like the Greeks, who cannot possibly help us against the Turks who can do us infinite damage'.[60] In a later letter to Sackville-West, Wilson added that a Greek defeat 'would have the enormous advantage of bringing our "frocks" slap up against it and forcing them to make friends with the Turks'.[61] Sackville-West, with the British delegation at Versailles, echoed Wilson's hostility: 'I wish we could clear out of Constantinople and leave it to the Greeks, the Turks and the French to fight it out amongst themselves.'[62] Rawlinson, the British military representative in Ankara, wrote to his brother, Lord Rawlinson, 'Why, Oh why, can't we pose as their [the Turks'] champions – take them in hand ourselves – make an "Egypt" of them . . . and incidentally earn an invaluable debt of gratitude from <u>all</u> Islam.'[63] Passed on to Curzon by way of Wilson, this letter articulated the view of a military establishment keen to avoid needless foreign entanglements.

Even the British Cabinet was divided on the Turkish settlement. In Curzon's view, the lifelong 'Radicals' such as Lloyd George, Edwin Montagu and George Barnes were the most imperialistic, while the 'Conservatives' such as himself, Lord Milner and Austen Chamberlain opposed involvement in the unfolding war in Asia Minor.[64] It has also been suggested that the Foreign Office as well as the military were markedly Turkophile.[65] Lloyd George's secretary, Frances Stevenson, noted in her diary that Lloyd George and Balfour were the 'only pro-Greeks' in the Cabinet: 'All the others have done their best to obstruct & the W.[ar] O.[ffice] have behaved abominably.'[66] The Turkish settlement also upset the India Office, understandably concerned with appeasing India's large Muslim population. At a conference held at 10 Downing Street in January 1920, the Secretary of State for India and the Secretary of State for the Colonies opposed a plan to remove the Sultan, instead laying great stress on the 'effect that the expulsion of the Turks would have in India'.[67] Curzon was forced to explain to Venizelos how the 'spokesmen of India and the Secretary of State for India . . . had stated that the expulsion of the Turk from Constantinople would be regarded as an intolerable insult to Islam, and would be followed by disturbances and rebellions in all parts of the Eastern world'.[68]

Economic weakness compounded Britain's lack of common purpose over Turkey. Britain was simply not economically strong enough to provide sustained support for the invasion of Anatolia. The postwar years were a time of retrenchment and cost cutting. As Curzon wrote to Balfour in August 1919, the expense of large overseas garrisons was one that 'could no longer be sustained'.[69] The First World War had drained British coffers and it was essential to reduce imperial commitments to fit a smaller, peacetime army. By the summer of 1919, it was becoming impossible to match up Britain's overseas commitments with budget constraints and a reduced army.[70] This was precisely the moment when Greek troops were pushing inland from Smyrna. By 1922, the year that the Chanak crisis erupted, Britain was firmly set on its interwar path of limited overseas military commitment. In the same year, Eric Geddes drastically cut British public expenditure and the 'Geddes Axe' fell disproportionately on the armed services whom Geddes felt were profligate spenders. It was all very different to the war years when the military had, 'in effect, a blank cheque from the exchequer'.[71] In the context of financial retrenchment and military cutbacks, Britain was forced to rely on outside support for enforcement of the Turkish settlement. This could come in varying forms: the Greeks, wartime allies such as France, Italy and America, or from the British empire. In the end, all would be found wanting.

The difficulties of enforcing the peace terms were apparent to British generals. The CIGS wrote to the British commander in

Istanbul in 1920, 'You have already seen the Terms of the Turkish Treaty, and you know as well as I do that if they refuse to accept we are quite unable to enforce our terms.'[72] In the meeting at San Remo in April 1920, where the peace terms of Sèvres were first agreed, the Allied leaders realized that they did not have the power to enforce the entire settlement on Turkey. Marshal Foch of France stated bluntly that without additional troops 'the treaty could not be enforced'.[73] The British army, which was in the process of demobilizing, simply did not have the military resources to supply the twenty-seven extra divisions needed to impose the peace terms on the Turks.[74] Neither were sufficient troops forthcoming from the other major powers such as France, Italy or America. The CIGS advised Lloyd George that without a full-scale invasion of Asia Minor, Mustafa Kemal could not be defeated: 'from a military point of view, it was as impossible to deal with Mustapha Kemal by merely holding a position at Constantinople or Smyrna as it was to deal with Sinn Fein by sitting at Dublin'.[75] Nonetheless, Lloyd George persevered. In March 1920, the British promised Venizelos that, while Britain could not help him with troops, it was 'prepared to render such assistance as she could in arms and munitions'. Turkish battlefield success shattered Venizelos's optimistic response to this offer of support.[76]

HOW STRONG WAS GREECE?

While something of a regional power, Greece did not have the political unity, economic and financial strength, or military power to defeat the Turks. As one contemporary commentator wryly observed, Greece 'combined the appetite of a Russia with the resources of a Switzerland'.[77] To make matters worse, as the Greek army advanced on Ankara, there was political upheaval on the Greek home front. Bitten by a pet monkey, the Greek king, Alexander, died in October 1920 after blood poisoning set in. This bizarre death sparked off a chain of events that toppled Venizelos and brought the ex-King Constantine I back to power. His supporters promptly purged the army of pro-Venizelos officers, precisely at the moment when Greek forces were engaging Turkish forces in battles west of Ankara. The political moves in Athens proved to be a disaster, as politically inspired changes swept through the Greek army in Asia Minor, lowering morale and reducing military effectiveness.[78] The Greek officers under Venizelos had had combat experience on the Macedonian front in 1918 but the Royalist officers appointed after the fall of Venizelos 'had had no training in the latest developments of warfare'.[79] The fall of Venizelos boosted the fortunes of the Kemalist forces, as he had been an important factor keeping the Allies together over the Turkish settlement. The pro-German Constantine attracted little backing from reluctant supporters of the Greek invasion such as the French. Now that Venizelos was gone, the French and Italians, who had been 'dragged unwillingly in the wake of Lloyd George's Philhellene schemes', seized the opportunity to make their peace with the Kemalists.[80] Therefore, in 1921, both Italy and France made settlements with the new regime in Ankara. These deals prompted the Soviets, with their own set of priorities in the region, to send a delegation to Ankara to negotiate a similar settlement. Undeterred by their political and military weakness, the Greeks refused at the London Conference in February–March 1921 to consider any modifications to Sèvres and, instead, launched a new offensive.[81]

France's support for Sèvres was never strong. With the change in regime in Athens after Alexander's death, France had the excuse it needed to escape any obligations to Britain over the Turkish peace. Consequently, Curzon was forced to accept a decision of the Supreme Council, 'backed by France and Italy', to cease all allied financial assistance and supplies of war material to the Greeks. He later agreed a declaration of strict neutrality.[82] This declaration, however, did not stop France, Italy and the USSR from sending covert military aid to the Kemalists in the hope of gaining favour with what looked to be the winning side in the Graeco-Turkish War. Greece's problem was that it was unable to prosecute the war with Turkey without external support. Granville, the British Minister in Athens, reported how 'Greece cannot possibly maintain the struggle in Asia Minor without financial assistance from the Allies and that there is even some doubt whether she can carry on at all unaided.'[83] By 1921, as the Greeks' supply of equipment dwindled, France, Italy and the USSR were sending supplies to the Kemalists.

Britain and Greece could not expect support from Italy, France and America to enforce a peace settlement designed to promote British and Greek interests. From the beginning, Italy was unhappy with the Turkish settlement. Feeling themselves ill-used, the Italians, according to Balfour, wilfully obstructed proceedings.[84] Kinross states that the Italians were 'implacably' opposed to Lloyd George's support of the Greeks and quietly began to re-establish contacts with Mustafa Kemal's government in Ankara.[85] In late 1920, the Italian Under-Secretary for Foreign Affairs visited Galib Kemali, a former Ottoman officer, to inform him that the Italians would help with modifications of the peace terms.[86] In April 1921, Horace Rumbold, the High Commissioner at Constantinople, wrote to Curzon at the Foreign Office about 'considerable' Italian arms and munitions supplies being sent to the nationalists.[87] The Italians felt little disposed to support a settlement that benefited Greece and Britain while excluding them from a region in which they felt they had a long-standing claim.

Equally, France obstructed implementation of the terms of Sèvres. Britain's representative at Versailles wrote back to say how the French were 'most averse to any measures being taken . . . towards enforcing the Treaty of Sèvres. This would be in accordance with French public opinion, as expressed in the press, which favours a modification of the treaty' in view of the fall of Venizelos.[88] In April 1919, Curzon reported on the 'constant trouble' caused by the French General Franchet d'Esperey in Constantinople.[89] Admiral De Robeck, based in Constantinople, reported to Curzon that, in his opinion, 'some of our Allies would be quite resigned to see us discredited in the Near East and are already working to undermine our position in ways which we cannot stoop to counter'.[90] In January 1920, Curzon circulated to the Cabinet a paper in which he recorded that the French hoped to cause Britain 'difficulties' with the Turkish settlement.[91] Wilson complained that French support for Turkey was a 'break of faith', while Rumbold in Constantinople described the French as 'dreadful allies' following their support for Mustafa Kemal.[92] British anger at France boiled over after an article appeared in the Turkish press containing an interview with France's representative in Ankara. As Lancelot Oliphant wrote home, 'If the words attributed to this officer were true, it would be hard to exaggerate the disloyal nature of such a speech made by the representative of an ally to a common enemy.'[93] The French seized on the fall of Venizelos to abandon the Greeks completely and, following the October 1921 Franco-Kemalist treaty, the French supplied the Turks with guns and aeroplanes. This helped to establish the military strength and raise the morale of the Anatolian army.[94] By the London Conference in early 1921, the French and Italians were actively courting the Kemalists and they made little attempt to hide the fact that they were going to ignore the Treaty of Sèvres.

The United States' involvement in the Turkish settlement could have helped make a workable peace but America remained undecided until Congress finally decided on an isolationist course in foreign policy. This removed America from the peace process altogether and left Britain even more isolated and reliant on Greek military success. As Lloyd George recalled in his account of the peace settlement, he was forced to wait on a decision from Wilson on American participation in the peace with Turkey: 'We knew only too well that without Wilson's powerful advocacy there was no hope of persuading the United States to undertake the previous responsibility of a mandate for the Straits.'[95] Curzon warned Balfour that the Turkish settlement could not be postponed 'till the date at which Wilson may have persuaded, or failed to persuade, the Senate to make up its mind about a Turkish mandate'.[96] But America proved unable to provide Britain with support for the Turkish settlement and this imposed further delays on an already postponed peace settlement. President Wilson's poor health placed additional strains on the by now complicated peace negotiations. The American leader almost certainly had a small stroke in late April 1919, one month before the Smyrna landings, and then a major stroke in the autumn. These illnesses put immense strain on Wilson and the peace process throughout 1919.[97]

Meanwhile, Soviet support gave the Kemalist forces a much-needed military advantage. In 1920, at the moment that Sèvres was being signed, the Russians joined forces with Mustafa Kemal in a joint invasion of Armenia. A pact between the Kemalists and Soviets in 1921 followed this division of territory between the two sides in eastern Anatolia and Armenia. After this successful attack ended any hopes of an independent Armenia or Kurdistan, the Soviets supplied the Kemalists with arms and ammunition that arrived via the ports of Sinope, Samsun and Inebolu.[98] The Kemalist alliance with Turkey's long-standing Russian enemy was mutually advantageous for both sides and left Mustafa Kemal's forces free to concentrate their attacks upon the Greeks, safe in the knowledge that their eastern flank was secure.[99]

The opposition of sections of the British decision-making elite, the hostility of the French, Italians and Soviets, and the indecision of America might not have proved fatal for Sèvres if the Turks had been willing to agree to the peace terms. The Turks, however, were unwilling to acquiesce in the destruction of Turkey and revived their military strength and political unity under the leadership of Mustafa Kemal.

THE REBUILDING OF TURKISH FORCES

Once the armistice at Mudros was agreed in October 1918, the Turkish army was ordered to demobilize. This, however, proved to be a very partial process and one almost impossible to enforce effectively. The problem was partly one of geography. As Milne, the British commander of the army of occupation, reported to the War Office:

> The task of disarming the Ottoman army presented peculiar difficulties. The main TURKISH armies were many hundreds of miles away and were sullenly withdrawn into the great tangle of mountains which forms the massif of ASIA MINOR. One of these armies had never been beaten at all, but, on the contrary, had recently carried out a victorious advance into the coveted Moslem territories of the CAUCASUS.[100]

The problem, however, was not just adverse terrain but also the fact that, as Milne noted, the Turks, rather like the German army in 1918, did not perceive themselves to be a defeated force: 'The fact that the Turk does not really realize that he is in disgrace may give trouble in the future, and if the peace terms are going to be severe, it appears to me essential that our forces in the town [Constantinople] are strengthened.'[101] Across Anatolia, arms and ammunition were being stored for a possible war with Greece.[102] The incomplete demobilization process left the Turkish army potentially ready for battle. Rawlinson commented on this in August 1919, the eve of the full-scale war with Greece: 'On the demobilization of the Turkish armies in Eastern Anatolia the demobilized troops have almost universally remained in the districts where they were demobilized.' Rawlinson went on to report how Mustafa Kemal disregarded orders from the Sultan's government in Constantinople that he should comply with the demobilization terms of the peace settlement.[103] Once the Greeks occupied Smyrna, any pretence at demobilization disappeared.[104] Instead, with the news of the Greek invasion, the Kemalist movement spread 'rapidly west' from Ankara, picking up support from ordinary Turks fearful of Greek occupation.[105] In this struggle, the Kemalists saw Britain as their enemy. The Acting High Commissioner in Constantinople sent back a translation of an article in the Turkish press that showed the 'extent to which the Kemalists persist in identifying His Majesty's Government with the activities of the Greeks in Asia Minor. The article illustrates the strength of feeling against Great Britain as well as against Greece.'[106] On the night of 14/15 June 1920, Turkish nationalist units challenged the British army for the first time by attacking British forces in the Ismid area. This was the beginning of a military confrontation that culminated in a crisis in 1922 when Kemalist forces confronted British troops at the town of Chanak by the Dardanelles. At the Chanak crisis, Britain called for help from the once-dependable empire, only to discover that the 'white' dominions were little interested in supporting Britain's clash with Kemalist Turkey. Only plucky little New Zealand offered unequivocal support.

ENDGAME

Nemesis for Lloyd George and the Greeks came with the defeat of Greek forces in Anatolia, the destruction of the city of Smyrna by Turkish forces in 1922 and the expulsion of the Greek population of Anatolia.[107] As a consequence, little or nothing remains today of the once-thriving Christian communities of Smyrna: not just the people have gone but the buildings of the old city were also destroyed in the fire that consumed the old city in 1922.[108] Widespread atrocities accompanied the burning of Smyrna as Turkish troops took revenge on the Greek population of the city and surrounding area. The Greek population fled from the Smyrna region and the Pontus district of northern Anatolia. The Graeco-Turkish War concluded with a huge, traumatic population transfer, as Greeks who had lived for thousands of years in Turkey, many of whom only spoke Turkish, were forced to move to Greece, while Turks living in Greece were made to go to Turkey. The Graeco-Turkish War uprooted and under coercion transferred some 1.5 million people who had to leave once the war ended.[109] The war concluded with a new treaty at Lausanne, one that recognized Turkey's new-found strength under Mustafa Kemal. The Treaty of Lausanne in 1923 succeeded where Sèvres had failed. It proved to be not just one of the most successful treaties of the First World War but one of the most enduring international treaties of the twentieth century. The population transfers and new boundaries after Lausanne marked the end of both Ottoman imperialism and the 'great idea' of a greater Greek empire. Lausanne also ruined Lloyd George's scheme to solve the 'eastern question' by establishing Greece as the pre-eminent power in the region. Neither just nor enforceable, Sèvres was an unfair and unrealistic settlement that must rank as one of the biggest failures of the Paris Peace Conference.

FIVE

An Elusive Peace Settlement in Palestine: the Peace Talks Following the 1948–9 Arab–Israeli War

Since its formation in May 1948, Israel has fought seven major wars with its Arab neighbours – in 1948–9, 1956, 1967, 1969–70, 1973, 1982 and 2006. Tracing the roots of the Arab–Israeli conflict back to the first Arab–Israeli war, from 1948 to 1949, this chapter seeks to answer the question of why, following the first Arab–Israeli war, the Rhodes armistice talks and Lausanne peace talks of 1949 ended with uneasy armistices but no overall peace settlement.[1] The failure to agree peace treaties between Israel and the Arab front-line states in 1949 after the first Arab–Israeli war led to a series of wars, starting in 1956, in which both Israel and the Arabs sought a military solution to the political questions of the legitimacy of Israel and its borders, and the fate of the 7–800,000 Palestinian refugees who had lost their homes in Israel's 'War of Independence' – what for the Palestinians was the 'catastrophe', *al-Nakba*, of 1948. If at all possible, the issues of the right of Israel to exist and Palestinian self-determination should have been resolved in 1949. Had they been settled early on, the depressing spiral of war in the Middle East could have been checked. Instead, the unresolved issues of 1948–9 remained to complicate Arab–Israeli relations, and it was only after the war of 1973 that Israel and Egypt finally entered into a political dialogue that resulted in the first peace treaty between the two sides in 1979 – thirty years after the first Arab–Israeli war.

THE HISTORIOGRAPHY ON 1948 AND AFTER

The unwillingness of the Arab states to come to terms with Israel has been the traditional explanation for the failure to forge a peace settlement. As Avi Shlaim recently recounted, according to this version of history, while Israeli leaders tried to broker a peace in 1949, all their efforts 'foundered on the rocks of Arab intransigence. Israel's leaders were desperate to achieve peace, but there was no one to talk to on the other side.'[2] This perspective on why peace failed crystallized soon after the creation of Israel. In the 1950s, the Israeli diplomat, Walter Eytan, put the blame firmly with the Arab states for refusing to recognize Israel. The Arabs expressed their hostility to Israel in their basic policy which aimed 'at the ruin and ultimate extirpation of Israel'.[3] Therefore, a peace was impossible because the Arab objective was the destruction of Israel, something the Israelis, obviously, could not countenance. In the 1970s, the editor of a selection of Israeli documents reiterated the view that while Israel wanted 'peaceful co-existence and friendly cooperation with its neighbours', the Arabs 'blocked any attempt to reach understanding on a practical solution of the Arab refugee problem, thus deliberately perpetuating the suffering of their own kin, using them as pawns in their fight against Israel'. However, notwithstanding this antipathy, Israel still persevered in its efforts to seek peace with the Arabs. This one-sided viewpoint absolved Israel of blame as it was the 'relentless hostility' of the Arabs and their unwillingness to engage in a dialogue that ruined any chance of peace.[4] The notion that the Arabs were somehow to blame for the failed peace dominated the English-language historiography on the Arab–Israeli conflict up until the 1980s.

This all changed in the 1980s with the arrival of what became known as the 'new' or 'revisionist' historians who offered radically different perspectives on the formation of Israel, the causes of the Palestinian refugee crisis and the reasons for the failed peace of 1949. The 'new' historians argued that the historiography on Israel had for too long been dominated by an 'old' or 'mobilized' history, written by Israeli scholars in the 1950s, 1960s and 1970s, that portrayed Israel as under serious threat from the Arabs and so forced into a series of wars for survival.[5] This 'old' history also sought to exculpate Israel from the charge that it stole Palestinian land and forcibly evicted the inhabitants. The 'new' or 'revisionist' historians, headed by Simha Flapan, Benny Morris, Ilan Pappé and Avi Shlaim, challenged the 'old' history.[6] They argued that Israel was responsible in some measure for the Palestinian refugee crisis, the Arab–Israeli wars and the failed peace of 1949, and that the image of Israel put forward by the 'old' historians was both misleading and determined by the political need to be pro-Israeli. The debunking by the 'new' historians of long-held shibboleths provoked a furore among the 'old' historians (who now became the 'new-old' historians) and the debate soon spilled over into the public domain. In articles and books, the 'new-old' historians counter-attacked. Aharon Megged charged the 'new' historians with writing history in the spirit of Israel's enemies; Efraim Karsh accused Morris and Shlaim of falsifying and recycling history.[7] Attack and counter-attack ensued as both sides slugged it out.[8] Meanwhile, some pro-Palestinian historians attacked the 'new' historians for not going far enough in their analyses.[9] The debate goes on in books and journals such as *Middle Eastern Studies, Journal of Palestine Studies, International Journal of Middle Eastern Studies, Middle East Journal, Studies in Zionism* and *Commentary*. This chapter will assess the validity of the claims of the 'old' and 'new' histories, drawing evidence from each camp to examine the failed peace of 1949.

ARAB PEACE OVERTURES

In line with the findings of the 'new' historians, it is not apparent that, following its creation in 1948, Israel actively wanted peace. There was both a lack of will on the part of Israel's leaders, notably the Prime Minister David Ben-Gurion, and little strategic impetus for Israel to sign peace treaties with the Arabs after its 'War of Independence'. The Arab states of Syria, Transjordan – renamed Jordan in 1950[10] – and Egypt all made attempts after the

1948–9 war – some more serious than others – to broker a peace. (The case of Lebanon is more problematic and work is now being done to examine Israel's relations with Lebanon in this period.)[11] Israel ignored or rejected these offers from the Arabs. Therefore, it would seem, contrary to the traditional historiography, and in line with the findings of the 'new' historians, that the blame for the failed peace in 1949, and subsequent Arab–Israeli conflict, lies with Israel.

It was Syria, one of Israel's most implacable foes, that made the most interesting and constructive offer in 1949. On 30 March 1949 a new leader, Colonel Husni al-Zaim, came to power in Syria. Zaim was keen to develop Syria's economic potential and one of his top priorities was to make peace with Israel. To make his peace feeler attractive to Israel, he offered to resettle 300,000 Palestinian refugees in Syria. As the question of the settlement of the 7–800,000 Palestinian refugees displaced in 1948–9 from what was now Israel had bedevilled the negotiations at Rhodes and Lausanne, with Israel resisting any right of return and the Arabs insisting on the right of refugees to return home, Syria's offer was a real opportunity to break the impasse.[12] In May 1949 the US Minister in Syria, James H. Keeley, noted Zaim's desire for a 'quick solution' to the Palestinian problem and how Zaim was ready to absorb 250,000 Palestinian refugees.[13] As recent scholarship has noted, Zaim's stance towards Israel in 1949 was indeed a 'positive and extraordinarily unusual position' for an Arab leader to adopt.[14] He and his main successor, Colonel Adib al-Shishakli, who between them ruled Syria from 1949 to 1954, both adopted 'pragmatic attitudes' towards Israel, hoping to conclude political agreements with Israel rather than again go to war. Therefore, during the armistice talks in early 1949, Zaim offered to sign a full peace treaty with Israel rather than just a basic armistice agreement.[15] According to Syria's Foreign Minister, Amir Adil Arslan, Zaim was even willing to meet with Ben-Gurion.[16] For an Arab leader, this was a ground-breaking offer and Zaim's willingness to compromise when it came to negotiating with Israel excited United Nations (UN) and American officials involved in the various Arab–Israeli negotiations.

Considering Zaim's offer, the US Secretary of State, Dean Acheson, informed the US Legation in Syria that Zaim's willingness to accommodate Palestinian refugees was of 'particular importance since Syria only Arab country except already willing Transjordan which can assimilate such number within reasonable time. If this opportunity can be exploited back of refugee problem can be broken.'[17] As Keeley, the US Minister in Damascus, noted, everyone who had discussed the peace offer with Zaim was impressed by his 'sincerity and broadminded' attitude towards Israel. The window of opportunity was, however, not going to remain open forever and, as the US Legation in Syria concluded, Zaim's ardour was 'cooling in face of Israeli insatiability'.[18] Keeley, frustrated by Israeli stubbornness, reported back to Washington on the requirement to impress upon Israel the need to seize this opportunity for peace: 'Yet unless Israel can be brought to understand that it cannot have all of its cake (partition boundaries) and gravy as well (areas captured in violation of truce, Jerusalem and resettlement Arab refugees elsewhere) it may find that it has won Palestine but lost the war.'[19]

The Americans felt that Zaim was someone with whom they could do business. Miles Copeland, a US intelligence operative in Syria, recalled how America had helped direct the coup that brought Zaim to power in the hope that he would liberalize Syria. Copeland concluded that one of Zaim's key priorities on coming to power was to do 'something constructive' about Syrian–Israeli relations.[20] Other senior American figures involved in the Middle East peace talks came to similar conclusions about Zaim. George McGhee, the American coordinator on Palestine refugee matters and roving US ambassador to the 'Middle World', recalled Zaim's agreement, in April 1949, to accept 250,000 refugees for settlement in Syria in return for economic assistance for Syria. Naturally, McGhee and his staff, 'elated' at this olive branch, tried to firm up the Syrian offer. However, as McGhee concluded, the problem lay with Israel and its unwillingness to respond positively to Zaim's offer:

Zaim had great difficulties in working out a ceasefire with Israel and felt he could not make concessions on refugees without a quid pro quo from Israel. These were not forthcoming and time ran out on him. . . . I have often thought how drastically the course of Middle East history would have been changed if one of these possibilities had materialized, and wondered if there was not something we could have done to push one of these proposals through.[21]

What exactly was Israel's response to the Syrian offer? In May 1949, Brigadier-General William E. Riley, the American Chief of Staff of the UN observers in Palestine, told Shabtai Rosenne, legal adviser to the Israeli Foreign Ministry and a member of the Israeli armistice delegation, that Zaim wanted peace so that he could concentrate on developing Syria. Zaim had asked Riley to speak to the Israelis about his proposal, within the context of the Lausanne talks, for the resettlement of 300,000 Palestinians in Syria and the settlement of the disputed Israeli–Syrian border. Riley also pointed out that Zaim wanted a joint force reduction on both sides of the new frontier. What was Rosenne's response to this intriguing offer? As the archival record shows, his 'reaction to the proposal was negative, and he told Riley that Ben-Gurion's reaction would in all probability be the same. . . . Rosenne said that Israel was in no hurry and that Syria was in far greater need of an agreement. Moreover, Israel did not fear the [UN] Security Council's reaction.'[22] On being pressed by the UN Palestine Conciliation Commission (PCC) to offer something constructive, Israel announced that it was prepared to consider the repatriation of 100,000 refugees. The PCC considered the Israeli figure derisory and it did not even officially communicate it to the Arabs.[23] Forced to consider a meeting with Zaim, Ben-Gurion made sure a suitably low-level delegation was put forward with the proviso that should the Syrians ask for a meeting with more senior officials this should be postponed.[24]

Later in May 1949, Reuven Shiloah, Adviser on Special Affairs with the Israeli Foreign Ministry, also saw Riley who again reiterated Zaim's offer to absorb the Palestinian refugees. Riley emphasized the importance of a *tête-à-tête* meeting between Zaim and Ben-Gurion, an encounter Zaim was willing to arrange, and regretted that Ben-Gurion refused to meet Zaim as 'only such meeting will produce results'. As Shiloah reported back to Moshe Sharett (Shertok), Israel's Foreign Minister (and Prime Minister from 1953 to 1955), Riley felt that Zaim, as the Syrian leader, should meet personally with Ben-Gurion as no other Israeli leader could commit Israel to such a daring peace move. Shiloah agreed with Riley and recommended that Ben-Gurion should respond favourably to any peace offer by Zaim.[25] However, as will be shown, Ben-Gurion, for various reasons, was uninterested in a peace that would involve compromise by both sides. Ben-Gurion was only willing to sign a peace treaty that involved the Arabs making concessions. As one of the editors of *Documents on the Foreign Policy of Israel* noted, Israel's starting point for negotiations was known to the UN negotiator Ralph Bunche and to the Syrians prior to the opening of any talks: 'uncompromising demand for Syrian withdrawal to the international border, and fixing of that border as the armistice line. Israeli delegates categorically rejected every solution that did not include a total Syrian withdrawal.'[26] This uncompromising attitude did not change with time. In 1952, Zaim's successor, Shishakli, also offered to sign a peace agreement with Israel. Ben-Gurion, however, was still intransigent, refusing to make any territorial concessions to Syria in return for a peace treaty.[27]

For the 'new' historians, Israel's stance in 1949 confirmed their view that Israel's hostile attitude to its Arab neighbours was the major cause of the Arab–Israeli conflict. In *The Birth of Israel: Myths and Realities* (1987) Flapan argued that Israel's reaction to Zaim's offer 'ranged from indifference to distrust to contempt'.[28] Morris concurred, recounting in his book on the Arab–Israeli conflict, *Righteous Victims: A History of the Zionist–Arab Conflict, 1881–1999* (2000),

> Of course, it was not Za'im's sincerity or seriousness that was of paramount concern. Israel's leaders simply refused to contemplate a concession of territory or water to achieve peace. As in their dealings with Abdullah [of Jordan], they were remarkably single-minded and rigid, convinced that the Arabs would eventually

agree to make peace without Israel having to make such concessions. Meanwhile, the armistice agreement would suffice.[29]

What of the other major Arab front-line states? Was Israel as intransigent in its talks with Jordan and Egypt as it had been with Syria? The Hashemite ruler of Jordan, King Abdullah, had made contact with Zionist leaders prior to the 1948 war. In November 1947, Abdullah met the future Israeli leader, Golda Meir (Meyerson), then acting head of the political department of the Jewish Agency, and the talks with Meir 'began negotiations in earnest' as Abdullah and the Zionists colluded to divide up Palestine once the last British forces left in 1948.[30] The controversial 'collusion across the Jordan' between Zionist and Arab forces allowed Abdullah to conquer the 'West Bank' of Palestine, in return for which he restrained his army, the well-trained British-commanded Arab Legion, from an all-out assault on the nascent Israeli army.[31] This understanding worked to mutual advantage. It was only over particularly tricky issues, such as the status of Jerusalem, that the Israeli army and the Arab Legion came to real blows. Otherwise, Israel and Jordan worked together to maximize their gains from the division of Palestine.[32] When the Arab–Israeli war had ended, and once Israel and Jordan had concluded an armistice agreement in April 1949, Abdullah attempted to transform the armistice into a comprehensive peace with the Zionist state.

The prospects for a Jordanian–Israeli peace were promising. As has been mentioned, Abdullah, undeterred by Arab opposition, had already made contact with Zionist leaders and arranged for the division of Palestine. These contacts were now extended and he gave the go-ahead for senior Israeli leaders to travel to Jordan to discuss a peace deal both with himself and his advisers. Israel's contacts with Jordan in the late 1940s and early 1950s were the closest it had with any Arab state. This allowed for a fruitful dialogue and in February 1950 the two sides initialled a peace treaty. The treaty, however, was never ratified. Why not? For the 'new' historians, Israeli battlefield success was part of the problem, as it established military prowess as the dominant discourse rather than diplomatic negotiations. Therefore, while Abdullah 'vigorously' pursued peace 'it was not easy. For one thing as Israel grew in strength, so did her appetite for land and lack of readiness for compromise.' While Israeli military victories undoubtedly played their part, the problem also lay with Abdullah who, increasingly isolated by his pro-Israeli position, was unable to prevail upon his own government to accept a peace with Israel. Abdullah not only had to contend with opposition within his own kingdom to a treaty with a state blamed for the expulsion of the Palestinians, but he was also under attack from other Arab states who were angry at his connivance with Israel and what had been done to the Palestinians. The Arab League, responsible for coordinating a united Arab response to Israel, looked on with horror as Abdullah annexed the West Bank in April 1950 *and* proposed a peace with Israel. As the ruler of a small desert kingdom, Abdullah was not sufficiently powerful to ignore the entreaties of the wider Arab community to cancel his proposed treaty with the Zionist enemy. Therefore, in 1950, with his 'customary realism', Abdullah, aware that he could not defy the Arab League indefinitely, agreed to suspend the talks with Israel in order to secure the Arab League's acceptance of his annexation of the West Bank.[33] If this is the case, responsibility for the failed Jordanian–Israeli peace, that came so close to success in 1950, lies more with Jordan than Israel. It was Abdullah's greed to control parts of Palestine that let the peace treaty slip with Israel. His desire to extend his kingdom was also his undoing when, in July 1951, an Arab nationalist, angry at Abdullah's policies, assassinated the Hashemite ruler as he left the al-Aksa Mosque in Jerusalem.

What of Egypt's reaction to Israel in this period? As Flapan recounted, in September 1948, King Farouk of Egypt contacted Elias Sasson, the Syrian-born Israeli diplomat, about a possible peace with Israel. Sasson reacted promptly and submitted a plan for a separate peace with Egypt. For Flapan, the Egyptian reaction to Sasson's offer 'confirmed Israeli expectations that there was some common ground for an alliance and separate peace'.[34] As a result of these tentative contacts, in October 1948 Sasson went to Geneva to meet Mohammed Hussein Heikal, chairman of the

Egyptian Senate. The response of Ben-Gurion to these inchoate peace feelers was to launch a military operation, 'Yoav', to expel the Egyptian army from southern Palestine and the Negev desert. In a clear reference to Israel's tough approach, Operation Yoav was also codenamed 'Ten Plagues', an allusion to the wrath of God visited on the Egyptians in the Passover story.[35] As Michael Oren concluded, while some Israeli leaders such as Sharett were 'inclined to respond favorably to Egypt's approach. Ben-Gurion . . . believed that the fate of the Negev would be determined by military, and not diplomatic, means.'[36] Ben-Gurion's preference for a military over a political solution, a policy supported by large sections of the Israeli population, ruined Sasson's chances of pursuing a dialogue for peaceful negotiation. When Egypt, under the new leadership of Gamal Abdul Nasser, again put out peace feelers in the early 1950s, a bellicose Ben-Gurion was again hostile to talks, and he worked successfully to undo the efforts of the more conciliatory Sharett to establish a dialogue with Egypt prior to a peace treaty.[37]

Ben-Gurion's hawkish, martial approach when it came to dealing with Egypt seems misplaced considering the four subsequent Israeli–Egyptian wars. But to ascribe the failure of the Israeli–Egyptian talks wholly to Ben-Gurion is misleading. The talks never developed beyond tentative contacts so it is hard to know how they would have turned out. Had they been pursued, domestic politics in Egypt and hostile Egyptian public opinion could well have combined to deflect an Egyptian leader from a peace with Israel. And the assassination of Abdullah was a salutary lesson to Arab leaders who ignored the wishes of their people. It was also the case that, under Farouk, Egypt was half-hearted about a peace settlement: there was not the willingness to make bold offers as with the mercurial Zaim, or the goodwill and pragmatism of the wily Abdullah. As Morris conceded, Farouk, unlike Zaim or Abdullah, was 'at best luke-warm' to the idea of a peace with Israel.[38]

Egypt and Israel also had serious differences that extended beyond the issues of the Palestinian refugees and control of the Gaza Strip, and would have been hard to resolve in 1949. There was, for instance, the question of the Negev desert. Control of the

Negev desert was an issue of considerable strategic importance for both Israel and Egypt. Israel wanted more land for the new Jewish state and, crucially, felt it required a land corridor to the sea at the Gulf of Akaba from which Israeli ships could trade with Asia. Meanwhile, Egypt, prompted in some measure by Great Britain, saw the Negev as a possible land-bridge from Egyptian-held Sinai and Gaza to Jordan. Therefore, at the Lausanne talks, the Egyptians demanded the Negev desert as a quid pro quo for a peace with Israel. While the Israelis rebuffed the idea of territorial concessions in the Negev desert, they did express an interest in exchanging land in the Negev for the Gaza Strip. But Egypt turned down this Israeli offer for fear of the impact that it would have on domestic Egyptian opinion that would view the swap as more Palestinian land going to Israel.[39]

ISRAEL AND THE 'IRON WALL'

For the 'new' historians, the answer to Israel's intransigence in the late 1940s and early 1950s originated in the 1920s with what has been described by Shlaim as the 'Iron Wall' in Israeli policy-making. Shlaim traced this idea back to the extremist Jewish nationalist agitator and thinker Ze'ev (Vladimir) Jabotinsky. In 1923, Jabotinsky published two works under the title *The Iron Wall*. In these pieces, Jabotinsky argued that the 'sole way' to an agreement with the Arabs was through an 'iron wall, that is to say, the establishment in Palestine of a force that will in no way be influenced by Arab pressure. In other words, the only way to achieve a settlement in the future is total avoidance of all attempts to arrive at a settlement in the present.' As Shlaim points out it was, therefore, pointless to talk to the Arabs as the 'Zionist program had to be executed unilaterally and by force'.[40] But as Shlaim stresses, Jabotinsky's plan involved two stages. After the first stage of the 'Iron Wall' there was a second stage that involved negotiations for a peace once the Arabs accepted Israel's existence. For the 'new' historians the problem was the fact that Ben-Gurion followed Jabotinsky's thinking up to stage one but failed to move on to stage two.[41] With the first part of the 'Iron Wall' driving strategy, Israel, after 1948, opted for military rather than political solutions when dealing with the Arabs. As a result, Zionist–Arab relations foundered and, at times, descended into war. The 'Iron Wall' concept challenges the notion that the Zionists wanted an accommodation with the Arabs and the Palestinians, but Arab obstinacy ruined any deal. In fact, the critical interchange was within Israel between those wanting to follow the 'Iron Wall' policy versus those seeking a more peaceful, political solution to the Arab–Israeli impasse.

Israeli battlefield success in the 'War of Independence' proved the relative value of the 'Iron Wall' of military victory over political dialogue. As one American Zionist leader noted, this triumph was a welcome psychological boost for a Jewish population traumatized by the horrors of the Second World War. Indeed, military victory over the Arabs in 1948–9

> . . . offered such a glorious contrast to the centuries of persecution and humiliation, of adaptation and compromise, that it seemed to indicate the only direction that could possibly be taken from then on. To brook nothing, tolerate no attack, cut through Gordian knots, and shape history by creating facts seemed so simple, so compelling, so satisfying that it became Israel's policy in its conflict with the Arab world.[42]

Ben-Gurion was undoubtedly tough when it came to negotiations with the Arabs. He famously told Kenneth Bilby, the correspondent of the *New York Herald Tribune*, that, while he was 'prepared to get up in the middle of the night in order to sign a peace agreement . . . I am not in a hurry and I can wait ten years. We are under no pressure whatsoever.'[43] With this in mind, Israel repeatedly used its growing military power to achieve its political objectives. For instance, in October 1948, Israel broke a UN ceasefire and attacked Egyptian forces in the Negev desert around the town of Beersheba in southern Israel/Palestine. Therefore, as John Bagot Glubb, the British commander of the Arab Legion, emphasized, southern Israel was won, not in the general fighting from May to June 1948, but by a deliberate Israeli violation of a UN ceasefire in October 1948.[44] In March 1949, during talks with the Jordanians on Rhodes, Israel again used the tactic of military action, this time to expel Jordanian forces from a lodgement in the southern Negev desert. The Israelis then moved south to capture what would become the Israeli town of Eilat at the head of the Gulf of Akaba. For those such as Glubb, Israeli policy went against the letter and spirit of the armistice talks on Rhodes and confirmed Israel's lack of interest in negotiating a solution:

> . . . after so long denying any military movement in the south, and after five days of prevarication in Rhodes, during which they constantly postponed signing the cease-fire agreement, the Israeli delegation came out in the open. They informed the Jordan delegation that the area extending southwards to the Gulf of Aqaba had been allotted to them by the 1947 partition plan and that they proposed to occupy it. This was in direct contradiction of the assurances they had been giving us for the previous fortnight. It will be seen that, in this respect, the Israeli policy was one of 'heads I win and tails you lose'.[45]

Although they upset the peace talks, the operations against Egypt and Jordan in the Negev altered the situation on the ground in Israel's favour and allowed it to emerge from the peace talks with control of the Negev desert and a port with access to the Red Sea. Military figures within Israel argued successfully that Israel had no other choice as negotiations with those such as Abdullah would only 'undermine Israel's military option'.[46] And this policy paid dividends: Zionists had only to look at the map of Israel in 1949, compared to the Jewish state envisaged by the UN partition plan of 1947, to see how military success had won the day. Israel's aggressive military operations from 1948 to 1949 lend weight to the 'Iron Wall' idea: before a political dialogue could be established and its usefulness tested, the Israeli Defence Forces (IDF) went into action against the Arabs so as to present negotiators with a military *fait accompli*.

It was also the case that 'hawks' predominated in the Israeli political apparatus at this time. It has been suggested by Moshe Ma'oz that in the Israeli Cabinet only Sasson, the Syrian-born diplomat, was 'unequivocally opposed to the policy of using military force rather than diplomacy'.[47] While Foreign Minister Sharett was another senior figure calling for political solutions in the face of Ben-Gurion's desire to press home Israel's military advantage, the momentum at the time within Israel was with Ben-Gurion.[48] On 2 November 1948, Yaacov Shimoni, the deputy head of the Foreign Ministry's Middle East department, wrote to Sasson to complain how Ben-Gurion sought 'to solve most of the problems by military means, in such a way that no political negotiations and no political action would be of any value'.[49] One of Ben-Gurion's key supporters was Moshe Dayan, who would become chief of staff and defence minister, and whose saying 'if only the men of the Foreign Ministry were like the tanks of the IDF, all Israel's international problems would be solved' reiterated the hard-line approach of Israeli decision-makers.[50]

There was little impetus for Israel to talk because its key issues – borders, refugees and Jerusalem – were non-negotiable. Expanded borders, a Jewish majority within Israel's population and some control over Jerusalem were the basic minima for a viable Jewish state and the armistice agreements, which confirmed the expanded borders of Israel, were far superior to any deal that limited Israel's borders or allowed hundreds of thousands of Palestinians back into Israel. It was a question of demography and Israel had no intention of negotiating away its population advantage now that the Palestinians had been expelled. With approaching 1 million Palestinians given the right to return home, the survival of a Jewish state was uncertain. With these national desiderata paramount, Israeli diplomats at the Lausanne conference worked hard at 'rendering this conference futile' because they knew that a settlement was unlikely to favour Israeli short-term goals.[51]

For Israel, postponing a peace treaty in 1949 made good sense as the new Zionist state concentrated on building up the economy and absorbing Jewish immigrants. Within three years, new migrants would double the Jewish population of Israel. The armistice agreements were effectively *de facto* peace agreements that obviated the need for Israel to pursue a comprehensive peace settlement; one that would undoubtedly reignite the thorny questions of borders and refugees.[52] This was the cause of Israel's stubbornness at the peace talks in the face of serious peace offers from Arab leaders. As Aryeh Shalev observed, peace was not an immediate goal because of the high price Israel would have to pay in two areas: absorption of Palestinian refugees and border concessions.[53] Therefore, Ben-Gurion and the Israelis stalled and obstructed UN, US and Arab peace offers. For the Americans, Israeli intransigence was exemplified by Ben-Gurion's 'uncompromising refusal' to meet Zaim, as a consequence of which 'stalemate seems likely to continue indefinitely'.[54] But this stalemate suited Israel. When the Turkish delegate on the PCC tried to convince Ben-Gurion of the Arabs' good intentions and of the need for Israel to make a comparable gesture to help the Arabs overcome their psychological barrier in negotiating with Israel, Ben-Gurion

> . . . could evade the trap set in this question only by attaching his answer to specific conditions: he said that the resolution in question spoke about refugees wishing to 'live in peace' with the Israelis, while it was far from certain whether the would-be returning Arabs would indeed have peaceful intentions. . . . He concluded by repeating Israel's standard argument namely that the refugee question could be solved only within the wider context of a peace settlement.[55]

Ben-Gurion had far more pressing issues in 1949 than making peace with the Arabs. Speaking at the Foreign Ministry in April 1949, Israel's Prime Minister emphasized the importance of Jewish immigration to the new Zionist state:

> On immigration hung also the fate of Israel. All our conquests, whether in the Negev, the Galilee or Jerusalem were meaningless without settlements. *Settlement was the true conquest.* If we were

to consider the three foundations on which the state was built – the ingathering of the exiles, the settlement of the land, and the security of the country – we would find that all three depended on a single factor: the absorption of immigration. It stood above all, and should it ever conflict with other interests, it had to take preference.[56]

Given Ben-Gurion's priorities, surrendering land or accepting anything but a token number of Palestinians to return home, were anathema, when, as he admitted, 'the absorption of immigration was the central issue'.[57] Peace with the Arabs was a priority but not of the first order, at least not in 1949. Ben-Gurion's top priorities were state building, immigration, economic growth and security for the new Zionist state. As Shlaim concluded, Ben-Gurion's position meant that while Israel was interested in peace, it was 'not prepared to pay a price for it'.[58]

Those opposed to the 'Iron Wall' concept have put forward a more sympathetic explanation for Ben-Gurion's actions in 1949:

Is it reasonable to dismiss out of hand as 'mistakes' Ben-Gurion's unwillingness to allow a large number of Arab refugees to return to their homes or his refusal to cede a territorial corridor in the Negev to Jordan or to give Syria half of Lake Kinneret? Ben-Gurion's reasoning cannot be understood without a conceptual approach. The fact is that he acted solely on the basis of his interpretation of Israel's national security interest and was broadly backed by Israeli public opinion. In this view the refugees would become a 'fifth column', the Negev might be cut off from the rest of the country if Jordan received a corridor, and the implications of giving Syria a critical water source like the Kinneret . . . were fraught with unacceptable risks. Naturally, in the light of the five costly wars Israel has fought since 1948, it is tempting to argue that an opportunity was missed at the outset. If Ben-Gurion rejected peace, however, it was not from a desire for future expansion but because he viewed the armistice lines as the essential minimum for sheer survival.[59]

It has to be said that this counter-revisionist argument does not absolve Israel from blame for the failed peace of 1949. It merely points out that Ben-Gurion had good reason to act the way he did and that he felt that he could not accept a peace in which Israel would have to concede land and refugees. Ben-Gurion's policies reflected what was probably, *for Israel*, seen to be the best strategy, *at the time*, to ensure its survival. But this is a point conceded by Morris, one of the leading 'new' historians:

> I am not arguing that Ben-Gurion was wrong; perhaps land and water resources were more important for a tiny, immigrant absorbing country than peace. I am, however, arguing Syria offered peace terms and that Ben-Gurion, apparently with Sharett's full support, failed to give negotiations a chance; decided this without bringing the matter before Cabinet; and then, for decades lied about the Syrians' (and, more generally, the Arab leaders') willingness to talk peace.[60]

In step with Morris, Shlaim drew a similar conclusion on Ben-Gurion: 'He knew that for formal peace agreements Israel would have to pay by yielding territory to its neighbors and by agreeing to the return of a substantial number of Palestinian refugees, and he did not consider this a price worth paying. Whether Ben-Gurion made the right choice is a matter of opinion. That he had a choice is undeniable.'[61]

THE ARABS AND ISRAEL

The 'Iron Wall' thesis presupposes that there were options available other than the ones taken by the decision-makers at the time. For this to be the case, the Arab peace offers of 1949–50 had to be substantive enough to become accepted, lasting peace treaties. If, on the other hand, the Arab peace offers were a will-o'-the-wisp, then the matter of Israel's non-response is less important. The viability of the Arab peace feelers needs to be assessed not just in light of Israeli intransigence but also with regard to the Arab politics of the period, and to the status of the Palestinian refugees. Perhaps peace in 1949 was a more elusive option than the 'new' historians would have us believe and, therefore, the question of Israel being at fault for the failed peace is something of a distraction to the real causes of the Arab–Israeli conflict.

Was, for instance, the Syrian peace offer of 1949 a credible one? Zaim, the Syrian leader, was a military dictator with all the qualities of an unelected military officer who had seized power by force. Subject to 'attacks where he would lose all logic', he and his ilk were poorly equipped to tackle Syria's problems.[62] Having served under French colonial rule, Zaim and his fellow officers came from the 'pre-ideological generation' unprepared for the radical change of the post-1945 Middle East. Neither were these leaders in power for very long: of the three colonels who seized power in quick succession in 1949 – Zaim in March, Sami al-Hinnawi in August and Shishakli in December – only Shishakli remained in power for any length of time, until he, too, was overthrown in February 1954.[63] In his short period in office, Zaim progressively alienated his supporters and lost touch with his powerbase within the Syrian military as he moved into the 'rarified air of untrammelled personal authority' and broke with the small number of officers with whom he had planned his coup.[64] Greed was also a motivating factor as Zaim hoped for personal pecuniary reward in addition to funds from America for Syria if he signed a peace. This funding even included a possible $1 million from Israel. Knowing of these shady dealings and Zaim's reputation as an adventurer, Ben-Gurion was wary of striking a deal with what proved to be a 'here today, gone tomorrow' politician.[65] Bearing in mind Zaim's reputation and the shifting sands of Syrian politics in the 1950s, would Syria's offer, had it been pursued by a more pacific Israel, have metamorphosed into a peace treaty?

While Ben-Gurion undoubtedly killed off any potential peace with Syria, the evidence available suggests that Zaim's offer of peace might have failed the test of time. To gain power, Zaim had allied himself to a group of nationalist officers determined to carry on the war with Israel. Therefore, it came as a shock when Zaim suddenly displayed an eagerness to negotiate with the enemy. When Zaim then went a step further and secretly entered into talks for a high-level meeting with Ben-Gurion, his aides were horrified at what was effectively Syria's recognition of Israel, an act they were unwilling to countenance. In such a hostile environment, a meeting with Ben-Gurion might well have hastened Zaim's departure from Syrian politics. Zaim balked at meeting the doveish Sharett for fear of the impact such an encounter would have on the Arab world, so one can only speculate at how Syrian (and Arab) public opinion would have reacted to a meeting with the bellicose Ben-Gurion.[66] In light of the hostile climate in the region, Zaim was unable to deliver the goods. Instead, as the 'new' historian, Ilan Pappé, admitted, his peace feelers

> . . . should be treated with caution. His short term in office and the inevitability of his downfall are bound to raise questions about the sincerity and, more important, the viability of his proposal. . . . But it was not money that Zaim needed in the first place, rather sufficient political support in his own country for his unusual scheme. Failing that support, it would prove impossible for Zaim to stay in power, and in August 1949 he was overthrown by another officer of the Syrian army.[67]

Ben-Gurion's fundamental reason for ignoring Zaim was because his concept of Israeli strategy precluded a deal with Syria. But when contextualized within Syrian politics, it is debatable, had Ben-Gurion shown more interest, whether the Syrian–Israeli negotiations had any future. In this sense, even though Syria showed a willingness to talk, both sides in 1949, and not just Israel, were culpable.

Across the Arab Middle East, leaders ready to communicate with Israel ran the risk of alienating their own population as well as fellow Arab rulers. Jordan was a case in point as Abdullah's collusion with Israel provoked a wave of hostility among the Palestinian population of Jordan and led to his assassination in 1951. Worried about the staying power of Arab interlocutors such as Abdullah, Israel moderated its response to peace offers.[68] A year after Abdullah's death, a revolution of young army officers in Egypt brought the charismatic Nasser to power. There followed a wave of pan-Arab revolutionary fervour that swept across the Arab world, toppling the old order of monarchical rule and landed privilege. The rise of 'Nasserism' split the Arab world into opposing sides, with a radical pro-Nasser camp versus conservative pro-Hashemite regimes. Hatred of Israel became one of the few issues that the Arabs could agree on. This militated against a peace settlement as neither Nasser nor the Hashemites could be seen to be openly dealing with Israel. It was also the case that had treaties with Israel been signed prior to 1952, would the new radical Arab regimes have honoured them? The emergence of a radical, divided Middle East in the 1950s transformed intra-Arab politics and threatened the peace process. Even before the revolutions of the 1950s, Arab leaders avoided negotiations with Israel for fear of the backlash at home; after 1952, states built on pan-Arabism found it even more difficult to reconcile their radical ideology with negotiations with Zionist Israel.[69] Arab governments could not resist the 'clamour for revenge' from populations desperate to hit back at Israel and were forced to choose between a dialogue with the enemy or remaining in power. As Rony Gabbay detailed, Arab leaders were on the horns of a dilemma:

> As long as the Arab states did not come to terms with Israel, or sign an armistice with it, they did not urge for Arab repatriation. As long as the possibility of resuming military operations in Palestine remained, there was no motive for advocating the return of the refugees. To where should they be returned? To Israeli territories, to become Israeli citizens? That meant recognition of Israel! Moreover, how could they approach their own people or even the refugees and request them to return while Palestine was still under Jewish occupation and not yet liberated! . . . The result was simple. The Arab delegation could ask for international relief, presenting the misery, suffering, destitution and distress of the refugees to the world, but they would not request their repatriation to their homes and lands, to be under Jewish control.

On the contrary, they should demand that the whole country be given back to its people, and that the Jews should be ejected and repatriated to their countries of origin in Europe.[70]

THE PALESTINIAN REFUGEE CRISIS

Even if Israel and the Arab states had settled their differences and come to an arrangement in 1949, what of the fate of the Palestinian refugees? Israel's expulsion of 7–800,000 Palestinians presented an almost insurmountable hurdle to any peace treaty. Although they were careful not to declare it openly, Israeli leaders firmly opposed any full-scale repatriation, preferring, as has been seen, to evade the issue in the hope that it would disappear.[71] But the question of the future status of hundreds of thousands of Palestinians, forced to live in wretched conditions in neighbouring Arab countries, would not go away. Any peace treaty needed to resolve the issue of recognition and rights for the Palestinians. Even if peace treaties with Syria, Jordan and Egypt had been signed, would the Palestinians have been willing to give up their former homes and make new lives and forge new identities on the West Bank, the Gaza Strip or in some part of Syria or Lebanon? The border clashes of the 1950s, when Palestinians attempted to cross the border to reoccupy their homes and tend their fields, suggest otherwise.

Much as some Arab leaders wanted to strike a deal with Israel, this was difficult because the Arab League created a common consensus that pushed the issue of the Palestinians to the fore in any settlement. The pan-Arab view was that Israel should not be allowed to evade its responsibility to the Palestinians; Israel claimed that the Arabs started the war of 1948–9 and encouraged the Palestinians to flee prior to a wholesale Arab invasion. The Palestinians became a convenient propaganda tool for Arab states eager to castigate Zionism in international fora such as the UN. While often uninterested in the plight of the Palestinian refugees, no Arab state was able to proceed with a separate peace with Israel without being seen to take into account the rights of the Palestinians for fear of the negative reaction from other Arab states.[72] But Israel, militarily strong, was determined to block any transfer of Palestinians wishing to return home. This made any comprehensive peace almost impossible as an acceptable home had to be found for the displaced Palestinians. The failure to solve the question of the rights of the Palestinians scuppered any chances of a peace and proved over the years to be one of the key motors of the Arab–Israeli conflict. It came as no surprise that when Egypt finally signed a peace treaty with Israel in 1979, it effectively absolved itself from the question of rights for the Palestinians, preferring to sign a treaty that benefited Egypt while marginalizing the question of a Palestinian state. By doing so, Egypt earned the opprobrium of the Arab world.

THE ROLE OF GREAT BRITAIN

The policies of the former imperial power in the region, Britain, compounded the already fraught situation. Britain encouraged Jordan to sideline the Palestinians and divide up Palestine with Israel in the hope that this would prevent an anti-British Palestine emerging under the leadership of Hajj Amin al-Husseini – the Grand Mufti of Jerusalem. As Abdullah became more reliant on Britain, he lost support from neighbouring Arab states.[73] This meant that Abdullah had to be careful when dealing with Israel so as not to be seen to be doing Britain's bidding. British strategy depended on control of the Suez Canal and Jordan. As Sir John Troutbeck, the head of the Middle East office in Cairo, argued, an Israeli–Jordanian peace treaty would be viewed unfavourably by the Egyptians, with whom Britain wanted good relations, and might jeopardize an agreement over British control of the Suez Canal. As control of the Suez Canal and good relations with Egypt were concerns of the first order, Britain did little to encourage Abdullah to sign a treaty with Israel that might have damaged Britain's position in Egypt.[74]

CONCLUSION

Israeli intransigence, intra-Arab politics and the question of the Palestinians combined to block a peace in 1949. Beneath the façade of secret talks there were too many unresolved issues and too much 'posturing and maneuvring' as Israel worked to consolidate the *status quo* and the Arab states tried to revert to the *status quo ante* the war of 1948–9.[75] Both positions were incompatible with a peace settlement. While leaders such as Zaim and Abdullah were willing to give ground, Arab domestic politics and Israeli stubbornness worked together to block these brief chances for peace. The victims of this failure to find a solution were the Palestinians, who were left without a state. Muhammad Nimr al-Hawwari, representing a group of Palestinians, recalled how the Palestinians were caught in the middle, reliant on Arab states that 'stalled and procrastinated, believing that keeping Israel under threat would lead to its economic collapse, since it would be forced to keep its army in a constant state of alert'.[76] When Israel's economy failed to collapse, when its military strength failed to wane, and when the Arab states proved unable to defeat Israel in battle, the Palestinians were forced to reassess their position and, in the 1960s, establish a Palestinian national movement to fight for a Palestinian state. After Egypt's treaty with Israel in 1979, other Arab states began to normalize relations with Israel and, from the late 1980s, the Israelis and Palestinians entered into a serious dialogue to try and settle the question of a Palestinian state that could coexist with Israel. It is to be hoped that both Israel and the Palestinians can find ways to accommodate the other and so arrest the move to conflict and war that has been such a characteristic feature of Arab-Israeli relations since the formation of Israel in May 1948.

PART THREE

The Far East

SIX

The Yalta Accords and the Origins of the Chinese Revolutionary Civil War, 1946–9

'[The] Japanese surrender has also paved the way for [the] final settlement between [the] Chinese Communists and [the] Central Government or an outbreak of large scale hostilities between them . . .'

Patrick J. Hurley, 20 August 1945[1]

On 14 August 1945, following two devastating atomic strikes against the cities of Hiroshima and Nagasaki, the Japanese government indicated its willingness to accept the terms of the Potsdam Declaration and thereby end its war against the United Nations. Although the surrender ceremony, which was held in Tokyo Bay on the quarterdeck of the American battleship the USS *Missouri*, would not take place for another three weeks, this decision 'to endure the unendurable' effectively marked the close of the Second World War in the Pacific.[2] Thus ended, in one fell swoop, eight years of Sino-Japanese rivalry on the Chinese mainland, four years of conflict between America and Japan among the islands of the Pacific Ocean, and a week of battle in Manchuria between the forces of the Soviet Union and the demoralized soldiers of Japan's once much-vaunted Kwantung Army.

As the fighting in these battle zones ceased, the victorious Allies inevitably found themselves faced with the task of bringing peace to the region. Fortunately this was not an activity for which they were totally unprepared. During the course of the war, the Allied leaders had engaged in many discussions about the shaping of the postwar world, agreeing in the process to a variety of principles and measures, the most famous expressions of which were the Atlantic Charter and the numerous protocols from the various inter-Allied conferences. Yet, of these many accords, easily the most important with respect to the settlement that would be implemented in China were the terms which collectively constituted what Akira Iriye has described as 'the Yalta system of international relations'[3] – namely the Cairo Declaration of 1 December 1943, the Yalta accords of 11 February 1945 and the Sino-Soviet Treaty of 14 August in the same year.[4] In addition to eliminating Japan as a power factor on the Asian mainland, these agreements also explicitly committed the Soviet Union to recognize the Guomindang (GMD) Party led by Generalissimo Jiang Jieshi (Chiang Kai-shek)[5] as the sole legitimate government of a unified China, and thereby implicitly to deny the legitimacy of the rival claims to governance of the Chinese Communist Party (CCP). In theory, therefore, the proposed peace settlement was one that ended the threat from Japan, China's main external enemy, and cut the ground from under the feet of the CCP, the Chinese government's only internal enemy. As such, it contained all the ingredients that most contemporary observers believed were necessary to form the basis for a durable and lasting peace.

However, this was not to be. Within weeks of the Japanese surrender, fighting was once again a feature of the Chinese landscape, as numerous small local skirmishes broke out between GMD and CCP forces. Slowly, the military momentum grew. Within months, the minor local incidents of late 1945 had given way to bigger clashes. Then in April 1946, in an event that heralded the unambiguous onset of civil war, a full-scale battle took place outside Siping (Ssuping). From this point there would be no turning back and the civil war quickly intensified. Soon large armies, boasting hundreds of thousands of front-line combat troops, as well as armour and artillery, found themselves fighting intense positional battles, and then massive campaigns, across the length and breadth of China.

Why was it that the end of the Second World War did not bring tranquillity to the Chinese mainland, but was instead followed almost immediately by an extremely bitter and hard-fought civil war?

TRADITIONAL EXPLANATIONS FOR THE ORIGINS OF THE CIVIL WAR

The answer most commonly given to this question is that the renewed conflict was the inevitable outcome of the deep and mutual ideological and personal hostility that existed between the GMD and CCP, an antipathy which went all the way back to April 1927.

Prior to that time, relations between the GMD and CCP had always been amicable. For the most part, this was because the GMD had a policy, first implemented by Dr Sun Zhongshan (Sun Yat-sen), the movement's founder, of accepting the right of communists to join the party. However, from the very start, this decision, which was an integral part of Dr Sun's strategy of obtaining aid from the Soviet Union, had not been universally popular among his colleagues. Indeed, many prominent figures within the nationalist movement – particularly those with commercial or banking interests – had long been hostile to the formation of an alliance with a party, the ultimate aim of which was to usurp their place in the socioeconomic order. For no one, however, was this hostility greater than for Dr Sun's successor, General Jiang Jieshi, the former commandant of the Whampoa Military Academy, who doubted the communists' loyalty to the nationalist cause (i.e. him) and found their message of class struggle unpalatable. Following Dr Sun's death in March 1925, he would soon find the opportunity to demonstrate just how intense his feelings on this matter actually were. On 12 April 1927, after he had willingly used CCP-organized strikes and demonstrations to facilitate a Guomindang takeover of the city of Shanghai, Jiang turned on his erstwhile allies. Troops loyal to Jiang, supplemented by members of the local underworld organization, the Green Gang (Qing Ban), rounded up the CCP cadres and leadership, along with their supporters in the trade union and worker's movements, and slaughtered them. The Shanghai Massacre was but the herald of things to come. Following rapidly on its heels, Jiang launched other anti-communist measures, including five military strikes, or encirclement campaigns, against the communists' key strongholds in the countryside, the so-called 'base areas'. The last of these attacks sent the communist forces fleeing to the north in a fighting retreat to Yan'an (Yenan) that has subsequently become known as 'the Long March'. Harassed every step of the way by pursuing nationalist armies, the situation looked bleak at this stage for the communists.

That Jiang never completed his anti-communist crusade was not due to any abatement of animosity on his part, but can be attributed instead to Japanese imperialism. By 1936, the Japanese, who had already conquered Manchuria five years earlier, were showing alarming indications that they had designs on more of northern China. In the face of this common national emergency, the GMD and CCP agreed to shelve their differences in order better to defend their homeland. Yet, even the manner in which they formed this united front speaks volumes about their underlying hostility. Until 1936, Jiang, whose motto was 'internal pacification before resistance to foreign invasion',[6] had kept up his attacks on the communists despite the increasing signs of Japanese activity. This order of priorities was only reversed when, in the pre-dawn hours of 12 December 1936, while he was at the army headquarters in Xi'an (Sian) trying to motivate his forces in Shaanxi province for a final assault against the communists, Jiang was kidnapped. The perpetrator of this action, which soon became known as the Xi'an incident, was Zhang Xueliang (Chang Hsüeh-liang), the warlord leader of Manchuria, the province that had been conquered by Japan in 1931. Bitterly hostile to the Japanese as a result of their usurpation of his territory, Zhang had long wanted to strike back. However, Jiang's preoccupation with the communist threat had forced him instead into a series of campaigns against people who were, in essence, fellow Chinese. Disillusioned by the endless fratricidal strife, but unable to alter Jiang's priorities by persuasion, Zhang decided that it was time to resort to other means. That this tactic succeeded in forcing Jiang to promise that in the future he would resist the Japanese rather than attack the communists should not obscure the fact that this volte-face was not voluntary, but resulted from coercion.[7] Even though Jiang cooperated with the communists during the war against Japan – and there were strict limits to such cooperation – he remained convinced throughout that it was the CCP that was his real enemy. 'The Japanese', he was fond of saying, 'are only lice on the body of China, but communism is a disease of the heart.'[8] Accordingly, despite being at war with Japan, he held back his best forces – perhaps as many as sixteen divisions or 400,000 troops – for use against the CCP.[9] This was not an attitude that boded well for future peace.

However, it was one that was fully reciprocated by the communists and their leader Mao Zedong (Mao Tse-tung). Just as Jiang had agreed to form a united front against the Japanese less out of desire than out of necessity (in his case protection from Marshal Zhang's irate Manchurian soldiers) so, too, did the adherence of the CCP to the common cause spring from ulterior motives. In their case, the sudden transformation of policy – exemplified by the change in the party slogan from 'oppose Jiang' to 'unite with Jiang to resist Japan' – was less a matter of conviction than a strategy designed to protect them from the nationalist armies that were poised to annihilate them.[10] As the well-known commentator on the Chinese Revolution, Lucien Bianco, has written: 'In 1936 the Communists had their backs to the wall; their position was . . . at times downright desperate.'[11] Yet, by agreeing, however insincerely, to accept GMD leadership of a united front, the communists were able to ensure that the nationalist forces ceased their attacks on the CCP and focused – at least initially – on the Japanese. As Mao observed this meant that the threatened massacre of the communists in 1937 – a massacre that might have been as bad as the one they had suffered in Shanghai in 1927 – was averted. 'As long as the Sino-Japanese contradiction remains sharp', he wrote, 'the situation of 1927 can never be brought about, nor the incident of April 12 . . . be repeated.'[12] On the contrary, the united front brought just the respite that the communists needed to rebuild their strength, something, moreover, that they were now able to do not as rebels but as patriots. This plan was as clever as it was deliberate. 'Mao and his followers', as one recent commentator noted, 'knew that in a Sino-Japanese war they could claim, as patriots, a legitimate, honourable, and self-defined role.'[13] Yet, in reality, as Mao's own writing makes clear, beneath the rhetoric of the united front and the common goal of defeating the Japanese invaders, the CCP remained committed to supplanting the GMD by revolutionary means. As he told the delegates at the sixth plenary session of the Central Committee of the CCP on 6 November 1938: 'the central task and the supreme form of a revolution is the seizure of political power by force of arms and the solution of problems by war'. Despite the united front, he did not deviate from the belief that 'without armed struggle the proletariat and the Communist Party could not win any place for themselves . . .'. On the contrary, all actions taken under the united front strategy 'should always be regarded as part of the entire revolutionary policy, as an indispensable link in the revolutionary line . . .'.[14] This, too, did not bode well for future peace.

As we can see, in the GMD and CCP there existed two mutually hostile organizations which, despite briefly coming together for one very particular purpose, had never disavowed the idea of destroying each other. On the contrary, both parties, to cite the words of John King Fairbank, 'by their nature aimed at total power'[15] and were willing, if not actually desirous, of using military means to achieve their goal. Having resorted to force on previous occasions, there were many who thought that, given the opportunity, they would do so again. As the American diplomat John F. Melby recorded pessimistically in his diary on 9 November 1945, 'practically everyone now says there is little or no hope for bringing unity to China. . . . The issues and the bitterness are too deep for peace.'[16]

It is this situation that has led many commentators and historians to suggest that, despite the ending of the Second World War, a resumption of fighting in China was always likely, if not actually inevitable. As they see it, the Chinese Civil War was the unavoidable product of an ideological confrontation between two power-hungry parties, whose mutual detestation and incompatible goals made them incapable of reaching an amicable settlement. Obviously, in such an interpretation, the terms of the agreement at Yalta were, at best, a peripheral issue; the war was going to occur anyway.

Although a substantial number of historians regard the outbreak of the Chinese Civil War as the unavoidable consequence of the mutual hostility of the GMD and CCP, there are problems with this approach. One objection is the teleological notion that the war was somehow 'inevitable'. While natural disasters may be inevitable, wars are invariably the product of human agency – the Chinese Civil War included. Thus, we find historians such as Odd Arne Westad challenging the view that the civil war was foreordained by developments in the preceding decades and concluding that 'those who proclaim that a generation of GMD–CCP rivalry and conflict predetermined an all-out civil war have simply not studied the documents from the 1945–6 period closely enough'.[17] What causes him to draw such a conclusion?

One reason for contesting the idea that the GMD–CCP conflict made war inevitable is that, despite the gloomy predictions of some observers, the prospects for peace actually looked quite bright in late 1945 and early 1946. There existed a huge constituency that either wanted peace for its own sake or could, at the very least, see advantages in its occurrence. Significantly, this constituency included the world's two superpowers, the Soviet Union and the United States, as well as major elements in China itself. As Mao himself recognized in late 1945, 'Peace can be obtained [as] the Soviet Union, the United States, and Great Britain want peace, the people want peace, we want peace.'[18]

That the Soviet Union should have desired an end to conflict in China in 1945 often comes as a surprise to people aware that the communists would ultimately be swept to power in the Chinese Civil War. However, that only goes to show the impediment that hindsight can be to historical empathy. For, as the Soviet leaders looked at the situation in China in 1945, they concluded that nationalist strength was such that any resumption of the Civil War would lead to the total destruction of communist influence in China. As a result, their advice to the CCP leadership was to seek an accommodation with

123

the GMD. In their view, a coalition in which the CCP participated as junior partner was infinitely preferable to the communists' destruction and, thus, worth the price of a few concessions.[19]

Another reason for the Soviet desire to see peace in China stems directly from the Yalta agreements. At the Crimea conference, the Soviet Union was able to extract, as the price of its entry into the war against Japan, British and American consent to the return of those territories and concessions in China that Russia had lost in the Russo-Japanese War of 1904/5. However, for this to mean anything, it was still necessary for the deal to be ratified by a Chinese government that was internationally recognized as legitimate. Only the GMD administration led by Jiang Jieshi fitted this description, and they were hardly likely to come to terms with a Soviet regime that sponsored their destruction. But a Soviet government that recognized their legitimacy and worked for their preservation was another matter entirely. Hence, the ratification of the Yalta terms in the Sino-Soviet Treaty of 14 August 1945 gave Jiang a good reason to honour the concessions to the Soviet Union; and by doing so, he gave the Soviet leadership a good reason to hope for peace and stability in the region.[20] As General John R. Deane, the American Military Attaché in Moscow, explained, 'Stalin has what he wants in Manchuria – the Lushun base (Port Arthur) and his railway – and he isn't going to jeopardize that in a Chinese Civil War.'[21] This, therefore, provided Stalin with another good reason for instructing the CCP to negotiate with Jiang. Recently opened documents in the Russian archives make it clear that the Soviet leader was unambiguous in conveying this message.[22]

Significantly, if the Soviet Union had good reason for desiring peace and stability in East Asia, so, too, did the Americans, who had long sought to promote harmony between the GMD and CCP. Their efforts had originally been aimed at unifying the Chinese so that they could devote their full resources to fighting the Japanese rather than each other. However, as the end of the war came into sight, a new priority began to assert itself. At this point, American leaders became increasingly alarmed that, when Japanese power was finally extinguished, Soviet influence in the Far East would fill the vacuum.

The obvious solution was to build up China into a regional power that could act as a counterweight. However, so long as Chinese internal politics kept the country's energies focused on domestic discord, there would be no possibility at all of China fulfilling this vital external role. Thus, it became the American objective to restore peace and stability to China.

Considerable efforts were devoted to this task. In particular, three American missions went to China specifically to promote an accord between the GMD and CCP. The first of these, which took place in June 1944, was headed by no less a personage than Vice-President Henry A. Wallace. Following hard on his heels was Major-General Patrick J. Hurley who went to China as the Personal Representative of President Franklin Roosevelt. Finally, in November 1945, President Truman appointed the much-respected former chief of staff, General of the Army George C. Marshall, as his Special Representative in China.[23] Although these missions differed in their approach, their message was fundamentally the same. As Secretary of State James F. Byrnes wrote on 9 December 1945, the goal of the United States was 'a strong, united, and democratic China'. To this end, he observed,

> it is essential that the Central Government of China as well as the various dissident elements approach the settlement of their differences with a genuine willingness to compromise. We believe . . . that the government of Generalissimo [Jiang Jieshi] affords the most satisfactory base for a developing democracy. But we also believe that it must be broadened to include the representatives of those large and well organized groups who are now without any voice in the government of China.[24]

As such 'broadening' would only be meaningful if it included the CCP, the United States government, like the Soviet government, was essentially advocating negotiations between the GMD and the communists for the peaceful resolution of their differences.

In addition to the international momentum behind the promotion of a peaceful and stable China, a domestic dynamic for peace also existed. In part, this came from popular pressure; the Chinese people themselves, having just emerged from eight years of savage fighting against the Japanese, were in no mood to see a resumption of old conflicts. Any party that openly advocated civil war was, thus, likely to haemorrhage popular support. Even in the authoritarian setting of 1940s China, this was a consideration that could not easily be ignored.[25] However, more significant than the desire for peace among the populace was the fact that both the CCP and the GMD also had reasons for wanting an end to their internecine struggle and the resolution of their differences through negotiations.

Of the two, the Communist Party's motive for seeking a negotiated settlement was most straightforward. Despite their revolutionary doctrine which told them that the Chongqing (Chungking) regime of Jiang Jieshi was a reactionary force doomed to inevitable extinction, whereas they, as the forces of progress, represented China's future, they were nevertheless by no means certain of victory. On the contrary, by most of the available indices of comparison, the numerous American-trained and equipped nationalist divisions seemed self-evidently more powerful than Mao's rural guerrilla armies. An immediate military contest might well, therefore, have ended in a communist defeat, a judgement that the Soviet Union very publicly endorsed by signing the Sino-Soviet Treaty of 14 August 1945 with the representatives of the GMD government. The message from Stalin to the CCP could not have been clearer. In guaranteeing Moscow's exclusive recognition of the Chongqing regime, he was implicitly declaring that he saw the nationalists as the dominant force in China and suggesting that the CCP come to terms with them. As Mao described it, 'Stalin wanted to prevent China from making revolution, saying that we should not have a civil war and should cooperate with [Jiang Jieshi].'[26] Given the significance of the Soviet Union to the communist movement, this was not a message that could easily be ignored. Thus, CCP weakness combined with Russian pressure provided Mao and his followers with a motive to seek peace rather than civil war.

Very different calculations were driving Generalissimo Jiang to a similar conclusion. Seeking to unify China under his Guomindang regime, he was well aware that the communists were a major obstacle to that objective. So long as they remained an independent entity, exercising power outside the control of the national government in areas where the fiat of the central authority did not run, China would not be united. Paradoxically, however, undertaking military operations against them could also weaken the government's hold over the country. As the Xi'an incident had all too graphically demonstrated to Jiang – and at a personal level – protracted internal conflict provided opportunities for generals and regional strongmen to escape from government control. As many of the country's regional leaders already possessed only the most tenuous loyalty to the Chongqing regime and would welcome the chance to loosen their ties with it, fighting a civil war would expose the country to the threat of renewed fragmentation.[27] However, if he could attain his goals without armed conflict, this danger need not be faced, and Jiang believed that this could be achieved. In particular, he was encouraged in this belief by the treaty with the Soviet Union, the chief benefit of which was that, in denying the CCP external support, it gave them a reason to compromise with the GMD. As Stalin had told the chief Chinese negotiator, Song Ziwen (T.V. Soong), 'if China enters into an alliance with the Soviet Union nobody will overthrow the government'.[28] Song had understood the import of this announcement; so, too, did Jiang. If ever there was an opportunity for negotiation from a position of strength it was now.

And then there was American pressure. The United States was the principal source of external aid for the nationalist regime. Money, armaments, logistics and expertise all came from American sources. For the nationalist government, ruling over a poor and war-ravaged land, it was absolutely vital that this largesse be continued. In this context, it hardly seemed expedient to alienate the Americans by refusing to cooperate with their efforts to bring about peace and stability in China. At least by going along with American initiatives, Jiang could demonstrate his inherent reasonableness and hope to qualify for substantial American aid should civil war actually break out. As with his fear of regional separatism, American pressure acted as an impetus for Jiang's involvement in negotiations.

In late 1945, therefore, considerable international and domestic forces were coalescing in China to provide an environment in which negotiations with the GMD could take place, perhaps even with some prospect of success. The momentum behind this combination of Soviet and American pressure, when put alongside a Chinese willingness to engage in discussions, however disingenuous it might sometimes have been, would even show results. On 10 January 1946, much to the surprise of many observers, General Marshall, who had arrived in China only four weeks previously, succeeded in arranging a ceasefire between the contending parties. Even more startlingly, he followed this up by sponsoring a series of inter-party talks – the so-called Political Consultative Conference (PCC) – that actually managed to achieve a consensus over China's future. Resolutions were passed on constitutional arrangements, the calling of a national assembly, local autonomy and the broadening of the government into a coalition led by Jiang.

Reactions to this agreement were not only positive, they were even enthusiastic, and not only from the general public,[29] who could be counted upon to react favourably to any occurrence that diminished the prospect of war, but also from the parties involved. The communists, for example, hailed the PCC resolutions as 'a great victory for China's democratic revolution' and predicted that 'from now on China has reached the new stage of peace, democracy, and reconstruction'. Even more tellingly, the party's cadres were notified that, in the wake of this settlement, a change of strategy would occur. 'The most important form for struggle in the Chinese revolution from now on is not armed struggle', they were informed, but has 'changed to non-armed parliamentary struggle.' The message concluded that 'domestic issues will [now] be resolved through politics'.[30] Jiang, meanwhile, issued a statement pledging to 'uphold this program faithfully and . . . see to it that all the military and civilian subordinates follow it strictly'.[31] Peace, it seemed, was really in sight.

Of course, as the historical record makes only too clear, the PCC did not lead to a lasting settlement. Not surprisingly, the collapse of this agreement has provoked considerable interest, with much of the discussion focusing on the vexed issue of who was to blame for this missed opportunity. Naturally, while some hold the nationalists culpable, others judge the communists to be the guilty party.[32] However, the question of relative blame is not relevant to this discussion. What is germane is that the PCC agreements represented, even if only briefly, a genuine opportunity to reach a peaceful solution to the GMD–CCP conflict.[33] As such, they show that alternatives to civil war existed up to the spring of 1946. In other words, despite all assertions to the contrary, war was not inevitable. But if that is the case, why then did the civil war break out?

ALTERNATIVE PERSPECTIVES (2): THE ROLE OF YALTA

The proposition that will be advanced here is that the conflict arose because the agreements reached under the Yalta system for the postwar arrangements in China, far from being conducive to tranquillity, actually promoted war. This is not an entirely novel proposal. Testifying before the Senate Foreign Relations Committee in 1951, Patrick Hurley, the former American Ambassador to China, expounded the view that

> American diplomats surrendered the territorial integrity and the political independence of China, surrendered the principles of the Atlantic Charter, and wrote the blueprint for the Communist conquest of China in the secret agreement at Yalta.[34]

Hurley's argument about the deleterious effects of Yalta, with its stringent criticisms of the American China Service and its implications of a State Department betrayal of American interests, was very much a product of its times. The hearings at which he gave evidence took place in the aftershock of the so-called 'loss of China' and in the era of McCarthyesque paranoia about Soviet infiltration into America. They were doubtless influenced by this context. Given that many of the polemical assertions of that time have since been utterly discredited, it is necessary to treat such evidence with caution. Nevertheless, if subsequent inquiry has shown that critics of the State Department, Hurley included, were wrong to suspect a diplomatic conspiracy to betray China at Yalta,[35] his general assertion that the Yalta accords had a significant impact on the future of China is not so easy to dismiss. On the contrary, recent research has done much to substantiate it, albeit not on the grounds that Hurley had advanced in 1951.

The principal reason that the Yalta system acted as a stimulus for further warfare was in its provisions regarding the three north-eastern provinces – Liaoning, Jilin (Kirin) and Heilongjiang – that collectively constituted Manchuria. Although lying north of the Great Wall and not forming part of intramural China ('China proper' as it used to be called), these territories were nevertheless of enormous significance. To begin with, possessing major urban areas and a well-developed transport infrastructure, they were among the most industrialized and prosperous parts of the country. Self-evidently, they were of considerable importance to China's economic future and a major asset in any battle to control the nation. In addition, having been occupied for fourteen years by the Japanese, they were also a potent symbol of Chinese patriotism. Any party that wanted recognition from the Chinese people as to its legitimate right to govern would have to be able to show that it could restore these provinces to the nation.

While this combination of economic strength and emotional resonance was bound to make Manchuria significant to China's future political development, the magnitude of the role that this territory was to play after 1945 was blown out of all proportion by the Yalta agreement. For reasons that will be made clear, this settlement led nationalists and communists alike to conclude that they had a realistic chance of excluding their opponents from this vital region and winning this enormous prize for themselves. Realizing that control of Manchuria would give them a decisive advantage, and believing that such control was possible, the two rival groups invested heavily in Manchuria. However, having once mortgaged their future on their grasp over these provinces, neither side could contemplate withdrawal. Inexorably the region became the battleground from which neither side could retreat and over which neither side could compromise. In effect, Yalta ensured that Manchuria, which in the 1930s had been 'the cockpit of Asia' because of its centrality to the Sino-Japanese conflict, would in 1946 be 'the Anvil of victory' in the GMD–CCP rivalry.[36] How did this come to pass?

On the face of it, the Yalta system made few controversial decisions with respect to Manchuria. Although Russian control over the naval base at Lushun was restored, the accords specifically recognized that the region was an integral part of China and should be restored to Chinese rule. If that appeared uncomplicated, the mechanism by which this outcome was to be achieved also appeared relatively straightforward. The scenario envisaged by the Allied leaders when they met in the Crimean resort in February 1945 was that, following the Soviet declaration of war against Japan, the Red Army would be used to sweep Japanese forces out of Manchuria. The province could then be turned over to the nationalist government, while American forces previously deployed in the China and Pacific theatres moved to north China to help repatriate the defeated Japanese army. With the Japanese invaders removed, Soviet and American forces could then leave China to the Chinese.

The reality, however, was altogether different. To begin with, the Soviet attack on Manchuria, while certainly terminating Japanese rule over the region, did not lead to a restoration of Chinese administration; rather, it created a political vacuum. This was all too predictable. The Japanese had occupied the territory for fourteen years. Although it was clear in late 1945 that this state of affairs would eventually come to an end, the suddenness of the Japanese surrender took the Chinese authorities by surprise. They had not made adequate preparations for this eventuality.[37] As a result, they were barely in a position to retake control of intramural China, let alone reassert their authority over a region from which they had been expelled a decade and a half previously. This situation would have major consequences. By simultaneously creating a power vacuum in Manchuria and introducing foreign forces into the region, the Yalta system inadvertently created a new and explosive environment. Instead of a controlled transfer of power, communist and nationalist armies found themselves in 'a competitive race to take over [the formerly] Japanese-occupied territory'[38] in Manchuria, a race in which Russian and American actions, taken in accordance with their understanding of the Yalta system, exacerbated the possibilities for conflict. The actions and interactions of the various participants in this race therefore need to be examined closely.

CCP policy towards Manchuria in the wake of the Japanese surrender reflected the fact that, on the face of it, the area provided them with a tremendous opportunity for political advancement. Manchuria was just the sort of prosperous urban and industrial region that they had always longed to control but had never previously been able to seize. Yet, in August 1945, with Soviet forces expelling the Japanese – as they had agreed to do at Yalta – success finally seemed within reach. For one thing, the liberating armies were fellow communists; the CCP had every reason to expect that they would help them in bringing the revolution to this vital area. On top of this, for reasons of geography, the CCP leaders did not expect immediate opposition from their Guomindang rivals. Manchuria was a long way from the nationalist power centres in south-western China, over a thousand miles away, in fact, but it was very close to the communist concentrations in the country's northern provinces. The rapid deployment of CCP military effectives into Manchuria was, thus, an easy task and one, moreover, that would allow the communists literally to steal a march on their Guomindang rivals; they could be ensconced in Manchuria before the nationalists could hope to get there. As a result of such thinking, the Soviet declaration of war against Japan was followed with incredible rapidity by the mass movement of CCP forces out of their bases in Hebei (Hopei), Shandong (Shantung) and Shanxi (Shansi) and into Manchuria.[39] By December 1945, the communist armies in Manchuria totalled about 200,000 men.[40] This was a major investment of scarce resources and was symptomatic of the importance that the communists attached to the region. It also provided them with no incentive to compromise their bid for control of Manchuria. In a paradoxical manner, Russian actions would solidify this sentiment.

Contrary to expectations, Soviet assistance was much less forthcoming than the CCP had hoped. In accordance with the Yalta terms, Moscow had promised that the areas liberated by the Red Army would be transferred to GMD control; they would not be handed over to the CCP. Nor did the Russians cooperate greatly on minor matters. Peng Zhen (P'eng Chen), a senior member of the CCP's Northeast Bureau, encapsulated the matter when he reported that Soviet forces showed 'a cold and detached attitude' to the Chinese communists.[41] Most significantly, Soviet commanders kept a tight rein on captured Japanese arsenals. Contrary to what is often assumed, recent research has shown that CCP requests to obtain weapons from these stores were generally refused.[42]

Yet denying assistance to the CCP, as the Soviet forces were bound to do under the Sino-Soviet Treaty, was not the same as actively frustrating the Chinese communists in their efforts. This was where the Russians would draw the line, a fact that Stalin had always made clear. As he had informed the GMD delegates during the treaty negotiations, while he would recognize Jiang's government and abstain from providing direct aid to the CCP, he would not actually 'fight against Mao'. This importance of this distinction did not escape notice, as a State Department intelligence appreciation from November 1945 illustrates. 'There is nothing in the treaty', it reported, 'which specifically obligates the Soviets to exclude the Chinese Communists from Manchuria.'[43] Nor did they; CCP cadres descended on the region in droves throughout the Soviet occupation.

There were other ways in which the lenient Russian interpretation of their obligations under the Sino-Soviet Treaty proved advantageous to the CCP. For example, while Soviet commanders took charge of the towns and cities of Manchuria, and even prepared for the handover of these places to nationalist officials, they did nothing to prevent communist forces from occupying the countryside. In this way, rural areas in eastern and northern Manchuria quickly became CCP strongholds. Another example concerns the question of Japanese weapons. As was mentioned earlier, Soviet forces did not generally allow access to Japanese supply dumps. At the same time, however, the Red Army did nothing to prevent communist forces from disarming surrendering Japanese units. By such means large quantities of small arms found their way into the CCP armies.[44] Indeed, some estimates propose that a haul of around 300,000 rifles and 138,000 machine guns was acquired in this manner.[45]

Soviet implementation of the Yalta system in Manchuria was extremely influential in determining CCP policy. In accordance with its treaty obligations, the Red Army did not engage in overt cooperation with the Chinese communists, refused to arm them directly, and removed them from many of the major cities. This was disappointing for the CCP, who had expected much greater and more overt assistance. Nevertheless, when all was said and done, they had been allowed to gain a toehold in the north-east. While this was less than they had hoped for, it was a sufficient gain to be worth defending. And defend it they would. Here, too, Soviet behaviour would be decisive. Exiled by Russian compliance with the Sino-Soviet Treaty to the peripheral areas of the region, the communists were relieved of the temptation to undertake a conventional military strategy based upon holding fortified cities – those who felt otherwise changed their minds after the defeat at Siping. Forced into the countryside, they were instead placed once again in the familiar situation of having to advance by rural revolution and attritional guerrilla warfare. As Gao Gang (Kao Kang), a senior member of the communist Northeast Bureau, explained:

> The work in the Northeast should be deep in the countryside, mobilizing the masses, dividing the land, and broadening the resources for soldiers. We must lead the cadres out of the foreign houses, leave the cities, give up automobiles, take off leather shoes and go to the countryside.[46]

This was a sound judgement. Having developed such tactics to perfection in the years since 'the Long March', the CCP was ideally placed to defend Manchuria by such means. Indeed, the very fact that they could carry out such a strategy in their new area of operations was, in itself, a further incentive to develop their position there. In other words, the Yalta system gave the CCP a territory in Manchuria to defend and a clear *modus operandi* for doing so. Ironically, nationalist and American reactions to the Yalta system would provide the communists with additional reasons for believing in the viability of this approach.

As was the case with the CCP, nationalist policy towards Manchuria was conditioned by the belief that a unique opportunity existed to seize control of this vital region. For the GMD, this belief rested heavily on their interpretation of the Yalta system. Convinced that, without Soviet backing, the Chinese communists were incapable of resisting nationalist military strength – which included thirty-nine American-trained and equipped divisions – they regarded the Sino-Soviet Treaty as a masterstroke. This agreement, which they had secured by such expensive and unwelcome concessions, gave them sole recognition as the legitimate government of China and promised Russian compliance in a nationalist takeover of Manchuria. If the Russians kept to their word and turned the province over to the nationalists – and the concessions were designed to ensure this – then the CCP would be unable to expand in the north-east. Instead, they would become isolated and vulnerable and could be eliminated as a threat to the national government.

As ever, the reality did not fully synchronize with the plans. When the Japanese surrendered, the closest GMD armies were 600 miles from Manchuria, while the majority of the nationalist forces were well over 1,000 miles away. In such circumstances, irrespective of Soviet actions, there was little chance of them reaching the north-east in time to pre-empt the CCP, whose forces, being much nearer, naturally enough ignored Jiang's orders to stay in their base areas. If, at this stage, the GMD had been reliant upon their own resources, then their troops would never have made it to Manchuria, with consequences that, as we shall see, would probably have been beneficial to the nationalist regime. However, the Yalta system would ensure that they were not dependent on their own capabilities, but could also rely upon the Americans.

In early October, a little over a month after the Japanese surrender, 53,000 US marines, supported by tanks, aircraft and artillery, landed in northern China. This deployment reflected the American understanding of the Yalta system. Believing that the Soviets had agreed to limit their influence in Asia to those concessions obtained at the conference, the United States government had decided as early as mid-July to take steps to ensure that the Soviet leaders did not extend their sway beyond what had already been determined. As a military presence was seen by many in Washington as the best way of achieving this, and was, in any case, needed to repatriate the Japanese from China, available units were sent to the area.[47] This decision would have several consequences. In addition to securing important parts of north China – including Beiping (Peiping), Tianjin (Tientsin) and Qinqdao (Tsingtao) – for the nationalists, these forces also put the Americans in a position to offer the GMD major logistical support. This they did. Instructed by the Joint Chiefs of Staff to 'assist the Central Government in the rapid transport of Chinese Central Government forces to key areas in China',[48] American personnel airlifted and shipped nearly half a million nationalist troops to the north-east. By these means a GMD presence in the region was created.

While this boosted Jiang's confidence, the arrival of GMD soldiers in Manchuria actually placed the nationalists in a position of weakness rather than of strength. To begin with, the nationalist leaders, eager for their forces to reach Manchuria, had used the opportunity provided by American logistics to send their best armies to the region, without previously ensuring that the central government had consolidated its position in northern China. As a result, the connection between nationalist centres in intramural China and their citadels in Manchuria was, at best, a tenuous one. In such circumstances, were the communists ever able to disrupt the lines of communication in north China, the nationalist armies in the north-east would be completely cut off. Compounding this was the situation in Manchuria itself. Nationalist armies occupied most of the major cities in the southern and central parts of the province, as well as controlling the railway connections between them, but they did not hold the countryside. Since lengthy railway lines running through open countryside are easier to destroy than to protect, this, too, created a situation in which the isolation of nationalist forces was more than a distinct possibility.

The vulnerability of the nationalist armies to gradual encirclement and strangulation did not escape notice. On 14 November 1945, the American Commanding General of the China theatre, Lieutenant-General Albert C. Wedemeyer, informed his superiors that the 'Communists strongly dispute [the] North China area, threatening lines of communication.' As a result, he reported that the 'American evaluation of [the] situation indicates that the Chinese Central Government is completely unprepared for [the] occupation of Manchuria against Communist opposition.' It would be far better, he maintained, to concentrate instead on consolidation in intramural China, with a view to 'securing overland lines of communication'.[49] Such was the urgency of the situation that he reiterated this point less than a week later. As he stated on 20 November,

> Logistical support for National Government forces and measures for their security in the heart of Manchuria have not been fully appreciated by the Generalissimo or his Chinese Staff. These facts plus the lack of appropriate forces and transport have caused me to advise the Generalissimo that he should concentrate his efforts on the recovery of north China and the consolidation of his military and political position there prior to any attempt to occupy Manchuria.[50]

Sadly, this excellent advice, which would have meant forgoing the occupation of the north-east, was never taken. To the nationalist leadership, the opportunity provided by American transportation simply seemed too good to be missed. Accordingly, the GMD forces were sent as fast as possible to Manchuria, where they remained dangerously exposed.

Needless to say, this point was not lost on the communist military leaders, who believed that the nationalist military dispositions perfectly suited their intended strategy. The senior CCP commander in Manchuria, Lin Biao (Lin Piao), expressed the feeling of many in his party when he noted that Jiang Jieshi 'will have his men occupy the large cities. That does not matter. We can give all the cities south of the [Songhua river (Sungari)] to him. . . . When the enemy has many cities to defend, his forces will have to be decentralized and we can conquer them one by one.'[51]

The nationalists, of course, saw things differently. As with the CCP, the occupation of north-eastern territory gave them the belief that they were in a strong position in Manchuria. Backed by America, holding many of the key centres, and facing an enemy that was apparently in retreat, the GMD leadership saw no grounds for pessimism, let alone for offering concessions in this vital region. They believed that a major military effort mounted from their existing strongholds would be enough to round up the communist forces and destroy them. When it came to Manchuria, therefore, the same combination of optimism and intransigence that motivated Mao and his followers was also present in Jiang and his colleagues. They, too, thought that the Yalta system had given them the edge in the north-east.

ENDGAME

As we have seen, the actions of the various participants in the race for Manchuria were heavily influenced by the Yalta system. The nationalists, buoyed by their treaty with Stalin and aided by the Americans, were able to occupy most of the major cities south of the Songhua river as well as the principal lines of communication. Meanwhile, communist armies, unhindered by the Soviet Union, took control of the countryside and the far north of the province. Both sides were thereby endowed with a sizeable block of territory in a region they saw as of vital strategic importance. This was something that they would not give up without a fight. Yet far from fearing such a struggle, both sides saw their existing position as a springboard for victory. The GMD leaders expected that their divisions could control the environs around them from the cities. This was a strategy that had served them well up to 1936 and they saw no reason to tamper with a winning formula. In 1946, they envisaged once again using the urban areas as impregnable *point d'appui* for mopping up the insurgents in the countryside. By contrast, the CCP commanders were certain that by controlling the rural areas they could mount a successful war of attrition. When their opponents were worn down and they were strong enough, then they could use their hold over rural Manchuria to isolate and cut off the cities. This strategy had been successful in the war with Japan; they expected it to work just as well, if not better, when facing the nationalist armies.

Consequently, when the negotiations failed and the fighting resumed, neither side was especially distressed. The Yalta system had left them both in what they regarded as positions of strength, from which vantage points they were quite happy to resort to the *ultima ratio regis* that is war. Of course, they could not both be correct in their evaluation that they were poised for victory. As events would soon prove, it was the CCP whose leaders had made the more accurate appraisal of their position and capabilities. In contrast, Jiang's optimism turned out to be much misplaced. In using American logistics to transport his best troops to the north-east, he had, indeed, as General Wedemeyer warned in November 1945, led his cause into disaster. Historical evaluations, however divided they are on other issues, are unequivocal on this point. F.F. Liu, writing soon after the communist victory, recorded that 'of all the critical decisions of the postwar period, none seem to be of greater historical significance than the government's resolve to reoccupy Manchuria'.[52] A more recent evaluation by Suzanne Pepper boldly states that Jiang's fatal blunder was 'the strategic military error . . . of transporting his best American-equipped troops directly to the North-east . . . without consolidating control of the territory in between'. As a result of this decision, 'some of [Jiang's] best divisions entered the North-east never to re-emerge'.[53] Yet, without the Yalta system providing a treaty with Stalin and American logistical support, it is unlikely that they would have been there in the first place – and facing entrenched CCP opposition.

CONCLUSION

Given that there are no inevitable wars, the Chinese Civil War was not foreordained and could have been avoided. As this chapter has shown, peace, although by no means easy to accomplish, could have been brought to China in 1946. That this did not happen does not mean that it could not have happened. Rather, it tells us that, in the context of the times, the people making decisions in China preferred war to peace. The reason for this was the Yalta system. The agreements that made up the Far Eastern peace settlement were based on the best of intentions, there was no anti-democratic conspiracy, but they had one unfortunate side effect. They convinced the protagonists in China that Manchuria was the key battleground and then moved them there in force and provided them with weapons. In addition, the two parties to the GMD–CCP conflict arrived in Manchuria in circumstances that they perceived as favourable to them. The nationalists found themselves ensconced in the key cities and in control of the main railway arteries, a situation that suited their strategy of controlling China from prestigious strongholds. In contrast to this, the communists dominated the countryside and discovered that nationalist force dispositions gave them the perfect opportunity to wage an attritional guerrilla war against an overextended enemy. With both sides in control of something tangible, and believing they would be able to seize more through force, there was little incentive to negotiate. In this way, the Yalta system made both sides believe that civil war was their best option and should be ventured into as soon as was practicable. And so it happened.

SEVEN

The Peace Settlement in Korea and the Origins of the Korean War, 1945–50

On 8 August 1945, shortly before Japan's surrender, Soviet forces invaded Japanese-controlled Manchuria and occupied the northern part of Korea. In response, in September 1945, American troops from US XXIV Corps, commanded by Lieutenant-General John R. Hodge, landed on the southern part of the Korean peninsula. Following these occupations, America and the USSR settled on a temporary partition of Korea along the 38th parallel, prior to an international trusteeship for Korea that had been discussed by President Roosevelt and Marshal Stalin in talks at the Yalta conference in 1945. With what would become the two 'superpowers' of the post-1945 world either side of the partition border along the 38th parallel, the peace 'settlement' dividing the Korean peninsula into North and South Korea was viable: local rivalries could be managed to prevent escalation to war and a potential Cold War flashpoint could be checked by strong outside powers willing and able to control events in their zones of influence. While partition was not an ideal solution, it could provide, as in Germany, a temporary answer to the vexed question of what to do with occupied enemy territory. So why did partition fail to keep the peace in Korea?

The partition of Korea was mismanaged. It divided the country against the wishes of the inhabitants, established opposing, undemocratic regimes, and left them to fight a war. For partition to work, legitimate regimes needed to be established that could command popular support. If this was impossible, the major powers in the region – the USA, the USSR and also communist China after 1949 – had to control the peninsula to keep the two Koreas apart. But rather than keep a tight check on their client regimes in Korea, American and, more especially, Soviet (and communist Chinese) policies encouraged the two sides to seek a military solution to the political issue of unification. This chapter will argue that what upset the peace settlement in Korea was not the partition arranged in 1945 (unsuitable as it was in so many ways) but the manner in which internal divisions in Korea, external mismanagement and aggressive opportunism combined to turn an uneasy but workable peace settlement based on *de facto* partition of Korea into all-out war in June 1950. This chapter will examine these three factors in turn before concluding with a discussion of revisionist historiography on the immediate causes of the Korean War.

INTERNAL DIVISIONS

John Merrill and Bruce Cumings, among others, have argued that the Korean War was essentially a civil war between the forces of revolution and the forces of tradition and reaction in Korean society.[1] This was a battle between Left and Right, between those influenced by Marxism–Leninism, and those purporting to subscribe to western liberal ideas, Confucianism, or an amalgam of the two.[2] The division of Korea into two ideological camps began during the struggle against Japanese rule before 1945; tensions grew after the end of the Second World War, before exploding into all-out war in 1950. As Dae-Sook Suh observed, while the Left condemned the United States and the Right the Soviet Union for the division of Korea, 'in truth the people must re-examine the Korean revolution and seek a Korean answer to the age-old problem of their country'.[3] Without a definite vision for Korea, the superpowers were unable to translate the vague promises made during the Second World War into a peace settlement that would subsume these internal rifts. Instead, the ideological differences outlined above divided the peninsula and, allowed to fester, combined to ruin the idea of international trusteeship for the country and set Korea on the path to war. The division of Korea into two opposing camps so soon after 1945 made war increasingly likely as the goal of unification of the peninsula could only be achieved through a revolution in the South, or a counter-revolution in the North. Distracted by events elsewhere, America and the Soviet Union failed to arrest the slide to war that both North and South Korea felt was necessary for successful unification on their terms.

With the liberation of Korea, some 3 million Koreans seeking a home in an independent Korea returned from exile abroad. With this influx of repatriates came banished Korean leaders eager to secure political control in Korea. Having spent many years in exile in America, communist and nationalist China or the Soviet Union, these Korean nationalist leaders brought with them a volatile mix of personal aspirations and conflicting political ideologies. Factionalism within the contending political camps was common: the Left, for instance, subdivided into those trained and supported by the Soviet Union, and those whose allegiance was to the communists in China. While most Koreans were 'high' with expectation at the opportunities afforded by national independence and freedom from Japanese rule, their leaders would be competing with one another for power and would turn to whatever external support was available to make their case.[4] As William Stueck noted, by September 1945, when American troops finally arrived on the peninsula, 'the seeds of future conflict were firmly planted'.[5]

If the hardening of the American and Soviet occupation zones into separate ideological entities were to be averted, the superpowers had to contain the tendencies of Korean politics towards ideological polarization and political factionalism. If ideological polarization were not checked, it would magnify fears that Washington and Moscow each had that the other would dominate the peninsula, and would eliminate prospects for a compromise settlement in the form of trusteeship or neutralization (as happened successfully in Austria and Finland). At the same time, factionalism would subvert possibilities for establishing viable coalitions of Korean political parties and would encourage the occupying powers to choose sides in any political squabbles.[6] However, instead of uniting the disparate elements in Korea after 1945, the superpowers acted as a centrifugal force, exacerbating existing political, social and economic tensions in Korean life.

While the USSR established Kim Il Sung, a young Korean chosen by Stalin, as the leader of a pro-Moscow client regime, the Democratic People's Republic of Korea, in the North, the American commander, Hodge, set about managing the transition from Japanese rule to independence in the South.[7] Hodge was ill-equipped and poorly suited for the task. The surrender of Japan after the dropping of the atomic bombs was so sudden that America had no troops readily available to send to Korea, and certainly none with adequate training for the difficult task of occupation duties in an alien land. General Douglas MacArthur, commanding US wartime forces in the Pacific and thereafter the occupation forces in Japan, chose Hodge, a 'blunt' infantry officer, who had received no specific training for the new assignment, mainly because Hodge's XXIV Corps on the island of Okinawa was closest to Korea.[8]

The American State Department knew very little about Korea and so was unable to tell Hodge what challenges he would be facing once he arrived on the peninsula. Hodge proved unable to make up the shortfall and was 'abysmally insensitive' to Korean desires for independence from Japanese rule.[9] While he had distinguished himself as a hard-driving field commander in the Pacific island-hopping campaign, Hodge's profoundly conservative political instincts failed to appreciate the nuances of Korean political life in 1945. He sent 'packing' local representatives who came out to meet him while he was sailing to Korea: 'He did likewise with every other Korean he met on his arrival who laid claim to a political mandate.'[10] Hodge refused to recognize or consult the 'Korean People's Republic' (KPR), a self-proclaimed Korean government that, although dominated by the Left, tried to establish a broad political base by appointing to important positions representatives from across the political spectrum, including the right-wing leader Syngman Rhee who was made chairman (and who would later become the head of the Republic of South Korea (ROK)). By August 1945, 'People's Committees' functioned in 145 towns across Korea.[11] Hodge viewed such 'people's' organizations with extreme suspicion and, with the support of MacArthur in Japan, his military administration in the South Korean capital, Seoul, targeted the KPR and labour organizations considered to be Left-leaning. A product of small-town America, Hodge saw the Left as a monolithic bloc. As Max Hastings concluded, Hodge made 'no attempt to examine closely the communist ideology of the Leftists, to discover how far they were creatures of Moscow, and how far they were merely vague socialists and nationalists who found traditional landlordism repugnant'.[12] Because of his fear of communism, Hodge relied on an older, conservative generation of Koreans to run the country. The essential qualification for entry into this group was anti-communism. Therefore, when the Americans in October 1945 created an eleven-man Korean 'Advisory Council', only one nominee, Yo Un-hyong, came from the Left. At the first meeting of the council, Yo Un-hyong took one look at the unrepresentative panel and walked out. In discouraging these early attempts to form a Korean-wide political movement, Hodge ended the first and most promising effort at national cohesion.

Instead, Hodge chose to rule through the Japanese colonial authorities detested by so many Koreans. At the war's end, the Japanese governor in Korea had cabled the Americans asking for authority to maintain control and complaining that 'Communist and independence agitators are plotting to take advantage of this situation to disturb peace and order.' This request met with an immediate and affirmative reply from the Americans: 'It is directed that you maintain order and preserve the machinery of government in Korea.' The Japanese commander replied that he was extremely 'grateful' to have been given the American mandate.[13] Indeed, when Japanese troops fired on crowds of jubilant Koreans welcoming American occupation troops arriving at the town of Inchon, killing two and wounding ten, the Americans did nothing to charge those responsible. Actions such as these discredited the American occupation and were propaganda coups for the Left.

Hodge's approach was 'dictatorial' and lacked tact. Quoted in the press comparing Koreans to the Japanese ('same breed of cat'), Hodge foundered in his job as political supremo.[14] He appointed Major-General Archibald V. Arnold, commander of the US 7th Division, to be the executive officer of the American Military Government (AMG). Arnold might have tempered Hodge's excesses but for the fact that, like Hodge, he 'lacked the experience that might have helped to avert some of the cardinal errors perpetrated, albeit in good faith, by the Americans in the following months'.[15] Hodge's parochial fixation with fighting communism blinded him to the subtleties of Korean life and, as his unchecked military administration became divorced from Washington, it also became increasingly unrepresentative and repressive.

As has been mentioned, to maintain order the Americans relied on the only established force they found when they arrived – the Japanese, whose 'impeccable correctness' was easier to deal with than the rivalries of the local Korean factions.[16] Hodge proclaimed that Japanese personnel would remain in administrative posts south of the 38th parallel until there were sufficient numbers of qualified Koreans to replace the departing Japanese. As a consequence, on 10 September 1945, crowds of Koreans took to the streets of Seoul to protest at Hodge's decision. Koreans who had suffered under the much-hated Japanese rule were horrified at the open camaraderie between American and Japanese officers.[17] An American naval officer in Korea, Ferris Miller, later recalled how the Americans' willingness to use the Japanese colonial authority as a means of maintaining order was 'one of the most expensive mistakes we ever made'.[18] When the Japanese officials finally left, they were replaced by Americans and conservative Koreans, many of whom had held administrative positions in the previous regime. These Koreans who had served the Japanese were loathed by many of their fellow countrymen, who viewed them as collaborators deserving punishment rather than employment. In 1949, Britain's consul-general in Seoul, Captain Vyvyan Holt, reported on how the proceedings under the National Traitors Law, charged with prosecuting collaborators, 'continued in a desultory manner . . .

no further arrests were made'.[19] This compares poorly with, say, Germany, where the Allies' war crimes trials and denazification policies, haphazard as they may have been, went some way to healing Germany and bringing it back into the world of liberal democracy.

But Hodge's policies, influenced by the unfolding Cold War, meant that erstwhile informers, torturers and anti-nationalists suddenly found themselves in positions of authority. The Americans even barred recruits to the Korean national police who had been imprisoned by the Japanese. Indeed, the first chief of staff of the South Korean army was a former colonel in the Japanese colonial army.[20] With the continuing growth of the People's Committees, the Americans relied on the powerful South Korean police force to keep order and, by the summer of 1946, the force had grown to 25,000 officers. These officers were keen to aid US occupation and the Korean Right. One American officer tasked with running the Korean police told the journalist Mark Gayn in 1946 how it was an 'ideal setup. All you have to do is push the button and somewhere some cop begins skull cracking. They've been learning the business under the Japs for 35 years.'[21] As a paramilitary addition to the new police force, Hodge sanctioned the creation of a force of young Koreans into a 'Rightist Youth Army' to aid the police.[22] Needless to say, government-run forces comprised of young toughs ready to fight political battles on the streets of South Korea did little to establish the credibility of the new regime across a broad spectrum of the Korean population.[23]

Basic language difficulties further skewed American policy in South Korea. When the Americans replaced their military officers in Korea with civil affairs officers, these had been trained for service in Japan and most did not speak Korean. The shortage of American Korean-language speakers meant that the Americans recruited local Koreans who spoke English to make up the shortfall. These were chosen by Hodge's Korean-speaking aide, George Z. Williams, the son of a missionary, from the Christians of Korea. Too often, this group was comprised of members of the Right and/or former collaborators with the Japanese. As a result of Williams' decision, the Americans received partisan advice on what was happening in Korea.

As a consequence of the mismanagement of the transition to Korean independence, extreme politically based violence became commonplace. A mob in the city of Taegu dealt out summary justice to police officers they captured: thirty-eight were murdered, 'tortured to death, burned at the stake, skinned alive. And once dead, their homes and families became objects of attack.'[24] The Korean police and army responded in kind, setting off a vicious spiral of violence and counter-violence. Torture in police custody in the South was commonplace. Holt, the British representative in Seoul, reported in 1949 how the opportunities

> . . . for the abuse of authority were many and seldom neglected, and the corruption and oppression of the police has become an outstanding feature of the life of the country. Torture is regularly applied to those arrested on political and other serious charges, and 'died under torture' is a routine entry in the police records. The Government indeed finds itself in a perplexing predicament for without employing harsh repressive measures it cannot withstand communism and yet these very measures, by disgusting and antagonising many elements of the public, constantly make new converts to the Communist cause.[25]

As Cumings outlined, Hodge misunderstood why so many ordinary Koreans hated the American-backed police. Instead, Hodge equated the Korean police with those in his home town of Golconda, Illinois: 'He made, in effect, the usual distinction. . . . But many Koreans viewed former colonial policemen as *ipso facto* illegitimate; their monopoly on the means of violence in postwar Korea was improper, inappropriate, and therefore, by that definition of legitimacy, unsanctionable.'[26] Corruption was also rife. 'Nothing can be done without bribery', reported Holt in Seoul and, as Hastings argued, while 'democratic political life' was revived in occupied Europe, in South Korea America created a 'fundamentally corrupt' society.[27] Corruption, police brutality and mob violence did little to establish the legitimacy of the ROK, and this lack of legitimacy paved the way for a war in 1950 as North Korea exploited the unrest in the South for its own ends.

While sanctioning state repression, Hodge and his administration rejected the economic and social reforms that proved so useful in winning over the populations of Germany and Japan to the new order of the postwar world. When the American occupation authority in Tokyo sent a representative to outline some of the positive policies implemented in Japan, Hodge's governor general, A.L. Lerch, rejected the advice offered: 'He comes from Tokyo, and tells me there are too many little children working in factories, and we must change this and change that. I told him, "As long as I am Military Governor, we change nothing."'[28] As American Marshall Aid rebuilt Europe, the American Congress, influenced by fiscal conservatives suspicious of America's expanding role abroad, discouraged the State Department from sending economic aid to Korea. The consequence of economic and social neglect was widespread poverty in South Korea. Miller, the US navy officer, returned to Seoul as a civilian contractor in 1947 to discover 'Koreans wearing clothes made of army blankets; orphans hanging around the railway station; people chopping wood on the hills above Seoul, the transport system crumbling. It was a pretty bad time.'[29] To add to the economic difficulties, rampant inflation slashed the living standards of ordinary Koreans. It had been calculated that with 1937 as a base of 100, by July 1945 wages and prices had both reached 200; by November 1945 wages were 2,000 while prices had soared to 8,000. In January 1946, the American military authorities in Seoul passed an anti-inflationary law freezing wages but not prices. This hit poor Korean peasants hardest.[30] The economic hardship in the South drew in the communist regime in the North, which took full advantage of the depressed conditions to propagate its radical agenda among disaffected, poverty-stricken South Korean peasants and workers. This further divided the peninsula as the North seized the opportunity to achieve unification by supporting a revolution in the South.

As Hodge relied on a traditional land-holding elite in South Korea to maintain control, land reform was difficult. But land reform was vital to establish the legitimacy of the ROK. It was one of the first reforms offered by the communists in China, and proved to be a successful means of winning over peasant support. Walter Sullivan of the *New York Times*, one of the few journalists who tried to understand the popular discontent that spread across South Korea from 1945 in terms other than communist subversion from the North, saw poverty and land as two key issues. Sullivan reported on the 'great divergence of wealth' in the South, with both middle and poor peasants living 'a marginal existence'. Sullivan interviewed ten peasant families who owned no land. While the landlord took 30 per cent of their produce, additional demands in the form of government taxes and other contributions exacted a further 48 to 70 per cent of the annual crop.[31] But the American authorities in Seoul consistently opposed even modest land reform. In the end, the US State Department ordered the AMG to sell Japanese-owned land in Korea in late 1946. But the AMG sold the land to anyone who could pay. Therefore, the land passed to landlords, businessmen and racketeers.

By contrast, in the North, land was given to needy peasants. In March 1946, the North Korean government introduced land reforms that redistributed 2.5 million acres formerly belonging to Japan to 725,000 landless or land-short peasants. Landlordism disappeared as land was redistributed; major industries were nationalized and radical reforms eliminated the worst abuses of the Japanese colonial period. North Korea also established nominal equality for women. The transformation of the North meant that by late 1946 'one of the first examples of revolutionary nationalism in a postcolonial "Third World" setting was in place'.[32] Unchecked, this revolutionary regime was likely to seek a military confrontation with conservative South Korea. As will be seen, the Soviets and Chinese did little to dissuade Kim Il Sung from taking aggressive action, and it was not long before border clashes along the 38th parallel, and guerrilla actions in the South, escalated to dangerous proportions.

While formal hostilities were declared in June 1950, the war between North and South Korea began in the late 1940s with a sustained guerrilla war in South Korea that resulted in 100,000 casualties before 1950.[33] There were large-scale uprisings in the countryside and in the towns of the South. In November 1946, in the South Cholla region of South Korea, a total of forty-seven cities, towns and villages, and two-thirds of all counties, were affected by popular uprisings. Rural and urban conflict pitched the nascent ROK army and police against the people, and these uprisings brought into focus the discontinuous and fractured structure of postwar Korea. The South Korean army, supported by American military advisers, was on almost continuous duty suppressing internal revolts that carried the urban political turmoil and rural peasant protests of 1945–7 to the level of unconventional warfare by 1949. The scale and intensity of the peasant-based guerrilla war grew with repressive counter-insurgency operations by Rhee's forces. By the end of 1949, the North Koreans claimed that there were 90,000 guerrillas fighting in the south. While there were indigenous roots to the uprisings in the South, North Korea supported these disturbances as a means of extending its control without actually invading. As Kim Il Sung reported to North Korean officers: 'The only way to obtain a glorious victory is to cause disturbances on the 38th parallel line and have the South Korean Army devote all of its attention to that area while our guerrilla units attack the puppets from the rear. This is the only way to unify our separate country.'[34]

EXTERNAL MISMANAGEMENT

As Korea tipped into the abyss of war, major crises in Europe such as the Berlin blockade overshadowed what were seen to be petty squabbles in the backwater that was Korea. As Peter Lowe remarked, the United States and the Soviet Union saw Europe as the vital arena where the Cold War would be won or lost: 'This was an excessively Eurocentric view and seriously underestimated the importance of the world outside Europe.'[35] Eager to resolve the Korean imbroglio, America, as with Britain in Palestine in the same period, decided to take the matter of Korea to the United Nations. The military occupation in Korea was proving expensive for an administration in Washington keen to reduce military spending and cut heavy foreign aid outlays.[36] Therefore, before the Korean War, the United States in East Asia eschewed the commitment of resources and prestige made in Europe. Between 1947 and 1949, the Truman administration had avoided direct action in China to prevent a communist victory in the civil war. Then, at the beginning of 1950, it resisted strong domestic pressure to make a concerted effort to save Taiwan from a possible communist Chinese invasion.

Following an agreement at the UN, America and the Soviet Union began withdrawing their troops from Korea in 1948. As with the British evacuation of Palestine, the withdrawal of American and Soviet troops sent out the wrong message to the two sides in Korea, and it was no coincidence that the most serious violence began once the restraining presence of the USA and USSR had gone.[37] With American troops pulling out of Korea, America 'generally forgot' about Korea.[38] Meanwhile, the American refusal to intervene directly over Taiwan encouraged the Chinese communist leader, Mao Zedong (Mao Tse-tung), to support North Korea's planned invasion of the South as he assumed that the Americans would not react decisively. Again, in 1949, as the United States withdrew its last occupation troops from Korea, it responded coolly to requests from the Philippines, nationalist China and South Korea to create a 'Pacific Pact' along the lines of NATO in Europe.[39] Weak signalling in the context of a polarized Korea would prove to be fatal.

America was in a difficult position. The Truman administration feared that if it gave a binding undertaking to defend the South in the event of serious conflict erupting, a bellicose Syngman Rhee might regard such an agreement as an excuse to attack the North. But the lack of support meant that Kim Il Sung saw 1950 as the right moment to seize the initiative and invade the South.[40] Even when war broke out in 1950, many observers were doubtful as to whether US support for the South would be forthcoming. On 25 June 1950, as North Korean troops crossed the 38th parallel, R.H. Scott of the British Foreign Office concluded, 'Personally, I doubt whether they [the US] will intervene militarily.'[41] For Robert M. Blum, it was the Korean War that transformed American policy across East Asia from indecision to containment to rollback: 'Not until the Korean War did the administration speak with one voice on China policy. . . . Until the early fall of 1949, [Dean] Acheson [US Secretary of State] was unsure of what to do about China, and the uncertainty was reflected throughout the State Department.'[42]

One of the most striking examples of weak signalling by the US was a speech given by Acheson on 12 January 1950 at the National Press Club in Washington, DC. The speech was a response to complaints about American inaction over the nationalist Chinese regime on Taiwan. Fearing that support for the Chinese nationalists would push the Chinese communists closer to the Soviet Union, Acheson, supported by Truman, opposed unequivocal backing for the nationalists on Taiwan.[43] Acheson's speech accurately reflected American national security policy in Asia at a moment when the scope and nature of the Cold War was unclear. Not knowing Soviet or communist Chinese intentions, Acheson omitted South Korea from the American defence perimeter in the Pacific. Rather, he argued that, if attacked, the ROK should expect help from the United Nations: 'the initial reliance must be on the people attacked to resist it and then upon the commitments of the entire civilised world under the charter of the United Nations'.[44] This seemed to indicate that America would not respond if South Korea was invaded. Acheson's speech may have inadvertently signalled to the North Koreans that the United States would not intervene if there was an invasion from the North.

Cumings disagreed with this assessment, arguing that Acheson's speech was a distraction from the real causes behind the Korean War: 'let us assume that Acheson nonetheless unintentionally communicated the wrong signal, that the United States would do nothing in the event of an invasion . . . what was the North Korean reaction to Acheson's speech? . . . It turns out that the North Koreans thought Acheson *included* the ROK in his perimeter, a bit of a daunting fact for Acheson's presumed failure of deterrence.'[45] Whether Acheson did or did not give a green light to start a war, the speech stimulated Kim Il Sung and gave him added leverage over the Chinese and Soviets. As one senior North Korean recalled, Kim Il Sung was convinced that America would not enter the Korean War and, if it did, US entry would not be decisive. Acheson's speech also allowed Kim Il Sung to 'bolster his case with Stalin irrespective of what his "true" attitude to the speech may have been'.[46]

If America helped to create the fragile regime in Seoul and was subsequently indecisive over its policy towards South Korea, the USSR and communist China were guilty of supplying North Korea with Soviet equipment, a Chinese-trained army and a mandate to invade the South. When Soviet forces arrived in 1945, their commander, Colonel-General Ivan Chistyakov, a war veteran, like the US commander Hodge, and hero of the Soviet Union, replaced Japanese officials with Koreans who had returned from exile with the Soviet forces and who were untainted by association with the Japanese.[47] Chistyakov had served for much of the 1930s in the Soviet Far East and so had some knowledge of the animosity felt by many Koreans towards the Japanese. In January 1946, the Soviets purged non-communists in North Korea and established Kim Il Sung as the new leader in Pyongyang, the North Korean capital. When the Soviets finally withdrew their forces in 1948, they left behind a substantial quantity of military hardware for Kim Il Sung's new army. For instance, the Soviet Twenty-Fifth Army of more than 120,000 men handed over all its weapons to the newly formed Korean People's Army (KPA). Indeed, according to a Soviet source, Moscow's military assistance to North Korea in this period exceeded that given to Mao Zedong's People's Liberation Army (PLA).[48] In the months immediately prior to June 1950, the Soviets transferred to the North Koreans an offensive force of warplanes, T-34/85 tanks, trucks and artillery with which to launch an attack on the South.[49] This transfer of goods was not without its advantages for Moscow. While the North received a great quantity of Soviet Second World War era military equipment, the Soviets made the Koreans pay for everything, 'including a 220-million rouble loan at 2 per cent interest, which was about what mortgages returned to American banks in 1949 – that is there was profit in it'.[50] Once war began in June 1950, Soviet officers acted as military advisers and, according to a British Foreign

Office report, assumed command of the North Korean air force on 27 June 1950.[51]

While Soviet support was vital, Kim Il Sung's decision to attack in 1950 was also closely tied to the course of the Chinese Civil War where North Korean troops were deployed with Mao Zedong's communist forces. Sensing the immense strategic advantage of communist victory in China, in early 1947 Kim Il Sung began dispatching tens of thousands of Koreans to fight with Mao Zedong. Once the Chinese nationalists were defeated in 1949, Kim Il Sung's battle-hardened troops returned home. From the summer of 1949 to early 1950, the Chinese communists returned 50–70,000 fully equipped Korean soldiers. In July 1949, the PLA's 166th Division, commanded by Pang Ho-san, crossed into North Korea and was promptly transformed into the North Korean 6th Division. At the same time, the PLA's 164th Division, also made up mostly of Korean soldiers, crossed the Yalu river into North Korea and became the 5th Division. These civil war veterans gave the North the necessary offensive punch to attack South Korea, and both the 5th and 6th Divisions played a crucial role in the invasion in June 1950.[52] It is fair to say that this transfer gave Kim Il Sung both a 'green light' and the means to attack the South.[53] Like Syngman Rhee, Kim Il Sung aimed to unify Korea by military means if necessary, 'unlike Rhee, he had by 1950 assembled the wherewithal to do it'.[54]

As with the Soviet Union, Mao Zedong's new communist administration in Beijing did little to discourage a North Korean invasion. Indeed, Mao's experience in the Chinese Civil War seemed to prove that China could stand up to superior American military power should a conflict arise. In Mao's view, his PLA forces had compelled the Americans to evacuate China and, with a growing PLA air force and navy, and having secured an alliance with the Soviet Union, Mao became even more confident of military success should a war break out.[55] Despite immense social and economic problems within China in 1949–50, Mao's radical ideology and need to support a fellow communist regime in Pyongyang prevented him from turning inwards and ignoring Kim Il Sung's requests for support should there be a war.

OPPORTUNISM: THE RUN-UP TO WAR

Kim Il Sung, it seems, had been planning a war long before 1945. During the struggle against Japanese rule, Kim shared his vision of a united, independent Korea with his comrades from the anti-Japanese resistance movement. One of these fellow resistance fighters recalled how Kim, their new battalion commander, 'never believed in peaceful unification; he never had such an idea. He only stuck to the idea of armed unification.'[56] For Kim Il Sung, the objective of the Korean War had little or nothing to do with the expansion or containment of communism in Asia. Rather, unification was a means of securing his political ambitions and resolving the ongoing issue of the division of Korea.[57] As new sources from the Russian and Chinese archives reveal, the Korean War was, first and foremost, Kim Il Sung's war, 'which he initiated on the basis of judgment (or misjudgment) of the revolutionary situation existing on the Korean peninsula'.[58] Rather than being a Soviet puppet regime that would respond to 'an itchy Soviet trigger finger', North Korea was a client communist state dependent on Soviet and Chinese support that would have to convince Moscow and Beijing of the efficacy of going to war.[59] As John Lewis Gaddis rightly concluded, the North Korean invasion was impossible without 'some kind of Soviet authorization'.[60] It was the willingness of China and the USSR to accede to the aggressive opportunism of their client power in Pyongyang that would lead to war.

Considering the conjunction of circumstances inside and outside Korea, 1950 seemed to be the right moment for Kim Il Sung to decide on a military solution to his political problem. The withdrawal of US troops, guerrilla revolts in the South, the success of Mao Zedong's communists on mainland China in 1949, the return of Korean soldiers fighting in China and the Acheson Press Club speech all contributed to Kim's decision to attack, but the final decision was his own. For war to be averted, the Soviet Union and/or China had to put a decisive stop to Kim's decision for war. But while America reined in South Korea, the Soviets and Chinese, beguiled by Kim's promise of a quick, decisive war, gave him the go-ahead to launch an attack that would destroy the uneasy peace along the 38th parallel.

In Pyongyang in early March 1950, Kim Il Sung discussed the possibility of military action against the South. The consensus was that the North could win in three weeks, assuming that America did not intervene – and American intervention was regarded as highly unlikely.[61] Kim, however, needed the support of the USSR and China. Having been on at least one trip to the USSR between February and March 1949 to fix up a cultural and economic agreement, Kim now went on a second visit to Moscow from 30 March to 25 April 1950 to talk to Stalin about a possible invasion, before visiting Beijing in May 1950 for final talks prior to war in June.[62] These visits were integral to the launching of the Korean War. Without the agreement and support of China and the USSR, North Korea was unlikely to attack. Kim, it seems, played his hand well, skilfully exploiting the complicated relationship between Stalin and Mao so as to divide two leaders who already viewed each other with some suspicion.

The ruling elite in Moscow and Beijing knew at least as early as the end of 1949 that Kim Il Sung was planning to attack the South.[63] Indeed, according to Stalin's interpreter, at the meetings with Kim in early 1949 Stalin encouraged the North Korean leader to take tough action. After Kim complained about border clashes along the 38th parallel initiated by the South, Stalin concluded, 'What are you talking about? Are you short of arms? We shall give them to you. You must strike the southerners in the teeth . . . strike them, strike them.'[64] Whatever the truth of the interpreter's account, Stalin avoided committing the USSR to a war in 1949, fearing that a war in Korea could result in direct military conflict between the superpowers.

However, in early 1950 Stalin's attitude changed and, convinced that direct US military intervention in Korea was unlikely, agreed to Kim's demand for a war. A war in Korea suited Stalin. It allowed the Soviet Union access to captured US military technology, especially downed US warplanes. This was of great benefit to the Soviet armed forces, notably the Soviet air force that could gain access to cutting-edge aviation technology. The Korean War also served as a substitute for a Third World War and allowed for the establishment of parameters for managing superpower conflict that remained in place throughout the Cold War.[65] Stalin, however, had reservations about two key issues if there was a war in Korea. Firstly, he was not going to commit Soviet forces to the war; secondly, he insisted that Kim travel to China so that Mao would share some of the responsibility for the war.[66] Kim charmed Stalin, diminished the threat of a superpower confrontation and, as one observer noted, insisted that the attack would be a decisive *blitzkrieg* that would be over in three days. He also argued that an uprising of 200,000 communist supporters and guerrillas in the South would facilitate victory. Finally, because of the speed and completeness of the attack, the United States would not have time to intervene.[67] While Stalin was impressed by Kim's plan, he made it clear that direct Soviet intervention would not be forthcoming and that Kim would have to look to Beijing for military support if he ran into trouble. Stalin did, however, order that North Korea's requests for military equipment be met and shortly after Kim's trip, confirmation also came in the form of a team of Soviet advisers sent to oversee the preparations for the attack. Stalin's opportunism in the run-up to the Korean War was such that, once the attempt to unify Korea had failed and the war bogged down into stalemate, he lost interest in Korea and hoped for a ceasefire. As the 'game was up', Stalin preferred to concentrate once again on more important matters in Europe.[68]

Stalin might have hoped that Mao would turn down Kim's request for war but, as Odd Arne Westad noted, the Chinese leader's 'personality as well as his ideology blocked such an option: Kim came to him to seek the liberation of his country – one of China's traditional clients; he had Stalin's OK; and he had reasonable chances of success'.[69] As Chen Jian has outlined, Kim's visit in 1950 tied in with Mao's concept of confronting the United States. Korea was moving centre stage for the Beijing regime.[70] During his stay in Beijing from 13–16 May 1950, Kim played on China's wish to confront America and manipulated the differences between Mao and Stalin. Naturally, he told Mao that Stalin had approved his plans to attack the South and that all that was needed was Mao's agreement. When Mao asked if North Korea would need Chinese assistance, Kim optimistically replied that the North Korean army operating in conjunction with communist guerrillas in the South could achieve victory and so Chinese military involvement was unnecessary. This facilitated China's acceptance of the decision for war, although the PLA's eventual intervention across the Yalu in October 1950 would prove just how wrong Kim's sanguine assessment of May 1950 was.[71]

WHO REALLY STARTED THE KOREAN WAR? REVISIONIST HISTORI-OGRAPHY FROM STONE TO CUMINGS

In 1952, I.F. Stone published *The Hidden History of the Korean War*, a controversial, revisionist account that blamed certain American officials and South Korean leaders for the war. Stone argued that an invasion suited Rhee's regime in Seoul, and that the notion of an unprovoked North Korean invasion is too simple an explanation. Rather, for hard-liners such as Rhee and MacArthur in Japan, a war in Korea, blamed on the North, threw a lifeline to South Korea and also to the nationalists in Taiwan under threat from a communist invasion from mainland China. A war in Korea would transform the strategic balance by bringing America directly into the fight against communism in East Asia.[72] Discussing Stone's thesis, Merrill concluded,

> Seeing an invasion coming, South Korean spokesmen issued a series of warnings in early May, Stone says, but then fell uncharacteristically silent. Seoul made no further efforts either to alert world opinion or to warn off the North. Short of war, according to Stone, Rhee had no way of escaping the deepening domestic and international crises facing his regime. Stone suggests that Rhee may have been advised by MacArthur, who held similar hard-line anti-Communist views . . . to remain totally silent about the North Korean threat.[73]

This line of argument was developed by Joyce and Gabriel Kolko in *The Limits of Power: The World and United States Foreign Policy, 1945–1954* (1972) and by Karunakar Gupta in an article in *China Quarterly* entitled 'How did the Korean War Begin?'[74] For the Kolkos, Pyongyang's attack was less important than its subsequent exploitation by Tokyo, Washington and Seoul.[75] Meanwhile, Gupta concluded that an analysis of the military situation along the 38th parallel in June 1950 'should convince any detached scholar that a prima facie case for the South's invasion of the North does exist'.[76] As the American Ambassador in Seoul, John Muccio, reported in August 1949, the ROK army was 'eager to get going. More and more people feel that the only way unification can be brought about is by moving "North by force".'[77]

More recently, Bruce Cumings, in his magisterial two-volume *The Origins of the Korean War* (1981, 1990), articulated the idea of a conspiracy by right-wing elements to provoke a North Korean attack. For Cumings, both North and South wanted a fight but it was a question of when: 'the North was not ready to fight in 1949 when the South was, and . . . the North was ready to fight in 1950 when the South also was'.[78] Cumings' conclusion revived Stone's thesis and opened up the debate on the origins of the Korean War. For Cumings, the conspiracy to drag America into a war in South Korea was masterminded by Colonel M. Preston Goodfellow, ex-deputy director of the wartime Office of Strategic Services (which became the CIA in 1947), in conjunction with like-minded American officers and elements within Korea and Taiwan. In an intriguing argument, Cumings concluded that the South, as much as the North, was responsible for war in 1950:

If one knew the Korean situation for years, and one knew what happened in the summer and fall of 1949, and one was well connected with intelligence apparatuses that would know, or at least suspect, that the North Koreans would wait, in the summer of 1950, for the first major southern provocation and then take off southward; and one understood that the United States would respond only to an attack that could be presented as unequivocal and unprovoked, and one had journeyed to Seoul to tell this to Rhee, and to Washington to tell it to [V.K. Wellington] Koo, and to Tokyo to tell it to MacArthur, and to Taipei to tell it to Chiang, in other words if one were Colonel Goodfellow, one might have reason to join the army on June 12, 1950, at the age of fifty-nine. Then one makes a first, deep cut, 'pulls a trick' that will suck in the North Koreans. And, perhaps, a few days earlier someone draws up a report projecting an imminent invasion, and then destroys the report, and lets an unwitting and sincere president stew.[79]

To buttress his argument, Cumings quoted from the diary entry of V.K. Wellington Koo (Gu Wei-jun), the Chinese nationalist representative in Washington, who, in late 1949, following a visit from Goodfellow just back from a trip to South Korea, wrote: 'G[oodfellow] said U.S. Govt. Position is this: avoid any initiative on S. Korea's part in attacking N.K., but if N.K. should invade S.K. then S.K. should resist and march right into N.K. with III World War as the result but in such a case, the aggression comes from N.K. and the Am[erican] people would understand it.'[80]

Cumings also recalled an exchange in 1987 with North Korean officials with whom he was negotiating for a visit by a British television crew to North Korea. These talks suggested that both sides were in some measure responsible in 1950. During the protracted talks, he was pressed time and again by the North Koreans to answer the question of who started the Korean War:

. . . at length I remarked that I thought the war in 1950 was intimately linked with the near-war in 1949, but that because crack soldiers were not back from China, the North did not want to fight in 1949 even if the South did. In 1950 the expeditionary force had returned, and perhaps then the North awaited the first southern provocation to settle the hash of the Rhee regime. This was met with a memorable, eloquent silence, as the officials exchanged glances and hard faces suddenly turned soft. They said nothing more about it.[81]

While strongly argued, Cumings' case is not proved. And until more archives are opened up for examination the debates will rage on. Many still argue that North Korea was directly responsible for the war. Stanley Sandler firmly put the blame on the North, arguing in the *Times Literary Supplement* that a 'myth about the opening of the war developed over the decades among some scholars of the left, has it that the invasion of the Republic of Korea on June 25 wasn't really an invasion at all . . . but more probably a riposte by the North Korean forces. . . . Yet, from the very outset, all the evidence . . . argues that there was no evidence of any ROK military build-up in the days just before the invasion.'[82] While there is good evidence that Rhee was considering an invasion of the North, possibly in 1949 or early 1950, lack of support from America scuppered the plan to attack the North.[83] At the same time, the collapse of the ROK in June 1950 does not suggest a force ready to attack. Also, while some officers such as Goodfellow might have acted beyond their brief, many Americans did their best to stop a war. In May 1949, during intense battles at Kaesong, the American commander in Korea, Brigadier-General W.L. Roberts, ordered the South not to attack and threatened to remove US support if it did. This was a decisive act of de-escalation. In early January 1950, Roberts publicly informed the ROK government that any aggressive action by the South would be followed by an immediate 'termination of all aid, both military and economic, from the US'.[84] America's Ambassador in Seoul, John Muccio, was also a key player in holding back the South, as Muccio's warnings to cut US aid also prevented a ROK attack across the 38th parallel.[85] Other experts have pointed to the fact that it was extremely doubtful whether the leader of South Korea, Rhee, was psychologically capable of hatching such a plan for a war. When war erupted in 1950, Muccio cabled Washington that the ageing President was 'so overwrought by the attack that he was almost incoherent'.[86]

The available evidence strongly suggests that both North and South Korea were willing to use military means to unite the Korean peninsula. Had the two sides known in advance just how long and bitter the war to unite the peninsula would be, and how much subsequent animosity it would create, they might have pulled back from the military option. But this was not to be. The war started in August 1949 with intense battles along the 38th parallel as Rhee's forces tried to seize jumping-off points for a possible future invasion. Any attack by the South, however, would need US agreement and, notwithstanding the efforts of those such as Goodfellow, this was not forthcoming. Meanwhile, in the North, with troops back from China, and new equipment from the USSR, Kim got the necessary go-ahead from Moscow and Beijing for an invasion. He, therefore, awaited the next assault by Rhee's forces that would be followed by a devastating riposte that would chase the ROK army south and liberate South Korea. While American restrictions limited what the South could do, by 1950 Soviet and Chinese restrictions on the North had been lifted. The North was preparing for a conflict in 1950, and something important was planned for 25 June 1950. It seems that Kim wanted a war to start in August 1950, but intense political rivalry in the North from those such as Hon-yong Pak, and appeals from guerrillas in the South, forced him to accelerate the momentum for war and start it six weeks early.[87]

CONCLUSION

Ignoring, for the moment, who actually started the Korean War, it is clear that the run-up to war shows that there was little impetus from all the parties involved in Korea to keep the peace. Even if Cumings and the revisionists overstate the case for Seoul's responsibility in the war, it is hard not to agree that the South was fundamentally bellicose and, with support from some Americans and Taiwanese leaders, willing to accept a military solution to the problem of Korean unification. Therefore, responsibility for war lies with both Koreas, the superpowers and China, all of whom mismanaged the tense situation on the peninsula.

Korea was on the brink of civil war in 1945, but the external powers with the ability to control Korea – the USA, the USSR and communist China – did too little to stop this internal conflict escalating into a full-scale war. Instead, the superpowers exacerbated the strained state of affairs. Having established an autocratic, unrepresentative regime in Seoul, the US then sent out a series of ambiguous messages about its commitment to East Asia in general and South Korea in particular. Washington also failed to balance the military strength of the two sides by making an unequivocal military commitment to Korea before war broke out in June 1950, after which it was too late. As Gye-Dong Kim observed, in this sense the Korean War was a failure of deterrence.[88] Meanwhile, Kim Il Sung's North Korea received increasing quantities of Soviet equipment, trained troops from China and, crucially, the agreement of Moscow and Beijing to go to war. In this sense, responsibility for the war lies firmly with the communist powers who gave North Korea the green light for war.

There were undoubtedly other strategies available that could have led to a more peaceful outcome to the question of a divided Korea. For instance, some form of neutralization for Korea based on partition, or a United Nations trusteeship over the whole peninsula, could have provided a temporary, interim solution prior to a final settlement. Even continued occupation by US and Soviet forces after 1948 was a better option than all-out war. But, unfortunately for the Korean people, these were roads down which the protagonists decided not to travel.

EIGHT

The Geneva Conference of 1954 and the Second Indochina War

On 7 May 1954, the curtain came down on a dramatic siege at the remote Vietnamese village of Dien Bien Phu. On that day, Vietnamese communist forces, the Vietminh, fighting for independence from French colonial rule, finally overwhelmed the 16,544 man (and one woman) French garrison after a long battle and a siege of 55 days.[1] Having suffered some 8,000 casualties, including 2,000 dead, the 8,000 survivors of the French garrison at Dien Bien Phu were marched off into captivity. The defeat was total. Only seventy-three men from the defeated garrison escaped through the jungle to be picked up by friendly forces in neighbouring Laos. The Vietminh simultaneously attacked Laos and, in June 1954, destroyed the French Expeditionary Corps' *Groupe Mobile* 100 on Route 19. The defeat at Dien Bien Phu was as much psychological as material. While the French High Command claimed that it could make up the losses and pointed to the heavy Vietminh casualties, a wave of defeatism swept through France after the battle. A strategic gamble by the French High Command to entice Vietminh forces into open battle had backfired disastrously and the First Indochina War ended in military catastrophe for the French. While there have been longer sieges in recent history, such as Leningrad, Stalingrad and Tobruk during the Second World War, France's defeat at Dien Bien Phu was special in that, as with the defeats by Japan of Tsarist Russia at Port Arthur in 1905, and Britain and America at Singapore and

165

Bataan in 1942, it proved that European armies could be defeated in conventional warfare by non-western armies. As the French commentator Bernard Fall aptly recorded, the 'Asians, after centuries of subjugation, had beaten the white man at his own game'.[2]

As the Vietminh and French army fought out their endgame at Dien Bien Phu, diplomats and politicians from China, the USSR, Britain, France, the USA and Vietnam gathered in Geneva to resolve the political questions surrounding the future status of Vietnam and Indochina.[3] On 21 July 1954, the delegates reached an agreement that instituted a ceasefire and partitioned Vietnam along the 17th parallel into a communist North Vietnam (the Democratic Republic of Vietnam (DRV)) and a South Vietnam supported by the west. This agreement, however, failed to resolve satisfactorily the key issues in Vietnam and Indochina and so led inexorably to a Second Indochina War as American forces replaced the French in the fight against communism. The two conflicts in Vietnam – French and American – finally ended in 1975 with a communist victory after a '10,000-day war' that devastated the region.[4]

Why did the Geneva Conference of 1954 lead directly from peace to war? This chapter will examine two sets of factors that combined to upset the peace arranged in Geneva in 1954. Firstly, the Geneva settlement ignored the military situation on the ground in Vietnam where the Vietminh had achieved a stunning victory. Instead, at Geneva, the Vietminh's allies – China and the USSR – convinced it to withdraw its forces from large areas of southern Vietnam and to accept partition of the country along the 17th parallel. Therefore, for the Vietminh, Geneva was, at best, a temporary settlement forced on it by China and the USSR just when it looked as though the French would be defeated militarily. Never reconciled to Geneva, the Vietminh soon started to campaign for the united Vietnam that had been denied it in 1954. Secondly, on the opposing side, the USA and South Vietnam were also unhappy with the Geneva settlement. America, in particular, keen to contain communism after the war in Korea, saw South Vietnam as a critical battleground in the Cold War. For America and South Vietnam, the Geneva settlement of 1954 gave far too much to the communists and, as with North Vietnam, they planned to sideline the Geneva accords. Because of this opposition, the Geneva settlement was a badly worded and incomplete compromise rejected by the two Vietnams and never accepted by the USA that failed to match up to the political goals of the protagonists. Because of this hostility to the Geneva settlement, the elections envisaged for 1956 that would decide the political future of Vietnam never happened. Instead, North and South Vietnam turned to military force. In the end, Geneva was not a peace settlement but a short armistice agreement between two wars.

DIEN BIEN PHU, THE VIETMINH AND THE MILITARY SITUATION IN VIETNAM

The Geneva settlement has been compared to the Treaty of Versailles in 1919 as it failed to 'clear the atmosphere of bitterness and resentment' and led to another war.[5] While it is true that Geneva, like Versailles, led to further conflict, it differed in that the victorious side, the Vietminh, was unable to dictate the peace to the power that lost the war – France. This seems strange as, by the time of Dien Bien Phu, a complete Vietminh victory across all of Vietnam was an almost certain outcome if the war had continued. Militarily, the Vietminh had the upper hand and if the Geneva Conference had not met immediately after the fall of Dien Bien Phu, it was more than likely that within a year the Vietminh would have taken over all of Tonkin, most of Annam and Cochin China, Laos and Cambodia.[6] The battle for Dien Bien Phu had galvanized the Vietnamese, awakening a 'fierce national pride' across the country, and was a potent symbol of what could be achieved through military action.[7] When the Vietminh leader, Ho Chi Minh, received news of the victory at Dien Bien Phu, he cabled his military commander, Vo Nguyen Giap: 'The victory is big, but it is only the beginning.'[8] After Dien Bien Phu, Ho Chi Minh and the Vietminh assumed that victory through armed struggle on the battlefield would translate into control over all of Vietnam.

If it is true that to the victor belongs the spoils, then the Vietminh was admirably placed to dominate the Geneva Conference and institute a peace that unified Vietnam under communist rule. France, desperate to end a colonial war in which it was well on the way to defeat, should have had little leverage over the Vietminh. Indeed, Georges Bidault, the French Foreign Secretary, confessed to his British counterpart, Sir Anthony Eden, that his hand consisted of 'a two of clubs and a three of diamonds'.[9] On 20 July 1954, a day before the delegates signed the Geneva settlement, the military situation in Vietnam was such that, in the north of Vietnam, the Vietminh could field 120 well-armed battalions against 80 French battalions, a third of which were Vietnamese units fighting for France.[10] Military logic dictated that France had to come to a settlement with the increasingly powerful Vietminh.

There has been considerable speculation over the years as to why the Vietminh accepted partition and a pro-western South Vietnam rather than pursue the military option and the united communist Vietnam that has always been its goal.[11] As has been mentioned, it was primarily pressure from the USSR and China that was decisive in de-escalating the war and getting the Vietminh to accept the Geneva settlement and partition. U. Alexis Johnson, one of the US delegates at Geneva, recalled how his impression was that the Soviets, and to a lesser degree the Chinese, 'acted as a restraining influence on the VietMinh who were flush with victory and saw no reason that they should not get all of at least Vietnam'. Johnson's view was that the Soviets used the prospect of an election in 1956 that the communists would win (the 'two-bite' approach) to coerce the Vietminh.[12] The Vietminh certainly gave ground at Geneva. Pressed by the Soviets and Chinese, the Vietminh accepted the 17th parallel division of Vietnam, a line of demarcation well to the north of its initial demand, and in doing so surrendered almost a third of the hard-won territory it held that lay south of the 17th parallel. Under Soviet pressure, the Vietminh also made concessions in Laos and Cambodia where the Vietminh not only withdrew its troops but also accepted that the communist movements in Laos and Cambodia, which the Vietminh had supported during the war with France, would now be denied a political role in the Laotian and Cambodian parts of the Geneva settlement.[13]

Why did the USSR act to restrict the Vietminh? Part of the explanation can be found in the fact that since Josef Stalin's death in March 1953 the Soviets had shown greater interest in negotiated solutions.[14] Moscow was also concerned because it knew that American entry into Vietnam to block a total Vietminh victory would probably, as in Korea, bring in the Chinese. Therefore, for the Soviets, while the Vietminh held 'all the aces', it needed to compromise to avert a Sino-US clash that could escalate into an unwelcome superpower confrontation.[15] This does not, however, fully explain the Soviet démarche at Geneva. The best explanation for Soviet behaviour lay in European politics where the USSR was trying to kill off a proposal – the European Defence Community (EDC) – that would have included West German troops. Moscow hoped to do this by offering the Left-Centre French government of Pierre Mendès-France, which had come to power in June 1954, a face-saver in the form of the 'two-bite' election proposal, which would preserve South Vietnam as a French ally, in the hope that Mendès-France would stifle the idea of the EDC. It was the EDC that was the Soviets' main priority.[16] The Soviets' calculation was that a satisfactory deal at Geneva would demonstrate to the French parliament that Mendès-France could deliver the goods. There has even been speculation that Mendès-France made a secret deal with the Soviet Foreign Secretary, V.M. Molotov, to trade the EDC for a favourable settlement in Vietnam; and France's subsequent rejection of the EDC on procedural grounds gives substance to the charge of collusion.[17]

The Chinese also pressured the Vietminh into accepting partition, warning that they might be persuaded to turn over Indochina to the United States if a deal were not reached. To avoid this happening, China pushed the Vietminh into agreeing a compromise with France.[18] Why did China act this way? After all, a deal with far-away France over the EDC was hardly a concern for communist China. China declined to support fully the Vietminh's fight for a united Vietnam for two reasons: firstly, Beijing was keen to avoid a head-on collision with a bellicose America angry at communist China and its intervention in the Korean War in 1950; secondly,

China did not want Vietnam to become a communist regional power in South-East Asia. Beijing's aim, therefore, was to keep Vietnam outside the imperialist orbit but dependent on China.[19] Chinese diplomats viewed with considerable apprehension Vietminh plans to create a military bloc of Vietnam, Laos and Cambodia once the French left that would, as the Chinese saw it, subordinate the interests of Laos and Cambodia to those of Vietnam. China's worry was not without foundation as, although separate communist parties had been established in Laos and Cambodia in 1951, the Vietminh still viewed Indochina 'as a single critical space' that a united Vietnam would lead as the strongest regional power.[20] In the end, China abandoned the Cambodian communist resistance as it had no common border with Cambodia and sabotaged the idea of a united Vietnam in order to block the formation of a strong regional power on its southern border.[21]

The actions of the USSR and China proved that it was the traditional concern with *realpolitik* rather than international communist solidarity that drove their foreign policies. As one critic of US foreign policy observed, China was the principal power broker on the communist side in the negotiations and the 'heady power broker's role soon revealed China's willingness to engage in classic big-nation diplomacy at the expense of Marxist internationalism, and in the end both it and the USSR, in their different ways and for their very diverse and mutually antagonistic reasons, prodded the DRV into accepting the Geneva Accords, particularly the "temporary" division along the seventeenth parallel'.[22] The Vietminh was well aware of the agendas of its Chinese and Soviet backers. As one Vietnamese communist organizer recalled, Geneva was like a 'warning shot, signalling that Vietnamese nationalism had now become hostage to the ideological and geopolitical conflicts of the great powers. The partition of the country had been agreed to by Russia's Molotov and China's [Foreign Minister] Zhou En-lai for reasons of their own national interest.'[23] While many within the Vietminh were angry at Ho Chi Minh's acceptance of the Geneva settlement, they also knew that behind the French loomed the Americans, and to avert American

170

intervention the Vietminh needed to play its hand carefully. Great Britain also played its part at Geneva as it checked American intervention plans in the hope that the communists would show a genuine willingness to compromise. Knowing that America was putting pressure on Britain to walk out of the conference, the Chinese were keen to find an acceptable solution that did not mean another war.[24]

While the Soviets declared that Geneva convincingly proved their peaceful intentions, Ho Chi Minh accepted the settlement as a matter of international communist discipline and because of his military dependence on China and the USSR. But Ho Chi Minh's basic attitude was unchanged. His statement after Geneva was: 'our country will surely be unified and our compatriots throughout the country will certainly be emancipated'.[25] The Vietnamese communists felt that time was on their side. Bernard Fall went to see the elderly Ho Chi Minh in 1962 and recorded their conversation:

'It took eight years of bitter fighting to defeat you French in Indochina,' said the slightly built grandfatherly man with the wispy goatee. 'Now the South Vietnamese regime of Ngo Dinh Diem is well armed and helped by 10,000 Americans. The Americans are much stronger than the French, though they know us less well. It may perhaps take ten years to do it, but our heroic compatriots in the South will defeat them in the end.'[26]

Senior Vietnamese communist leaders echoed Ho Chi Minh's sentiments and, bitterly resentful of the decision reached at Geneva, were determined to unify Vietnam by whatever means necessary.[27] The Vietminh leadership acquiesced in partition at Geneva, under heavy pressure from Beijing and Moscow, partly because it had no choice and partly because it calculated that it could control what it saw as a fragile, puppet regime in the South by political subversion, regardless of what it signed up to at Geneva. This was a recipe for more conflict as North Vietnam had little intention of keeping to the word, let alone the spirit, of a treaty more suited to defeat than victory.[28] Geneva was a galling conclusion to Vietnamese victory over the French at Dien Bien Phu. As they saw it, the Vietnamese communists had fought for the unity and territorial integrity of the countries of Indochina that were now being betrayed at Geneva by China and the USSR.

The Vietminh never saw the Geneva settlement as a permanent solution. Rather, Geneva was a temporary arrangement prior to the elections envisaged for 1956 that the communists were convinced they would win. Pham Van Dong, the Deputy Premier and Foreign Minister of North Vietnam, held that France was bound by the terms of the ceasefire agreement for Vietnam that said that partition was a temporary solution pending the elections to be held in July 1956. For North Vietnam, France was obliged to fulfil in full the provisions of the Geneva settlement, including the elections for 1956 that the communists were sure would bring about the unification of Vietnam.[29] The North Vietnamese saw the Geneva accords as compatible with unification and, in February 1955, issued the following statement:

> The restoration of normal relations between the two zones is in complete conformity with the spirit of the Geneva Armistice Agreement. The first sentence of the Agreement on the cessation of hostilities in Viet-nam stipulates that the demarcation line, on either side of which the forces of the two parties shall be regrouped after their withdrawal, is only provisional. The Final Declaration of the Geneva Conference clearly mentioned that: *'The military demarcation line should not in any way be interpreted as constituting a political or territorial boundary.'*[30]

The decision at Geneva to make the 17th parallel the border between the two Vietnams was far from ideal. The Vietminh wanted the dividing line farther south to reflect its military gains. Colonel Bui Tin, a Vietminh leader in the fight against France and the US, recalled how his comrades were 'forced to accept the partition of Vietnam along the 17th parallel, whereas we wanted it further south at Deo Ca. We believed that we could easily have gained all that territory if fighting had continued.'[31] Because much of South Vietnam was under

Vietminh control in 1954, the decision to divide at the 17th parallel meant that the Vietminh had to surrender hard-fought territory. It was, therefore, hardly surprising that the Vietminh viewed the 17th parallel as little more than a temporary demarcation line. In no way was it to be considered a political frontier.[32] Ho Chi Minh had argued for a division to be drawn at the 13th parallel but the delegates settled on the 17th parallel. Had Geneva agreed a border farther south, it is possible that this would have gone some way to meeting Vietminh demands for more of the spoils of war and so helped to avert another conflict. The territory between the 13th and 17th parallels, while thinly populated, contained the ancient and symbolic Vietnamese capital of Hue and saw some of the most bitter fighting in the 1960s and 1970s. It was also bordered by Laos, through which North Vietnam built the 'Ho Chi Minh Trail' in the 1960s to take war supplies for communist fighters in the South.[33] A smaller South Vietnam without Hue and with the 13th parallel as its northern boundary would have been a better option than the expanded South Vietnam created at Geneva in 1954. North Vietnam felt that it had been cheated territorially at Geneva in 1954. The elections promised for 1956 were never held and by the early 1960s North Vietnam was only interested in the total military victory that it had been so close to achieving in 1954.[34]

SOUTH VIETNAM AND AMERICA

As with the North, what would become South Vietnam was also strongly opposed to the Geneva settlement of 1954. The fact that the South had not procured any of the military victories of the communist North did not stop its vociferous and bellicose opposition to the political settlement. The South Vietnamese Prime Minister (and President from 1955), Ngo Dinh Diem, was emphatic in his refusal to accept the Geneva terms: 'Our delegation at Geneva has not signed that agreement, for we cannot recognize the seizure by Soviet China [sic] – through its satellite the Vietminh – of over half of our national territory. We can neither concur in the enslavement of millions of compatriots faithful to the nationalist ideal, nor to the complete destitution of those who, thanks to our efforts, will have succeeded in joining the zone left to us.'[35]

Vocal in his opposition to Geneva, the intransigent Diem was never reconciled to the territorial division along the 17th parallel.[36] His opposition to cooperation with the North was such that he refused coexistence in even its most basic forms. Therefore, in November 1954 he turned down the North's proposals for the re-establishment of normal postal communications between the two halves of Vietnam.[37] South Vietnam specifically dissociated itself from the final agreement at Geneva, which, among other things, laid down that elections were to be held in 1956 to decide on the reunification of Vietnam.[38] This was a disaster for the durability of the Geneva settlement as the promise of elections was one of the main enticements held out to North Vietnam.

It was not the only disaster to befall the settlement. The very nature of the South Vietnamese regime caused problems. The partition of Vietnam could have provided the space for South Vietnam to build a strong economy and a measure of popular support so as to establish itself as a convincing alternative to communist North Vietnam.[39] After all, a legitimate, prosperous and democratic South Vietnam would have been in a stronger position to resist communist encroachments and might have turned the 17th parallel into a viable border. But this was never done. Instead, as with South Korea, South Vietnam became a corrupt, repressive state reliant on US aid. Diem's record in agricultural and economic reform was abysmal. According to one authority: 'The bulwarks of a solid economy were simply never constructed. Despite an American aid program that was larger than any other save that granted Korea, the Vietnamese economy not only did not progress, it went backwards.'[40] Diem used murder to eliminate opponents and his regime became so brutal that, in 1963, America actually abetted in his assassination. Diem's assassination, paradoxically, made South Vietnam even weaker as it deprived the country of its last strong leader with the ability to maintain authority.

What of America's role in the Geneva settlement? Like the two Vietnams, the US was never reconciled to the peace settlement and its delegation 'crept like a snail unwillingly to Geneva'.[41] Long before the Geneva Conference, America had resisted calls for peace in Vietnam. In 1952, it had exerted strong pressure upon France not to respond to peace feelers extended by the Vietminh.[42] America saw the war in Vietnam as part of a wider picture of communist aggression that demanded a tough response. In his State of the Union address on 2 February 1953, US President Dwight D. Eisenhower referred to the war in Korea as 'part of the same calculated assault that the aggressor is simultaneously pressing in Indochina and Malaya'.[43] In response, America bankrolled France's war in Vietnam with a military aid programme that cost $1.1 billion in 1954, representing 78 per cent of the French war burden.[44] For the US, defeat in Indochina, coming so soon after the fall of nationalist China, would have had serious repercussions across Asia and the Pacific, making potential allies feel that friendship with the United States was a 'liability rather than an asset'.[45]

In April 1954, as the fate of Dien Bien Phu hung in the balance, threatening remarks made by US Secretary of State John Foster Dulles, the US navy and Vice-President Richard Nixon gave rise to fears that the US was even considering military intervention in Vietnam. Codenamed Operation Vulture – *Vautour* in French – there was discussion of US–French air attacks on Vietminh positions around Dien Bien Phu and even a possible tactical strike with nuclear weapons in an effort to relieve the beleaguered garrison. The arrival of two US nuclear-equipped carriers off northern Vietnam was evidence of American commitment.[46] In the end, it was only reluctance to become involved in another war so soon after Korea, along with British unwillingness to support a US strike, that resulted in the cancelling of Operation Vulture.[47] While the US eschewed a conventional strike in 1954, it was already considering covert action against the Vietminh. In January 1954, Dulles argued in the National Security Council, 'If we could carry out an effective guerrilla operation against this new Viet Minh government, we should be able to make as much trouble for this government as they had made for our side. . . . We can raise hell and the Communists will find it just as expensive to resist as we are now finding it.'[48]

175

Therefore, participation in the Geneva talks with communist states was anathema to a US administration committed to fighting communism in South-East Asia. In the first Indochina plenary session on 8 May 1954, the Americans rejected the validity of the diplomatic invitations to North Vietnam and 'non-existent so-called governments or states, such as the so-called Pathet Lao or free Cambodians'.[49] On 12 May, Eisenhower instructed the US team at Geneva not 'to deal with the delegates of the Chinese Communist regime, or any other regime not now diplomatically recognized by the United States, on any terms which imply political recognition. . . . The position of the United States in the Indochina phase of the Geneva Conference is that of an interested nation which, however, is neither a belligerent nor a principal in the negotiation.'[50] In his short stay in Geneva, Dulles refused to shake hands with the Chinese Foreign Secretary, ordered the US delegation to ignore the Chinese delegation and generally 'conducted himself with the pinched distaste of a puritan in a house of ill-repute'.[51]

In the Cold War atmosphere of McCarthyite anti-communism, US politicians opposed America's decision even to agree to *negotiate* the Indochina problem at the Geneva Conference. In a speech in early July 1954, Senator Mike Mansfield declared, 'At Geneva, international communism obtained by diplomacy what it had failed up to then to obtain by threats, bluster, propaganda, intimidation and aggression . . . Geneva was a mistake; and the result is a failure of American policy. It is a profoundly humiliating result.'[52] For Eisenhower the 'terrible agreement at Geneva' was unacceptable even before it was signed.[53] While publicly the United States paid some lip service to the Geneva agreement, it privately regarded it as a major defeat for western diplomacy and a potential disaster for US interests across East Asia.[54] America acceded to participation in the Geneva Conference largely because France needed it for domestic political reasons. But the overwhelming majority of American officials were certain that it would fail and were determined to make no concessions: 'They believed that any political settlement in Indochina, given the prevailing military situation, would amount to handing over control of the entire country to Ho Chi Minh.'[55]

Because of US hostility, the Geneva settlement was stillborn. When Mendès-France was elected French Premier on 17 June 1954, promising that he would obtain a ceasefire in Indochina by 20 July, US participation in the Geneva Conference was, to all intents and purposes, over, and thereafter America pursued an independent course in Indochina.[56] This independent course involved support for South Vietnam and rejection of the Geneva settlement. The loss of North Vietnam to communism strengthened American resolve to support the rest of Indochina and, especially, Diem's South Vietnam. This American policy was incompatible with the core idea of the Geneva settlement – the reunification of Vietnam through internationally supervised elections and the neutralization of Cambodia and Laos.[57] On 21 July 1954, the day of the signing of the Geneva accords, America reiterated its 'traditional position that peoples are entitled to determine their own future and that it will not join in any arrangement which would hinder this. Nothing in its declaration just made is intended to or does indicate any departure from this traditional picture.'[58] Likewise, in his news conference of the same day, Eisenhower told assembled journalists, 'The United States is issuing at Geneva a statement to the effect that it is not prepared to join in the conference declaration. . . . We also say that any renewal of Communist aggression would be viewed by us as a matter of grave concern.'[59] In the end, the Eisenhower administration reluctantly pledged to abide in principle to the Geneva agreement, but the warning that it would challenge any renewal of aggression would be the justification for President John F. Kennedy's intervention in Vietnam in the 1960s.[60] For America, the Geneva settlement was viewed as an 'Indochinese Munich'.[61]

The US strategic response to Geneva was swift: on 21 July 1954 Eisenhower issued a statement outlining how the US 'was actively pursuing discussions with other free nations with a view to the rapid organization of a collective defense in Southeast Asia in order to prevent further direct or indirect Communist aggression in that general area'.[62] Desperate to block the spread of communism, Dulles rapidly organized a meeting in the Philippines to create a US-backed security organization – the South East Asia Treaty Organisation

(SEATO) – to contain the spread of communism.[63] It was SEATO rather than Geneva that would provide the key to US policy over the coming years and which would drag America into the Second Indochina War in the 1960s.

Considering all the difficulties outlined above, can we really talk of a Geneva 'settlement' or 'accords'? As Robert R. Randle has observed, the term 'accords' implies a meeting of minds and a consensus among delegates. It also suggests that the settlement was sufficiently similar in form and content to be subsumed under term 'accords'. In fact, the Geneva settlement, as Randle noted, comprised a number of very different documents: six unilateral declarations, three ceasefire agreements, a final declaration, and the minutes of the last plenary session of the conference: 'Only in the case of the cease fire agreements can we speak of accords having been reached. . . . The final declaration was an accord only for the states that consented to observe its terms. Not all the participating states so consented. . . . Moreover, the language of most of the Geneva documents was unclear in rather crucial respects, implying the absence of a consensus.'[64]

The Geneva settlement was indeed a vaguely worded, legally defective and unsatisfactory compromise. In the rush to conclude a settlement and expedite France's withdrawal from Indochina, the parts of the Geneva settlement that could produce disagreement were simply glossed over.[65] The documentation at Geneva was ambiguous in its discussion of the political settlement and, while there was mention of elections, the wording was unclear with regard to the method for holding them, and even about their exact purpose. Geneva internationalized the peace without providing any effective policing for the terms of the settlement. It also failed to control the import of arms, munitions and military personnel across the rugged land and sea frontiers of Indochina.[66] An International Control Commission (ICC), composed of representatives from Canada, Poland and India, was to supervise the truce, but none of the great powers displayed any real interest in the functioning of the ICC after the conference adjourned in July 1954.[67]

America played a big part in the failure at Geneva. Had it signed the agreement and participated fully and fairly in the discussions at Geneva, China, the USSR, Britain and France might well have been willing to guarantee the settlement and enforce partition for an indefinite period. By refusing to deal with communist North Vietnam, America rejected a finite end to the First Indochina War. If Geneva had been presented as a settlement supported by all the major powers, the North Vietnamese might have been forced into a resentful coexistence, and North and South Vietnam 'could have gone their separate, authoritarian ways'.[68] But in the absence of any guaranteed agreement, the question of whether Vietnam was one state or two remained.

The term 'Geneva settlement' is a misnomer. All that was signed on 21 July 1954 was a series of armistice agreements that provided for a military separation of forces. It achieved little else. The irony is that the purely military terms of the ceasefire agreement signed by the French and the Vietminh at Geneva worked very well and were 'carried out with a precision worthy of congratulations on all sides'.[69] Hostilities ceased: in Vietnam the opposing forces regrouped on either side of the demarcation line, the Vietminh left Cambodia, and the Pathet Lao withdrew to northern Laos.

ELECTIONS AND THE SECOND INDOCHINA WAR

In the South, after the Geneva settlement, Diem ignored the call for elections and set about crushing opposition so as to consolidate his powerbase. When the last French troops left in 1955, he arranged a rigged referendum to confirm himself as President of South Vietnam. Diem had no interest in an election against Ho Chi Minh, and American officials encouraged him to avoid such a contest. Diem and the Americans maintained that there could be no free elections as long as the North, which had a larger population, would announce that 99 per cent of its votes had been cast in favour of whatever position the government endorsed. Therefore, even if a huge majority of southerners should vote against unification – unlikely considering the opposition to Diem in the South – North Vietnam would still win. For this reason, elections were a non-starter. Knowing this to be the case, Diem took his cue from the Americans who, after Geneva, made it clear they would disregard the election clause and support Diem. Indeed, on 7 July 1954, two weeks before Geneva was signed, Dulles wrote to the US Ambassador in Paris how the elections were best left *sine die*: 'Thus since undoubtedly true that elections might eventually mean unification Vietnam under Ho Chi Minh this makes it all the more important that they should be held as long after cease-fire agreement as possible . . . to give democratic elements best chance. We believe important that no date should be set now.'[70]

There are good reasons to suspect that the North Vietnamese leadership never really expected the nationwide elections to take place. But Diem's actions only confirmed the North's suspicions that its hopes for peaceful reunification would be delayed indefinitely unless it did something. With the Soviet Union unenthusiastic about pressing the elections agreed at Geneva, North Vietnam was forced to call for the overthrow of the Diem government.[71] Without the elections, the North would have to resort to force if it wanted to achieve its goal of a united Vietnam, and so it was not long before it started infiltrating communist cadres and troops into the South to unsettle Diem's regime. This, in turn, drew in America, keen to defend Indochina against communism. Inexorably, America replaced France in the fight to contain communism in South-East Asia.

CONCLUSION: AMERICA AND VIETNAM

While the Geneva settlement was successful as an armistice and disengagement document, it failed as a peace settlement. This was partly due to its vague and ambiguous wording, but this was a function of the fact that no form of words was likely to reconcile the differing aims of the protagonists involved. If America had been less suspicious and hostile to practically whatever the Geneva Conference produced, a durable settlement could have been a possibility. But a long-lasting settlement depended on US flexibility and the readiness of the North to accept partition of Vietnam. These were not forthcoming: the US was committed to fighting communism; North Vietnam, spectacularly successful at Dien Bien Phu and determined to unite the country, only accepted partition when forced to do so by China and the USSR. When Sino-Soviet pressure to accept the Geneva settlement was replaced in the 1960s by a willingness to support North Vietnam with military aid, conflict in some form was almost inevitable. Had Diem been unable to hold onto power in the South, which many thought likely, the North's ability to unify Vietnam by political subversion would have averted war. But Diem survived and the North, realizing that he was not going to fall, resorted to guerrilla warfare in the late 1950s. When this did not work it deployed regular North Vietnamese forces in the early 1960s to overthrow the South. In response, in 1965, the first regular US troops arrived to back up America's policy of containment of communism and the Second Indochina War began in earnest.[72]

The Second Indochina War was one of the most egregious mistakes of US foreign policy during the Cold War. In January 1973, after eight years' fighting, America and North Vietnam initialled an agreement to end the war in Vietnam. The aim of this agreement was much the same as that of the 1954 Geneva settlement. But this time the terms were very different, reflecting as they did the successes of the communist forces, something that the 1954 settlement had not done: the ceasefire was to be *in situ*, with no provision for the withdrawal of North Vietnamese forces from the South. This begs the question of why, in 1973, the United States accepted terms so much worse than those it had rejected nineteen-and-a-half years earlier. The answer is to be found in the loss of men and prestige America suffered in the Second Indochina War; in the domestic pressure within the US to end a war that was dividing the nation; and in the new realism by the US President, Richard Nixon, and his Secretary of State, Henry Kissinger, on US foreign policy.

But what is so bizarre is why US strategists opposed the 1954 settlement and got sucked into a war in Indochina in the first place. It is true that without US support Diem's South Vietnam would almost surely have fallen to communism, but was a united communist Vietnam such a bad thing? After all, the US would only have been in the same position as it found itself in 1975, but without the costly Second Indochina War that it subsequently lost, leaving 58,000 Americans and many more Vietnamese dead. As the Sino-Soviet and Sino-Vietnamese clashes of the 1960s and 1970s proved, left to their own devices, and without the war in Vietnam to unite them, China, the USSR and North Vietnam would probably have come to blows with one another sooner rather than later. The Second Indochina War actually helped to unite disparate communist powers around a common cause. US involvement in Vietnam in the 1960s also drained and distracted America, and this gave the Soviet Union the space in which to build up its armed forces to achieve a rough military parity with America.

Why did US decision-makers fail to foresee the consequences of their actions and choose to get involved in a war in Vietnam? Part of the explanation was that America, purged of experts on the region during the anti-communist McCarthyite hysteria of the 1950s, failed to see that Ho Chi Minh and the Vietnamese communists were, at heart, nationalists wanting to expel the French and unite and control their country, rather than agents of Moscow and Beijing. As Robert S. McNamara, the US Defense Secretary in the 1960s, wrote in his candid *mea culpa* published in 1995, in the polarized world of the Cold War the US saw the hand of international communism behind events in Indochina. Therefore, 'ill-founded judgements were accepted without debate. . . . We failed to analyze our assumptions critically, then or later. The foundations of our decision making were gravely flawed.'[73] McNamara, after the event, was right: America's hostility to the Geneva Conference of 1954 and its involvement in the Second Indochina War made little or no strategic sense and, by strengthening America's enemies, put back the date for America's eventual victory in the Cold War.

Conclusion
War and Peace – a Symbiotic Relationship?

'A bad peace is even worse than war.'

Tacitus, Annals, *III*

Covering the period 1870 to 1975, this study has shown that there is a relationship between peace and war. However, it is not always the relationship that people assume. Too often, peace does not terminate a war, as much as sow the seeds for another conflict. Even if the peace does not provide the immediate grounds for a resumption of fighting – as with the Treaty of Frankfurt of 1871 – it can determine the matrix of the subsequent war in terms of who fights the war and how it is fought. The same can be said for the Yalta Accords of 1945 which led to the Chinese Revolutionary Civil War and, also, crucially, like Frankfurt, established where and how the war would be played out. In this sense, peace settlements are complicated constructs that can and do lead to further conflict in a variety of different ways.

The other peace settlements discussed in this study all have a direct and immediate outcome in terms of another clash of arms, be it in Europe, the Near East or the Far East. So, as we have seen, Versailles did lead to the Second World War; the Turkish peace settlement did cause a war between Greece and Turkey; the Geneva Accords did produce the Second Indochina War; and the failure to forge a settlement for Palestine/Israel did make for a series of subsequent Arab-Israeli wars. Why is this so?

The answer to this question is complicated, but this study has suggested that there are certain common themes. What are these? Firstly, there is the question of whether or not a peace settlement is 'just'.[1] Treaties devoid of any sense of justice are liable to fail. The Graeco-Turkish War is illustrative of this phenomenon. It was a war that was sparked by a legitimate grievance by Turkey at a flawed peace settlement that many, including those within the British decision-making process at the time, felt was hard to justify, except in terms of naked self-interest. However, the notion of a just treaty should not be accepted uncritically as a cause of war. For some treaties, the question of justice deflects from the real issues. The Treaty of Versailles is a case in point. It was not, as it is often falsely depicted, a harsh or 'Carthaginian Peace'; and most modern commentators would strongly question whether the failure of Versailles was anything to do with whether it was just or unjust. Rather, they would emphasize that German claims of unfair treatment masked the real problem of German hegemonic desires over continental Europe, and beyond.[2] Therefore, justice can be an explanatory factor for the failure of a peace settlement, but equally it can be a red herring for the historian searching out the causes of modern wars.

And yet, the issue of justice and the Versailles settlement is not without interest, as it illustrates the next theme that emerges from this examination: the protagonists' acceptance or otherwise of a peace settlement. With Versailles, the fact that the Germans saw it – or pretended to see it – as unjust led to their refusal to accept its legitimacy and abide by its terms. This meant that Hitler's rejection of Versailles in the 1930s met with widespread approval from the German people. British and American acquiescence in Germany's unraveling of Versailles proved that it was not just the defeated power that felt that the treaty was unacceptable. This non-acceptance of the settlement proved its undoing. A similar scenario destroyed the Geneva Accords of 1954. The side that had emerged victorious – the Vietminh – was forced to agree to a humiliating climb down at Geneva that in no way corresponded to its military success against the French at the battle of Dien Bien Phu. In this instance, the victorious power only temporarily complied with the terms of the peace settlement. But the communist regime in Hanoi never actually accepted it. Like communist North Vietnam, neither the United States nor its protégé, the South Vietnamese government of Ngo Dinh Diem, had any intention of endorsing a peace settlement which was anathema to their goals. This ensured that the documents signed at Geneva led, sadly, to a conflagration that would last another decade and further devastate Vietnam, Laos and Cambodia. Equally, in the Middle East, after the first Arab-Israeli war, the peace talks in 1949 foundered because of Israeli unwillingness to accept a comprehensive settlement in the wake of their military successes on the battlefield in their 'War of Independence'. Meanwhile, on the other side, it is debatable whether the Arab population, regardless of what their leaders signed up to, would have agreed to terms that they felt sold the Palestinians down the river. Again, the issue of acceptance was the key.

If a settlement is neither just nor acceptable to the parties at the peace table, the only way it can be made to work is if it is enforced. The oft-discussed Treaty of Versailles is a classic case in point. After the Great War, it was left to war-torn France to enforce German compliance with the treaty terms, as Britain and American proved unwilling to fulfil their obligations in this respect. In the face of German recalcitrance, France proved unable, on her own, to enforce the terms agreed in the *Galerie des Glaces* in June 1919. Even when victorious powers show a willingness to enforce their terms, this does not necessarily mean that they will be successful. Sèvres is a good example of this problem. Britain, through its proxy, Greece, invaded Anatolia to force Turkish compliance with the peace settlement. But the Turks successfully resisted this military *démarche* and, in 1922, at the town of Chanak, went one step further and also forced Britain into a hasty retreat. Therefore, as these examples show, it is not simply a question of a willingness to enforce peace terms, but also of the military and diplomatic means available.

A final theme to emerge is mismanagement of the peace process. This can be a function of poorly written treaty documents or the way in which those tasked with implementing a workable settlement fail to do their job properly. Illustrative of the former is the Potsdam Protocol of 1945. Ambiguities and inconsistencies in the text ensured that bitter arguments about how the document should be interpreted erupted long before the ink was dry. The same problem can be seen with the Geneva settlement of 1954, which was a hastily drawn-up and badly worded conclusion to the First Indochina War. In terms of implementation, Korea shows how a functioning, *de facto* settlement was mismanaged by those on the ground, thus allowing warmongers in North Korea to seize the opportunity for war.

What of the period after 1975? The themes from this study continue to haunt the decision-makers involved in forging peace. A good example of this is the Second Gulf War of 1990–1991, a conflict that followed the Iraqi invasion of Kuwait in 1990.[3] Arguably, what made this war possible was the situation created by the termination of two previous conflicts. The first of these was the incredibly fierce struggle that took place between Iran and Iraq between 1980 and 1988 (The First Gulf War). This was a bitter and intense war that required the full resources and complete attention of the two participating nations. Clearly, therefore, while it was taking place, there was no possibility of the Iraqi leadership contemplating an armed intervention anywhere else. Thus, in a literal sense, the closing down of this war in a manner that left Iraq's military infrastructure and combat capability intact was a pre-requisite for any new military venture involving Iraq. This was, in fact, what occurred. The peace with Iran, essentially a restoration of the *status quo ante*, left Iraq with the military wherewithal to consider new battles elsewhere. It also provided Saddam Hussein's Iraq with an incentive to fight again. The financial cost of first attacking Iran and then of defending against the unexpectedly resolute Iranian resistance had proven so high that oil-rich Iraq had become heavily indebted. A successful invasion of Kuwait promised to ease this problem; not only would Iraq's financial obligations to Kuwait be wiped away by such a move, but the seizure of the Sheikhdom's oil reserves would provide a healthy monetary fillip that could restore Iraq to fiscal health. Saddam Hussein was further encouraged to undertake this action in the belief that no one would be willing or able either to oppose or to attempt to reverse the invasion once it had occurred. He was doubtless encouraged in this belief by the established practices of the previous forty years.

During the Cold War, the Kremlin, as is shown by their actions in the Arab-Israeli conflict, would never have permitted – indeed, would have actively blocked – an American-led assault on an ally, such as Iraq, in so strategically sensitive a region. However, it is important to note that the liberation of Kuwait by US-led coalition forces occurred in parallel with the collapse of the Soviet Union. These facts are inextricably linked. It was the end of the Cold War and the new international environment created in the immediate wake of this allowed operation 'Desert Storm' to take place. Thus, just like the ending of the Iran-Iraq War, the termination of the long-standing Soviet-American antagonism was an essential prerequisite for the conflict of 1990–1991.

The peace settlement that concluded this war was equally unsatisfactory, and would also lead to further fighting both in the short and the longer term. In the immediate aftermath of the war, this manifested itself within Iraq in revolts against Saddam's regime in both the north and the south of the country. In the south, in particular, these revolts were brutally suppressed leaving a recalcitrant Saddam Hussein firmly in control of the Iraqi central government. As it had been the hope of the coalition powers – especially the United States – that these revolts would do the job of overthrowing Saddam for them, thus bringing about a new and more favourable Iraqi government, when this did not happen, the United States found itself faced with enforcing a peace settlement on a regime, the very existence of which acted as a living reproach to American foreign policy. This situation was further complicated by the fact that the United States harboured the suspicion that Saddam Hussein aspired to acquire weapons of mass destruction and had a secret programme in place aimed at building up the capability to manufacture such devices. The production and possession of such weapons by Iraq had been forbidden in the peace settlement of 1991, but ensuring compliance with this was not easy. The highly secretive Saddam Hussein was not at all keen to open his country up to the kind of rigorous international inspection that would have conclusively proved to the American and other governments that Iraq had abandoned its illicit aspirations for chemical and biological weaponry. Over the next decade, various sanctions, including periodic attacks from Anglo-American warplanes, were undertaken to encourage Iraqi cooperation with the inspection process, but were not entirely successful in bending Saddam Hussein to their will. This was an untenable situation and it is, therefore, not wholly surprising that when a new American administration took office and acquired, in the wake of the attacks of 11 September 2001, an agenda of being proactive about ensuring American security, that Iraq was firmly in their sights. The war that began in March 2003 (variously known as 'Operation Iraqi Freedom', 'The Iraq War' and 'The Third Gulf War') was, thus, in many senses the direct consequence of the settlement of 1991, which left many more hawkish American politicians believing that there was unfinished business to be dealt with.

Unforeseen internal demographic and political change can also upset a peace settlement, as is shown by the war between Israel and Lebanon in the summer of 2006. As we saw in an earlier chapter in this volume, in 1949, after the first Arab-Israeli war, Israel and Lebanon never signed a peace treaty. This, however, did not immediately lead to another war, as the Christian-dominated government in Lebanon was willing and able to keep the peace with a neighbour, Israel, with whom it had relatively good relations.[4] This meant that there was an effective end to hostilities after the brief war of 1948–9. It was the influx of Palestinian refugees after 1948–9 and the rise in the numbers and political power of the indigenous (and poorer) Muslim Shia population of Lebanon that changed Lebanon and combined to break the *de facto* peace of 1949. After Jordan's crushing of Palestinian armed resistance in the 'Black September' fighting of 1970, many Palestinian fighters decamped to Lebanon, escalating attack and counter-attack between the Palestinians and the Israeli army along Lebanon's southern border. After 1975, Lebanon descended into civil war. In 1982, Israel invaded Lebanon and remained in occupation in the south of the country until 2000 when it unilaterally withdrew in the face of armed Shia resistance to the occupation. With Palestinian power shattered, a new power broker had emerged: the Shia political party, Hezbollah. A border demarcation issue between Israel and Lebanon over a small stretch of land known as the 'Shebaa Farms' was one issue but the real stumbling block was the enmity between Hezbollah and Israel. It was this and not the failed peace of 1949 that led to renewed war in 2006.

As the twenty-first century nears the end of its first decade, there are numerous on-going conflicts. It is to be hoped that they can be successfully terminated and a peaceful settlement forged. However, as has been shown in this study, if renewed fighting is not to break out at a later date and if the seeds of new conflicts are not to be sown, care has to be taken in the settlements reached. Peace is not only often fragile, but it often contains the essential foundations for future conflict.

Notes

Introduction

1   Carl von Clausewitz, *On War* (London: Penguin, 1968), p.400.

2   Lady Gwendolen Cecil, *The Life of Robert Marquis of Salisbury* (London: Hodder & Stoughton, 1921), II, p.34.

3   Michael Walzer, *Just and Unjust Wars: A Moral Argument with Historical Illustrations* (London: BasicBooks, 1992 [1977]) , p.56.

4   Psalms, 85, 10.

5   Donald Kagan citing Will and Ariel Durant. See Donald Kagan, *On the Origins of War* (London: Pimlico, 1997 [1995]), p.4.

6   Leo Tolstoy, *War and Peace* (London: Macmillan, 1943) first and second epilogues.

7   Sir Michael Howard, *The Invention of Peace: Reflections on War and International Order* (London: Profile Books, 2000).

8   Sir Michael Howard, *The Causes of Wars: and other Essays* (London: Counterpoint, 1983); A.J.P. Taylor, *How Wars Begin* (London: Hamish Hamilton, 1979); Jeremy Black, *Why Wars Happen* (London: Reaktion Books, 1998); Erik Goldstein, *Wars and Peace Treaties, 1816–1991* (London & New York: Routledge, 1992).

9   The authors in this Macmillan series include Volker Berghahn on Germany, John Keiger on France, Dominic Lieven on Russia, Zara Steiner on Great Britain, and Samuel R. Williamson, Jr. on Austria-Hungary.

10   Henry A. Kissinger, *A World Restored: Metternich, Castlereagh and the Problems of Peace, 1812–1822* (Boston: Houghton Mifflin, 1973).

11   Quoted in Robin Wright, 'How the Curse of Sykes-Picot Still Haunts the Middle East', *The New Yorker* (30 April 2016).

One

1.   Marquis de Montebello to Jean Casimir-Périer, 17 December 1893. Quoted in George F. Kennan, *The Fateful Alliance: France, Russia, and the Coming of the First World War* (Manchester, Manchester University Press, 1984), pp. 231–2.

2.   This apt but rather colourful phrase comes from Colin McEvedy, *Penguin*

Atlas of Recent History: Europe since 1815 (Harmondsworth, Penguin, 1982), p. 24.

3. Alistair Horne, *The Fall of Paris: The Siege and the Commune, 1870–1* (London, The Reprint Society, 1967), p. 38ff.

4. Michael Howard, *The Franco-Prussian War: The German Invasion of France, 1870–1871* (London, Rupert Hart-Davis, 1961), p. 234.

5. Bertrand Taithe, 'Reliving the Revolution: War and Political Identity during the Franco-Prussian War', in Bertrand Taithe and Tim Thornton (eds), *War: Identities in Conflict, 1300–2000* (Stroud, Sutton Publishing, 1998), p. 143.

6. Memorandum by Gladstone, 25 September 1870. Quoted in H.C.G. Matthew (ed.), *The Gladstone Diaries: Volume VII, January 1869–June 1871* (Oxford, Clarendon Press, 1982), pp. 368–9.

7. 'Germany, France, and England', *Edinburgh Review* (October 1870). Quoted in Karina Urbach, *Bismarck's Favourite Englishman: Lord Odo Russell's Mission to Berlin* (London, IB Tauris, 1999), pp. 52–3.

8. 'Terms of Peace', *Quarterly Review* (October 1870). Quoted in Lady Gwendolen Cecil, *Life of Robert Marquis of Salisbury* (London, Hodder & Stoughton, 1921), 2, p. 36.

9. Count Max Montgelas, *The Case for the Central Powers: An Impeachment of the Versailles Verdict* (New York, Alfred A. Knopf, 1925), p. 200.

10. Harry Elmer Barnes, *The Genesis of the World War: An Introduction to the Problem of War Guilt* (New York, Alfred A. Knopf, 1927), pp. 382–9.

11. Ibid., pp. 383–4.

12. Sidney Bradshaw Fay, *The Origins of the World War* (New York, Macmillan, 1929), 1, pp. 52–3.

13. Barnes, *Genesis of the World War*, p. 386.

14. Christopher Andrew, *Théophile Delcassé and the Making of the Entente Cordiale: A Reappraisal of French Foreign Policy, 1898–1905* (London, Macmillan, 1968), p. 19.

15. *New York Times* (2 January 1920). Quoted in John S. Ewart, *The Roots and Causes of the Wars (1914–1918)* (New York, George H. Doran, 1925), 1, p. 671.

16. E. Malcolm Carroll, *French Public Opinion and Foreign Affairs, 1870–1914* (Hamden, CT, Archon Books, 1964), pp. 112–13.

17. John F.V. Keiger, *France and the Origins of the First World War* (Basingstoke, Macmillan, 1983), pp. 10–11.

18. Marc Ferro, *The Great War 1914–1918* (London, Routledge, 1973), p. 28.

19. L.C.F. Turner, *Origins of the First World War* (New York and London, Norton, 1970), p. 20.

20. E.D. Morel, *Diplomacy Revealed* (London, The National Labour Press, 1921), p. 97. Quoted in Edward E. McCullough, *How the First World War Began: The Triple Entente and the Coming of the Great War of 1914–1918* (Montreal, Black Rose Books, 1999), p. 200.

21. Ibid., pp. 207 and 322.

22. Barnes, *Genesis of the World War*, p. 147.
23. M.B. Hayne, *The French Foreign Office and the Origins of the First World War, 1898–1914* (Oxford, Clarendon Press, 1993), p. 242.
24. J.F.V. Keiger, *Raymond Poincaré* (Cambridge, CUP, 1997), p. 125.
25. Ibid., p. 152.
26. Stephen R. Rock, *Why Peace Breaks Out: Great Power Rapprochement in Historical Perspective* (Chapel Hill, NC, University of North Carolina Press, 1989), p. 74.
27. David Starr Jordan, *Alsace-Lorraine. A Study in Conquest: 1913* (Indianapolis, IN, The Bobbs-Merrill Company, 1916), p. 6.
28. Quoted in Matthew S. Seligmann, 'Germany and the Origins of the First World War in the Eyes of the American Diplomatic Establishment', *German History*, 15 (1997), 322.
29. Lieutenant-Colonel A.V.F.V. Russell to Sir Edward Goschen, 3 March 1911. Quoted in G.P. Gooch and H. Temperley (eds), *British Documents on the Origins of the War, 1888–1914* (London, HMSO, 1926–38), 6, p. 594.
30. Mark Hewitson, 'Germany and France before the First World War: A Reassessment of Wilhelmine Foreign Policy', *English Historical Review*, 115 (2000), 584.
31. David A. Welch, *Justice and the Genesis of War* (Cambridge, CUP, 1993), p. 104.
32. Jordan, *Alsace-Lorraine*, pp. 19–20.
33. Keiger, *France and the Origins*, p. 15.
34. Jordan, *Alsace-Lorraine*, p. 83.
35. Dan P. Silverman, *Reluctant Union: Alsace-Lorraine and Imperial Germany, 1871–1918* (University Park, PA, The Pennsylvania State University Press, 1972), p. 3.
36. Keiger, *France and the Origins*, p. 40.
37. Carroll, *French Public Opinion*, pp. 87–8.
38. Ibid., p. 87.
39. Ibid., p. 185.
40. Jean-Jacques Becker, *1914: Comment les Français sont entrés dans la guerre. Contribution à l'étude de l'opinion publique printemps – été 1914* (Paris, Presses de la Fondation Nationale des Sciences Politiques, 1977), pp. 53–62.
41. Ibid., p. 62.
42. Andrew, *Théophile Delcassé*, p. 22.
43. Matthew S. Seligmann, *Rivalry in Southern Africa, 1893–99: The Transformation of German Colonial Policy* (Basingstoke, Macmillan, 1998), p. 115.
44. Ibid., p. 134.
45. Andrew, *Théophile Delcassé*, p. 173.
46. Quoted in G. Lowes Dickinson, *The International Anarchy, 1904–1914* (London, George Allen & Unwin, 1937), p. 51.
47. G.P. Gooch, *Franco-German Relations, 1871–1914* (London, Longman,

Green & Co., 1922), p. 5.

48. Niall Ferguson, *The Pity of War* (London, Allen Lane, 1998); Stig Förster, 'Der deutsche Generalstab und die Illusion des kurzen Krieges, 1871–1914. Metakritik eines Mythos', *Militärgeschichtliche Mitteilungen*, 54 (1995); David G. Herrmann, *The Arming of Europe and the Making of the First World War* (Princeton, NJ, Princeton University Press, 1996); John H. Maurer, *The Outbreak of the First World War: Strategic Planning, Crisis Decision Making, and Deterrence Failure* (Westport, CT, Praeger, 1995); Annika Mombauer, 'Helmuth von Moltke: A General in Crisis?', in Matthew Hughes & Matthew S. Seligmann (eds), *Leadership in Conflict 1914–1918* (Barnsley, Leo Cooper, 2000); David Stevenson, *Armaments and the Coming of War: Europe 1904–1914* (Oxford, OUP, 1996).

Two

1. Anthony Lentin, *Guilt at Versailles: Lloyd George and the Pre-History of Appeasement* (London, Methuen, 1985), p. 143.
2. Winston S. Churchill, *The Second World War, Volume 1: The Gathering Storm* (London, Cassell & Co., 1948), p. 7.
3. W.K. Hancock, *Smuts: The Sanguine Years, 1870–1919* (Cambridge, CUP, 1962), p. 524.
4. Lentin, *Guilt at Versailles*, p. 97.
5. Ibid., p. 128.
6. Barry Eichengreen, *Gold Fetters: The Gold Standard and the Great Depression, 1919–1939* (Oxford, OUP, 1992), p. 141.
7. As Modris Eksteins has noted, the economic catastrophe of 1929 occurred during the year that marked the tenth anniversary of the signing of the treaty, an unhelpful symbolism that was much remarked upon by the treaty's critics. See Modris Eksteins, *Rites of Spring: The Great War and the Birth of the Modern Era* (Boston and New York, Houghton Mifflin, 1989), p. 294.
8. See, for example, Fritz Stern's comment, 'How could National Socialism have triumphed in 1933 . . .? A people humiliated and disarmed by the vengeful Treaty of Versailles . . . saw in National Socialism a great temptation.' Fritz Stern, *Dreams and Delusions: The Drama of German History* (London, Weidenfeld & Nicolson, 1987), p. 14.
9. A.J.P. Taylor, *The Origins of the Second World War* (Harmondsworth, Penguin, 1964), p. 336.
10. Royal J. Schmidt, *Versailles and the Ruhr: Seedbed of World War II* (The Hague, Martinus Nijhoff, 1968), p. 243.
11. Niall Ferguson, *The Pity of War* (London, Allen Lane, 1998), p. 407ff.
12. Lentin, *Guilt at Versailles*, p. 132.
13. Hancock, *Smuts*, p. 522.
14. Jay Winter and Blaine Baggett, *1914–18: The Great War and the Shaping of the 20th Century* (London, BBC Books, 1996), p. 338. Similar views can be

found in Douglas Hurd, *The Search for Peace: A Century of Peace Diplomacy* (London, Warner Books, 1997), p. 37 and David Sinclair, *Hall of Mirrors* (London, Century, 2001).

15. Quoted in Gordon A. Craig, *Germany 1866–1945* (Oxford, OUP, 1981), p. 425.

16. Ferguson, *Pity of War*, pp. 395–6.

17. Sally Marks, *The Illusion of Peace: International Relations in Europe, 1918–1933* (London, Macmillan, 1976), pp. 18–20.

18. John W. Wheeler-Bennett, *The Forgotten Peace: Brest-Litovsk, March 1918* (New York, William Morrow & Co., 1939), pp. 269–75. Richard Pipes, *The Russian Revolution, 1899–1919* (London, Collins Harvill, 1990), p. 595.

19. Fritz Fischer, *Germany's Aims in the First World War* (New York, Norton, 1967), p. 104.

20. Sally Marks, 'The Myths of Reparations', *Central European History*, 17 (1978), 255.

21. H.A.L. Fisher, *A History of Europe* (London, Edward Arnold, 1936), p. 1161.

22. Lentin, *Guilt at Versailles*, pp. 132–3.

23. Brian Bond, *The Pursuit of Victory: From Napoleon to Saddam Hussein* (Oxford, OUP, 1996), p. 119.

24. Margaret MacMillan, *Peacemakers: The Paris Conference of 1919 and its Attempt to End War* (London, John Murray, 2001), pp. 492–3.

25. John Maynard Keynes, *The Economic Consequences of the Peace* (London, Macmillan, 1919).

26. Stephen A. Schuker, *American 'Reparations' to Germany, 1919–33: Implications for the Third-World Debt Crisis* (Princeton, NJ, Princeton University Press, 1988), p. 17.

27. Lentin, *Guilt at Versailles*, p. 24.

28. Schuker, *American 'Reparations'*, p. 120.

29. A.J.P. Taylor, *The Trouble Makers: Dissent over Foreign Policy, 1792–1939* (Bloomington, IN, Indiana University Press, 1958), p. 174.

30. Walter Hines Page to Edward M. House, 12 December 1914. Walter Hines Page Papers, bMS Am 1090.1, box 14; by permission of the Houghton Library, Harvard University.

31. Adolf Köster quoted in William Ebenstein, *The German Record: Political Portrait* (New York, Farrar & Rinehart, 1945), p. 191.

32. Churchill, *The Second World War*, 1, p. 5.

33. Quoted in Sally Marks, '1918 and After: The Postwar Era', in Gordon Martel (ed.), *The Origins of the Second World War Reconsidered: The A.J.P. Taylor Debate after Twenty-Five Years* (London, Unwin Hyman, 1986), p. 24.

34. David Woodward, '"Black Jack" Pershing: The American Proconsul in Europe', in Matthew Hughes and Matthew S. Seligmann (eds), *Leadership in Conflict, 1914–1918* (Barnsley, Leo Cooper, 2000), p. 153.

35. For appraisals of Dresel and his mission, see Klaus Schwabe, *Woodrow Wilson, Revolutionary Germany and Peacemaking 1918–1919: Missionary Diplomacy and the Realities of Power* (Chapel Hill, NC, University of

North Carolina Press, 1985), pp. 160–1; Arno J. Mayer, *Politics and the Diplomacy of Peacemaking: Containment and Counterrevolution at Versailles, 1918–1919* (New York, Alfred A. Knopf, 1967), p. 281.

36. Ellis Loring Dresel to William Phillips, 22 January 1919. Ellis Loring Dresel Papers, bMS Am 1549; by permission of the Houghton Library, Harvard University.

37. Ibid.

38. Henry L. Bretton, *Stresemann and the Revision of Versailles: A Fight for Reason* (Stanford, CA, Stanford University Press, 1953), p. 21.

39. Koppel S. Pinson, *Modern Germany: Its History and Civilization* (New York, The Macmillan Co., 1955), p. 429.

40. Marc Trachtenberg, 'Reparations at the Paris Peace Conference', *Journal of Modern History*, 51 (1979), 37.

41. For details of the latter issue, see James F. Willis, *Prologue to Nuremberg: The Politics and Diplomacy of Punishing War Criminals of the First World War* (Westport, CT, Greenwood Press, 1982).

42. Hugh Gibson to Ellis Loring Dresel, 18 August 1919. Ellis Loring Dresel Papers, bMS Am 1549; by permission of the Houghton Library, Harvard University.

43. Ferguson, *Pity of War*, pp. 419–20.

44. Among many works on this see Arthur S. Link, *Woodrow Wilson: Revolution, War, and Peace* (Arlington Heights, IL, Harland Davidson, 1979), ch. 5.

45. Ellis Loring Dresel to Christian A. Herter, 14 December 1921. Ellis Loring Dresel Papers, bMS Am 1549; by permission of the Houghton Library, Harvard University.

46. William Phillips, *Ventures in Diplomacy* (Boston, The Beacon Press, 1952), pp. 94–5.

47. Ellis Loring Dresel to Frank Polk, 12 April 1920. Ellis Loring Dresel Papers, bMS Am 1549; by permission of the Houghton Library, Harvard University.

48. Marks, '1918 and After', pp. 29–30.

49. House Diary, 9 February 1919. Quoted in Charles Seymour (ed.), *The Intimate Papers of Colonel House* (Boston, Houghton Mifflin, 1928), 4, p. 345.

50. Walter A. McDougall, 'Political Economy versus National Sovereignty: French Structures for German Economic Integration after Versailles', *Journal of Modern History*, 51 (1979), 12.

51. William R. Keylor, *The Twentieth-Century World: An International History* (Oxford, OUP, 2nd edn, 1992), p. 91.

Three

1. Quoted in J.F.C. Fuller, *The Conduct of War, 1789–1961* (London, Methuen & Co., 1972), p. 318.

2. Wilson D. Miscamble, *George F. Kennan and the Making of American Foreign Policy, 1947–1950* (Princeton, NJ, Princeton University Press, 1992), pp. 25–8.

3. George F. Kennan to the Secretary of State, 22 February 1946. Quoted

in Department of State, *Foreign Relations of the United States, 1946* (Washington, DC, US Government Printing Office, 1969), 6, pp. 699–700.

4. W.H. Parker, *Mackinder: Geography as an Aid to Statecraft* (Oxford, Clarendon Press, 1982), pp. 47, 165–6 and 187; John Lewis Gaddis, *Strategies of Containment: A Critical Appraisal of Postwar American National Security Policy* (New York and Oxford, OUP, 1982), pp. 57–8.

5. This is not to ignore the fact that there was a geopolitical dimension to Kennan's thinking, particularly in respect to how the United States should behave in global affairs. However, the principal configuration of his argument with regard to the Soviet Union was along ideological lines. For the background and basis of this view, see Daniel Yergin, *Shattered Peace: The Origins of the Cold War and the National Security State* (Boston, Houghton Mifflin, 1977), esp. pp. 17–41.

6. Adam B. Ulam, *Stalin: The Man and His Era* (London, IB Tauris, 1989), pp. 162–3.

7. Richard Pipes, *The Russian Revolution, 1899–1919* (London, Collins Harvill, 1990), p. 506.

8. This point has been clearly developed by Bukharin's biographer. See Stephen F. Cohen, *Bukharin and the Bolshevik Revolution: A Political Biography, 1888–1938* (London, Wildwood House, 1974), pp. 62–9.

9. Ulam, *Stalin*, p. 164.

10. John W. Wheeler-Bennett, *The Forgotten Peace: Brest-Litovsk, March 1918* (New York, William Morrow, 1939), p. 278.

11. William G. Rosenberg, 'Russian Labor and Bolshevik Power: Social Dimensions of Protest in Petrograd after October', in Daniel H. Kaiser (ed.), *The Workers' Revolution in Russia, 1917: the View from Below* (Cambridge, CUP, 1987), p. 117.

12. Dmitri Volkogonov, *The Rise and Fall of the Soviet Empire* (London, HarperCollins, 1998), p. 24.

13. Bernadotte E. Schmitt and Harold C. Vedeler, *The World in the Crucible, 1914–1919* (New York, Harper & Row, 1984), p. 197.

14. Leonard Schapiro, *The Origins of the Communist Autocracy: Political Opposition in the Soviet State. First Phase, 1917–1922* (London, G. Bell & Sons, 1955), pp. 92–5.

15. Pipes, *Russian Revolution*, p. 583.

16. Alan Bullock, *Hitler and Stalin: Parallel Lives* (London, HarperCollins, 1991), p. 68.

17. Pipes, *Russian Revolution*, p. 592.

18. Ibid., p. 567.

19. Adam B. Ulam, *Lenin and the Bolsheviks: The Intellectual and Political History of the Triumph of Communism in Russia* (London, Fontana, 1969), p. 508.

20. James Bunyan and H.H. Fisher, *The Bolshevik Revolution, 1917–1918: Documents and Materials* (Stanford, CA, Stanford University Press, 1934), p. 503.

21. Ibid., p. 500.

22. Orlando Figes, *A People's Tragedy: The Russian Revolution, 1891–1924* (London, Pimlico, 1997), p. 544.
23. Wheeler-Bennett, *Forgotten Peace*, p. xii.
24. This interpretation of the dispersal of the Constituent Assembly comes from Isaac Deutscher, *Stalin: A Political Biography* (Harmondsworth, Penguin, 1966), p. 191.
25. *Cold War: Comrades, 1917–45* (London, BBC, 19 September 1998).
26. David Reynolds, 'The European Dimension of the Cold War', in Melvyn P. Leffler and David S. Painter (eds), *Origins of the Cold War: An International History* (London and New York, Routledge, 1994), p. 136.
27. Arthur M. Schlesinger Jr, 'Origins of the Cold War', in Robert A. Divine (ed.), *Causes and Consequences of World War II* (Chicago, Quadrangle Books, 1969), p. 352.
28. For an interesting interpretation of the importance of some of the other conferences, see Keith Sainsbury, *The Turning Point: Roosevelt, Stalin and Chiang Kai-Shek, 1943: The Moscow, Cairo and Teheran Conferences* (Oxford, OUP, 1985).
29. A good guide to the details of this settlement as they applied to Germany can be found in Dennis L. Bark and David R. Gress, *A History of West Germany, Volume 1. From Shadow to Substance, 1945–1963* (Oxford, Blackwell, 1993), pp. 47–56.
30. Herbert Feis, *Between War and Peace: The Potsdam Conference* (Princeton, NJ, Princeton University Press, 1960), pp. 235–9.
31. 'Protocol of the proceedings of the Berlin Conference', 2 August 1945. Rohan Butler and M.E. Pelly (eds), *Documents on British Policy Overseas* (London, HMSO, 1984), Series I, Vol. 1, p. 1267.
32. Marc Trachtenberg, *A Constructed Peace: The Making of the European Settlement, 1945–1963* (Princeton, NJ, Princeton University Press, 1999).
33. 'Extract from Conclusions of a Meeting of the Cabinet held at 10 Downing St. on 13 September 1945 at 11 a.m.' M.E. Pelly and H.J. Yasamee (eds), *Documents on British Policy Overseas* (London, HMSO, 1990), Series I, Vol. 5, p. 114.
34. 'Draft Statement of Policy on Industrial Disarmament.' Ibid., p. 118.
35. Trachtenberg, *Constructed Peace*, p. 60.
36. Sir William Strang to Mr O.C. Harvey, 5 October 1945. M.E. Pelly and H.J. Yasamee (eds), *Documents on British Policy Overseas*, I, 5, p. 189.
37. Paul M. Kennedy, *The Rise and Fall of the Great Powers: Economic Change and Military Conflict from 1500 to 2000* (New York, Random House, 1987), p. 374.
38. Anne Deighton, *The Impossible Peace: Britain, the Division of Germany and the Origins of the Cold War* (Oxford, Clarendon Press, 1990), p. 108.
39. Jules Michelet, 'Légends démocratiques du Nord', *La Sorcière* (1851), p. 226. Quoted in G.F. Hudson, *The Hard and Bitter Peace: World Politics since 1945* (London, Pall Mall Press, 1966), p. 39.
40. Alexis de Tocqueville, *Democracy in America* (New York, Alfred A. Knopf,

1976), 1, p. 434.

41. Imanuel Geiss, *The Question of German Unification, 1806–1996* (London and New York, Routledge, 1997), p. 85.

Four

1. G.M. Trevelyan, *A Shortened History of England* (Harmondsworth, Pelican, 1967 [1942]), p. 373.

2. Until the establishment of the Turkish republic in 1923, there were two centres of power: one 'Ottoman' under Sultan Mehmed VI in Istanbul, the other a 'Kemalist Turkish' regime in Ankara under Mustafa Kemal. Readers will allow some imprecision in the use of the terms 'Ottoman' and 'Turkish'. Istanbul/Constantinople will also be used interchangeably.

3. While the Arab component of the Sèvres settlement has had considerable durability, the decision at Sèvres to allow Jewish immigration into Palestine laid the basis for the Arab–Zionist conflict that erupted into war in 1948.

4. Roderic H. Davison, 'Turkish Diplomacy from Mudros to Lausanne', in Gordon A. Craig and Felix Gilbert (eds), *The Diplomats, 1919–1939* (Princeton, NJ, Princeton University Press, 1953), p. 172.

5. Harry N. Howard, *The Partition of Turkey: A Diplomatic History, 1913–1923* (Norman, OK, University of Oklahoma Press, 1931), p. 243.

6. Quoted in A.L. Macfie, *Atatürk* (London and New York, Longman, 1994), p. 100.

7. For full details of the terms see H.W.V. Temperley (ed.), *A History of the Peace Conference of Paris* (London, Henry Frowde/Hodder & Stoughton, 1924), 6, pp. 29–31.

8. Howard, *Partition*, p. 222 and Salahi Ramsdan (or Ramadan) Sonyel, *Turkish Diplomacy: Mustafa Kemal and the Turkish National Movement* (London and Beverly Hills, CA, Sage, 1975), pp. 6–7.

9. See Michael Llewellyn Smith, *Ionian Vision: Greece in Asia, 1919–1922* (London, Allen Lane, 1973), pp. 72–3.

10. David Lloyd George, *Memoirs of the Peace Conference* (New York, Howard Fertig, 1972), 2, pp. 651 and 799.

11. Conversation between Wilson, Clemenceau, Lloyd George and Orlando, 1 April 1919. Arthur S. Link (ed.), *The Deliberations of the Council of Four (March 24–June 28, 1919). Notes of the Official Interpreter Paul Mantoux* (Princeton, NJ, Princeton University Press, 1992), 1, p. 111.

12. Howard, *Partition*, p. 248.

13. Lloyd George, *Memoirs of the Peace*, pp. 804–5.

14. Paul C. Helmreich, *From Paris to Sèvres: The Partition of the Ottoman Empire at the Peace Conference of 1919–20* (Columbus, OH, Ohio State University Press, 1974), p. 100.

15. Smith, *Ionian Vision*, pp. 84–5.

16. Sonyel, *Turkish Diplomacy*, p. 87.

17. Patrick Balfour (Lord) Kinross, *Atatürk: The Rebirth of a Nation* (London, Weidenfeld & Nicolson, 1964), pp. 139 and 140.

18. A.J.P. Taylor (ed.), *Lloyd George: A Diary by Frances Stevenson* (London, Hutchinson, 1971), p. 230.

19. Note of an interview between the Prime Minister and Venizelos at 10 Downing Street, 31 October 1919. Lloyd George Papers, House of Lords Record Office (HLRO), LG/F/92/12/5.

20. Erik Goldstein, *Wars and Peace Treaties, 1816–1991* (London and New York, Routledge, 1992), pp. 51–2.

21. Quoted in Smith, *Ionian Vision*, ch. 1.

22. Richard Clogg, *A Concise History of Greece* (Cambridge, CUP, 1992), p. 85.

23. Granville to Balfour, 17 November 1918. Public Record Office (PRO), FO371/3147.

24. Curzon to Granville, 21 October 1919. Curzon Papers, British Library (BL), Mss.EurF112/278.

25. Smith, *Ionian Vision*, p. 74.

26. Lord Beaverbrook (Max Aitken), *The Decline and Fall of Lloyd George* (London, Collins, 1963), p. 153; Joseph C. Grew, *Turbulent Era: A Diplomatic Record of Forty Years* (London, Hammond, 1953), 1, p. 497.

27. Wilson to Milne, 12 July 1920. Wilson Papers, Imperial War Museum (IWM), HHW2/37/18.

28. Quoted in Smith, *Ionian Vision*, pp. 12–13.

29. Conversation between Lloyd George, Wilson and Clemenceau, 13 May 1919, quoted in Link (ed.), *Deliberations*, 2, p. 57.

30. Beaverbrook, *Decline and Fall*, p. 152.

31. Harold Nicolson, *Peacemaking 1919* (London, Constable, 1933), p. 35.

32. Michael Dockrill and J. Douglas Goold, *Peace without Promise: Britain and the Peace Conferences, 1919–23* (London, Batsford, 1981), p. 183 (also p. 248).

33. Review of the situation in the Middle East, with special reference to the danger of delay in reaching a general settlement, by Curzon, 18 April 1919. Curzon papers, BL, Mss.EurF112/278.

34. Laurence Evans, *United States Policy and the Partition of Turkey, 1914–24* (Baltimore, MD, Johns Hopkins Press, 1965), p. 170.

35. Temperley (ed.), *History of the Peace Conference*, 6, pp. 28–9.

36. Quoted in David Walder, *The Chanak Affair* (London, Hutchinson, 1969), pp. 81–2.

37. De Robeck (Constantinople) to Curzon, 18 November 1919. Lloyd George Papers, HLRO, LG/F/59/12/7.

38. A. Rawlinson, *Adventures in the Near East, 1918–22* (London, Jonathan Cape, 1934), pp. 156 and 226–7.

39. Davison in Craig and Gilbert (eds), *The Diplomats*, p. 181.

40. Dockrill and Douglas Goold, *Peace without Promise*, p. 185.

41. Douglas Dakin, *The Unification of Greece, 1770–1923* (London, Ernest Benn,

1972), p. 224.

42. Curzon to Balfour, 20 June 1919. Curzon Papers, BL, Mss.EurF112/278.

43. Helmreich, *From Paris to Sèvres*, p. 98.

44. Evans, *United States Policy*, p. 181.

45. Walder, *Chanak Affair*, p. 70.

46. Smith, *Ionian Vision*, p. 90.

47. Balfour to King, Lloyd George and Hankey, 18 July 1919. Balfour Papers, BL, Add.Mss.49734, ff. 129–31.

48. Evans, *United States Policy*, pp. 179–81.

49. Ibid., p. 181.

50. Toynbee, quoted in Richard Clogg, 'King's College London and Greece, 1915–22', in *Greece and Great Britain during World War One* (Thessaloniki, Institute of Balkan Studies, 1985), pp. 208–9.

51. Maurice (Lord) Hankey, *The Supreme Control: At the Paris Peace Conference* (London, George Allen & Unwin, 1963), pp. 162–3.

52. Temperley (ed.), *History of the Peace Conference*, 6, p. 48.

53. Davison in Craig and Gilbert (eds), *The Diplomats*, p. 175.

54. Report dated 23 May 1919 from the Control Officer Ankara enclosed in Admiral Calthorpe (C-in-C, Mediterranean) to Lord Curzon, 11 June 1919. PRO, FO371/3158.

55. Milne to Secretary of State WO, 11 August 1920. Milne Papers, Liddell Hart Centre for Military Archives (LHCMA), Box 3.

56. De Robeck (Constantinople) to Curzon, 18 November 1919. Lloyd George Papers, HLRO, LG/F/59/12/7.

57. Ibid.

58. See Alistair Horne, *A Savage War of Peace: Algeria 1954–1962* (London, Papermac, 1996), p. 37.

59. Wilson to Harington, 29 April 1921. Wilson Papers, IWM, HHW2/46B/6.

60. Wilson to Sackville-West, 25 September 1919, in Keith Jeffery (ed.), *The Military Correspondence of Field Marshal Sir Henry Wilson* (London, Bodley Head/Army Records Society, 1985), p. 126. Smith in *Ionian Vision* (p. 124) sees the Foreign Office as hostile to the Turks.

61. Wilson to Sackville-West, 4 April 1921. Wilson Papers, IWM, HHW2/12G/23.

62. Sackville-West to Wilson, 31 March 1921. Wilson Papers, IWM, HHW2/12G/22.

63. Lieutenant-Colonel A. Rawlinson to Lord Rawlinson, 15 January 1920 enclosed in Wilson to Curzon, 27 February 1920. Wilson Papers, IWM, HHW2/20A/31.

64. Curzon to Balfour, 20 August 1919. Balfour Papers, BL, Add.Mss.49734, ff. 154–60. Curzon's assessment is questionable inasmuch as Montagu was usually pro-Turk.

65. Smith, *Ionian Vision*, p. 124.

66. Taylor (ed.), *Stevenson*, p. 230 (20 July 1921).

67. Draft conclusions of a Conference held at 10 Downing Street, 5 January 1920.

Curzon Papers, BL, Mss.EurF112/268.

68. Curzon to Granville, 21 October 1919. Curzon Papers, BL, Mss. EurF112/278.

69. Curzon to Balfour, 20 August 1920. Balfour Papers, BL, Add.Mss.49734.

70. See Keith Jeffery, *The British Army and the Crisis of Empire 1918–22* (Manchester, Manchester University Press, 1984), p. 160.

71. Roger Adelson, 'The Formation of British Policy Towards the Middle East 1914–1918' (doctoral thesis, Washington University, 1972), p. 483.

72. Wilson to Milne, 14 May 1920. Wilson Papers, IWM, HHW2/37/13.

73. British Secretary's Notes of a Meeting of the Supreme Council held at San Remo, 20 April 1920. Quoted in Rohan Butler and J.P.T. Bury, *Documents on British Foreign Policy* (London, HMSO, 1958), Series I, Vol. 8, pp. 54–5.

74. David Fromkin, *A Peace To End All Peace: Creating the Modern Middle East, 1914–22* (London, Penguin, 1991), p. 428.

75. Meeting held in PM's room at H(ouse) of C(ommons), 1 June 1921. Lloyd George Papers, HLRO, LG/F/206/5.

76. Notes of a conversation held in the Secretary of State's Room, WO, 19 March 1920. Lloyd George Papers, HLRO, LG/F/199/9/2.

77. Quoted in Clogg, *History of Greece*, p. 70.

78. Ibid., p. 95.

79. Edward S. Forster, *A Short History of Modern Greece, 1821–1956* (London, Methuen, 1958), p. 141.

80. Andrew Mango, *Atatürk* (London, John Murray, 1999), p. 306.

81. Davison in Craig and Gilbert (eds), *The Diplomats*, p. 189.

82. Sibyl Crowe and Edward Corp, *Our Ablest Public Servant: Sir Eyre Crowe, 1864–1925* (Braunton, UK, Merlin Books, 1993), pp. xii–xiv.

83. Granville to Curzon, 12 February 1921. Lloyd George Papers, HLRO, LG/F/55/3/10.

84. Brief Notes on the Present Conference Situation by Balfour, 25 February 1919. Balfour Papers, BL, Add.Mss.49750, ff. 110–14.

85. Kinross, *Atatürk*, p. 142.

86. Sonyel, *Turkish Diplomacy*, pp. 83–4.

87. Quoted in Martin Gilbert, *Sir Horace Rumbold: Portrait of a Diplomat, 1869–1941* (London, Heinemann, 1973), p. 239.

88. British Section, Allied Military Committee, Versailles (Y.H. Kisch) to Wilson, 23 November 1920. Wilson Papers, IWM, HHW2/12G/6.

89. Review of the Situation in the Middle East, with special reference to the danger of delay in reaching a general settlement, by Curzon, 18 April 1919. Curzon Papers, BL, Mss.EurF112/278.

90. De Robeck (Constantinople) to Curzon, 18 November 1919. Lloyd George Papers, HLRO, LG/F/59/12/7.

91. 'The Future of Constantinople', paper printed for Cabinet by Curzon, 4 January 1920. Curzon Papers, BL, Mss.EurF112/268.

92. Wilson to Lloyd George, 4 December 1920. Wilson Papers, IWM, HHW2/10;

Gilbert, *Rumbold*, p. 249.

93. Oliphant to Hardinge, 12 July 1922. Balfour Papers, BL, Add.Mss.49749, f. 243.

94. Beaverbrook, *Decline and Fall*, p. 154.

95. Lloyd George, *Memoirs of the Peace*, p. 818.

96. Curzon to Balfour, 20 August 1919. Balfour Papers, BL, Add.Mss.49734, ff. 154–60.

97. Link (ed.), *Deliberations*, 1, p. xxv.

98. Crowe and Corp, *Our Ablest Public Servant*, p. 409; Smith, *Ionian Vision*, p. 221.

99. Davison in Craig and Gilbert (eds), *The Diplomats*, p. 183; Gilbert, *Rumbold*, pp. 224–5.

100. Milne to Secretary of State WO, 11 August 1920. Milne Papers, LHCMA, Box 3.

101. Milne to Wilson, 1 December 1918. Wilson Papers, IWM, HHW2/37/4.

102. Erik J. Zürcher, *Turkey: A Modern History* (London and New York, IB Tauris, 1997), p. 140.

103. A. Rawlinson, 'Note on the situation in eastern Anatolia at the time of Erzerum conference, 11 August 1919', enclosed in War Office to Foreign Office, 4 September 1919. PRO, FO371/4158.

104. Rawlinson, *Adventures in the Near East*, p. 148.

105. Captain Perring to Vice-Admiral J. De Robeck, 1 October 1919. PRO, FO371/4160.

106. Frank Rattigan (Acting High Commissioner) to Curzon, 1 June 1921 (passed to Cabinet 25 June 1921), quoting article in *Hakimiet-i-Millié* of Ankara of 28 April 1921. Lloyd George Papers, HLRO, LG/F/59/12/10.

107. The destruction of Smyrna is detailed in Marjorie Housepian Dobkin, *Smyrna, 1922: The Destruction of a City* (Kent, OH and London, Kent State University Press, 1988 [1966]).

108. For a description of the little that remains of old Smyrna see Roderick Beaton, 'Letter from Smyrna', *Times Literary Supplement* (20 October 2000), 14–15.

109. Clogg, *History of Greece*, p. 101.

Five

1. The armistice negotiations began on the Greek island of Rhodes on 13 January 1949 and continued on Rhodes and elsewhere until July 1949. Israel secured armistice agreements in rapid succession: Egypt on 24 February, Lebanon on 23 March, Jordan on 3 April and Syria on 20 July. The Lausanne peace conference lasted from April to September 1949 but failed to come to a final settlement.

2. Avi Shlaim, *The Iron Wall: Israel and the Arab World* (London, Allen Lane/Penguin, 2000), p. 49.

3. Walter Eytan, *The First Ten Years: A Diplomatic History of Israel* (London,

Weidenfeld & Nicolson, 1958), p. 61.

4. Meron Medzini (ed.), *Israel's Foreign Relations. Selected Documents, 1947–74. Volume One* (Jerusalem, Ministry for Foreign Affairs, 1976), pp. 265 and 270.

5. For a cogent summary of the 'new' historians' perspective see Avi Shlaim, 'The Debate about 1948', *International Journal of Middle East Studies*, 27 (1995), 287–304; Bernard Wasserstein, 'Old Historians and New', *Jerusalem Post* (27 December 1999); and Eugene L. Rogan and Avi Shlaim (eds), *The War for Palestine: Rewriting the History of 1948* (Cambridge, CUP, 2001).

6. Benny Morris, *1948 and After: Israel and the Palestinians* (Oxford, Clarendon Press, 1994 [1990]), p. 8 (also discussed in the preface of Shlaim's *The Iron Wall*). Morris has also recently published his *Righteous Victims: A History of the Zionist–Arab Conflict, 1881–1999* (London, John Murray, 2000).

7. Aharon Megged, 'The Israeli Suicide Drive', *Ha-aretz Weekly Magazine* (10 June 1994), quoted in Efraim Karsh *Fabricating Israeli History: The 'New Historians'* (London, Frank Cass, 1997). See also Karsh's *Fabricating Israeli History: The 'New Historians'* (London, Frank Cass, 2000 [1997]), preface to the second revised edn, pp. xv–xxxix.

8. For instance, Morris's review of Karsh's *Fabricating Israeli History* entitled 'Refabricating 1948', in *Journal of Palestine Studies*, 27/2 (Winter 1998), 81–95.

9. For instance, Nur Masalha's essay 'A Critique of Benny Morris', in Ilan Pappé (ed.), *The Israel/Palestine Question* (London and New York, Routledge, 1999) (originally an article in *Journal of Palestine Studies*, 21/1 (Autumn 1991), 90–7); Norman Finkelstein, 'Myths, Old and New', *Journal of Palestine Studies*, 21/1 (Autumn 1991), 66–89; and Morris, 'Response to Finkelstein and Masalha', in the same issue of *Journal of Palestine Studies*. Prominent Palestinian scholars such as Edward Said have acknowledged the work done by the 'new' historians: see www.history.ac.uk/reviews/paper/shlaimavi.html.

10. The date for the change of name to Jordan is sometimes given as 1946. The name Transjordan was widely used until the early 1950s.

11. See the revised 2007 edition of Rogan and Shlaim (eds), *War for Palestine*, pp. 8–9.

12. For an account of the Syrian-Israeli dialogue see Avi Shlaim, 'Husni Za'im and the Plan to Resettle Palestinian Refugees in Syria', *Journal of Palestine Studies*, 15/4 (Summer 1986), 68–80. The right of return is still a contentious issue, with Palestinian negotiators still insisting on the right of displaced Palestinians to return to Israel/Palestine: Peter Beaumont and Ed Vulliamy, 'Middle East peace talks fail to end deadlock', *Observer* (24 December 2000). On the BBC News (4 January 2001) Ehud Barak, then the Israeli Prime Minister, emphatically rejected any right of return.

13. Quoted in Aryeh Shalev, *The Israel–Syria Armistice Regime, 1949–1955* (Boulder, CO and Jerusalem, Westview Press and *Jerusalem Post*, 1993), p. 28.

14. Shalev, *The Israel–Syria Armistice Regime*, p. 28.

15. Moshe Ma'oz, *Syria and Israel: From War to Peacemaking* (Oxford,

Clarendon Press, 1995), p. 20.

16. Andrew Rathmell, *Secret War in the Middle East: The Covert Struggle for Syria, 1949–1961* (London and New York, IB Tauris, 1995), p. 39.

17. Secretary of State (Acheson) to the Legation in Syria, 13 May 1949, in *Foreign Relations of the United States 1949. Volume 6. The Near East, South Asia, and Africa* (Washington, DC, US Government Printing Office, 1977), p. 1007 (hereafter *FRUS*).

18. The Minister in Syria (Keeley) to the Secretary of State, 19 May 1949, in *FRUS*, pp. 1031–2.

19. Ibid.

20. Miles Copeland, *The Game of Nations: The Amorality of Power Politics* (London, Weidenfeld & Nicolson, 1969), p. 42.

21. George McGhee, *Envoy to the Middle World: Adventures in Diplomacy* (New York, Harper Row, 1983), p. 36.

22. Shabtai Rosenne (Tel Aviv) to Ben-Gurion and Sharett, 18 May 1949, in Yemina Rosenthal (ed.), *Documents on the Foreign Policy of Israel. Volume 3. Armistice Negotiations with the Arab States, December 1948–July 1949. Companion Volume* (Jerusalem, Israel State Archives, 1983), p. 99 (hereafter *DFPI Companion*).

23. Pablo de Azcárate, *Mission in Palestine, 1948–52* (Washington, DC, The Middle East Institute, 1966), pp. 151–2.

24. Shabtai Rosenne to J. Robinson (New York) and the Israeli Delegation in Lausanne, 1 May 1949, in Rosenthal (ed.), *DFPI Companion*, p. 96.

25. Reuven Shiloah to Moshe Sharett, 31 May 1949, in Yemina Rosenthal (ed.), *Documents on the Foreign Policy of Israel. Volume 3. Armistice Negotiations with the Arab States, December 1948–July 1949* (Jerusalem, Israel State Archives, 1983), p. 592.

26. Foreword to Rosenthal (ed.), *DFPI Companion*, p. xxxv.

27. Ma'oz, *Syria and Israel*, p. 21.

28. Simha Flapan, *The Birth of Israel: Myths and Realities* (New York, Pantheon, 1987), p. 210.

29. Benny Morris, *Righteous Victims*, p. 265.

30. Ilan Pappé, 'British Rule in Jordan, 1943–55', in Michael J. Cohen and Martin Kolinsky (eds), *Demise of the British Empire in the Middle East: Britain's Responses to Nationalist Movements, 1943–55* (London, Frank Cass, 1998), pp. 201–2.

31. Avi Shlaim, *Collusion Across the Jordan: King Abdullah, the Zionist Movement and the Partition of Palestine* (Oxford, Clarendon Press, 1988).

32. Critics of the 'new' historians fiercely deny that there was collusion between Israel and Abdullah. See, for instance, Karsh, *Fabricating Israeli History*.

33. Shlaim, *Collusion*, pp. 435 and 620–1.

34. Flapan, *Birth of Israel*, pp. 205–6.

35. Ibid., p. 208.

36. Michael Oren, 'The Diplomatic Struggle for the Negev, 1946–56', *Studies in*

Zionism, 10/2 (1989), 203; see also Michael B. Oren, *Origins of the Second Arab–Israel War: Egypt, Israel and the Great Powers, 1952–56* (London, Frank Cass, 1992), p. 96.

37. Ahron Bregman and Jihan El-Tahri, *The Fifty Years War: Israel and the Arabs* (London, Penguin, 1998). See also Benny Morris, *Israel's Border Wars, 1949–56: Arab Infiltration, Israeli Retaliation, and the Countdown to the Suez War* (Oxford, Clarendon Press, 1993) and Motti Golani, *Israel in Search of a War: The Sinai Campaign, 1955–1956* (Brighton, Sussex Press, 1998).

38. Morris, *Righteous Victims*, p. 268.

39. Oren, *Origins of the Second Arab–Israeli War*, p. 96.

40. Shlaim, *The Iron Wall*, pp. 14 and 598.

41. Avi Shlaim, talk at RIIA, Chatham House London (1 June 2000).

42. Nahum Goldmann quoted in Shlaim, *The Iron Wall*, p. 40.

43. Shlaim, *The Iron Wall*, p. 52.

44. John Bagot Glubb, 'Violence on the Jordan–Israel border: A Jordanian View', *Foreign Affairs* (4 July 1954), 553–4.

45. John Bagot Glubb, *A Soldier with the Arabs* (London, Hodder & Stoughton, 1957), p. 231.

46. Foreword to Rosenthal (ed.), *DFPI Companion*, p. xxvii.

47. Ma'oz, *Syria and Israel*, p. 23.

48. Benny Morris paints a less favourable picture of Sharett, accusing him of encouraging the destruction of Palestinian villages to prevent a return of refugees: Benny Morris, 'The Crystallization of Israeli Policy Against a Return of the Arab Refugees: April–December 1948', *Studies in Zionism*, 6/1 (1985), 91.

49. Quoted in Shlaim, *The Iron Wall*, p. 41.

50. Quoted in Shlaim, *Collusion*, p. 445.

51. Shlomo Perla, 'Israel and the Palestine Conciliation Committee', *Middle Eastern Studies*, 26/1 (1990), 117.

52. Morris, *Righteous Victims*, p. 252.

53. Shalev, *Israel–Syria Armistice*, p. 29.

54. The Minister in Syria (Keeley) to the Secretary of State, 19 May 1949, in *FRUS*, p. 1031.

55. Perla, 'Israel and the Palestine Conciliation Committee' *Middle Eastern Studies*, 117.

56. Ben-Gurion speaking at a Political Consultation in the Ministry for Foreign Affairs (Tel Aviv), 12 April 1949, in Yehoshua Freundlich (ed.), *Documents on the Foreign Policy of Israel. Volume 2. October 1948–April 1949. Companion Volume* (Jerusalem, Israel State Archives, 1984), pp. 94–5.

57. Ben-Gurion speaking at a Political Consultation in the Ministry for Foreign Affairs (Tel Aviv), 12 April 1949, in Freundlich (ed.), *DFPI Companion*, p. 95. Ben-Gurion finished this sentence with 'and it obliged to Israel to achieve peace with the Arabs' – presumably a reference to the armistice agreements.

58. Shlaim, *Collusion*, p. 465.

59. Joseph Heller, *The Birth of Israel, 1945–1949: Ben-Gurion and His Critics*

(Gainesville, University Press of Florida, 2000), p. 306. The 'new' historians would challenge Heller's view that Ben-Gurion did not seek a 'greater' Israel.

60. Morris, *Righteous Victims*, p. 686, n. 20.

61. Shlaim, *The Iron Wall*, pp. 50–1.

62. Patrick Seale, *The Struggle for Syria: A Study of Post-War Arab Politics, 1945–1958* (New Haven, CT and London, Yale University Press, 1987 [1965]), p. 59.

63. Patrick Seale, *Asad of Syria: The Struggle for the Middle East* (London, IB Tauris, 1988), p. 46.

64. Seale, *Struggle for Syria*, pp. 59 and 61–2. Seale also observed that a deal with Israel could have been signed in April 1949 had not *Syria* held out for better terms.

65. Ma'oz, *Syria and Israel*, p. 22.

66. Shalev, *Israel–Syria Armistice*, p. 31. Itamar Rabinovich, *The Road Not Taken: Early Arab–Israeli Negotiations* (London and New York, OUP, 1991), pp. 221–2, disagreed: 'As for the negotiations with Husni al-Zaim: Even if he is seen as an eccentric and exceptional figure . . . the fact remains that Zaim's Syrian enemies generally did not denounce him for his dealings with Israel and for his efforts to come to terms with that country. . . . One wonders, therefore, what could actually have been achieved had all those concerned taken a much bolder stance at the end of the 1948 war.'

67. Ilan Pappé, *The Making of the Arab–Israeli Conflict, 1947–1951* (London and New York, IB Tauris, 1992), p. 227.

68. Uri Bar-Joseph, *The Best of Enemies: Israel and Transjordan in the War of 1948* (London, Frank Cass, 1987), p. 244.

69. Oren, 'Diplomatic Struggle for the Negev', pp. 206 and 208; Rabinovich, *Road Not Taken*, p. 210.

70. Rony Gabbay, *A Political Study of the Arab–Jewish Conflict* (Paris, Minard, 1959), pp. 269–70.

71. Gabbay, *Political Study*, p. 273; Morris, 'The Crystallization of Israeli Policy Against a Return of the Arab Refugees', 91–2.

72. Shlaim, *The Iron Wall*, p. 50.

73. Ilan Pappé, 'British Rule in Jordan, 1943–55', in Cohen and Kolinsky (eds), *Demise of the British Empire in the Middle East*, p. 205.

74. Wm. Roger Louis, *The British Empire in the Middle East: Arab Nationalism, the United States, and Postwar Imperialism* (Oxford, Clarendon Press, 1985), p. 579.

75. Neil Caplan, *The Lausanne Conference, 1949: A Case Study in Middle East Peacemaking* (Tel Aviv, Moshe Dayan Center for Middle Eastern and African Studies, 1993), p. 121.

76. Ibid., pp. 121–2.

Six

Notes

1. Patrick J. Hurley to the Secretary of State, 20 August 1945. Quoted in Department of State, *Foreign Relations of the United States: Diplomatic Papers 1945: Volume 7: The Far East* (Washington, DC, US Government Printing Office, 1969), p. 534 (hereafter cited as *FRUS*).
2. Robert J.C. Butow, *Japan's Decision to Surrender* (Stanford, Stanford University Press, 1954), pp. 241–50.
3. Akira Iriye, *The Cold War in Asia: A Historical Introduction* (Englewood Cliffs, NJ, Prentice-Hall, 1974).
4. The full texts of these documents can be found in the Department of State, *United States Relations with China with Special Reference to the Period 1944–1949* (Washington, DC, US Government Printing Office, 1949), pp. 585–604.
5. Throughout this chapter and the next, the transliteration of Chinese names will follow the *pinyin* system. On first use, however, where a more familiar Wade-Giles alternative exists, this may be indicated in parentheses.
6. Kai-yu Hsu, *Chou En-lai: China's Grey Eminence* (Garden City, NJ, Doubleday, 1968), p. 113.
7. Tien-wei Wu, *The Sian Incident: A Pivotal Point in Modern Chinese History* (Ann Arbor, University of Michigan Press, 1976), pp. 142–8.
8. F.F. Liu, *A Military History of Modern China, 1924–1949* (Princeton, Princeton University Press, 1956), p. 243.
9. Tang Tsou, *America's Failure in China, 1941–50* (Chicago, University of Chicago Press, 1963), pp. 150–1.
10. Gregor Benton, 'Communist Guerrilla Bases in Southeast China after the Start of the Long March', in Kathleen Hartford and Steven M. Goldstein (eds), *Single Sparks: China's Rural Revolutions* (Armonk, NY, M.E. Sharpe, 1989), p. 82.
11. Lucien Bianco, *Origins of the Chinese Revolution, 1915–1949* (Stanford, Stanford University Press, 1971), p. 150.
12. Tsou, *America's Failure*, p. 139.
13. Lyman P. Van Slyke in Lloyd E. Eastman et al., *The Nationalist Era in China, 1927–1949* (Cambridge, CUP, 1991), p. 177.
14. Tsou, *America's Failure*, pp. 131–3.
15. John King Fairbank, *The Great Chinese Revolution, 1800–1985* (New York, Harper & Row, 1986), p. 208.
16. John F. Melby, *The Mandate of Heaven: Record of a Civil War, China 1945–49* (Toronto, University of Toronto Press, 1968), pp. 29–30.
17. Odd Arne Westad, 'Could the Chinese Civil War have been Avoided? An Exercise in Alternatives', in Larry I. Bland (ed.), *George C. Marshall's Mediation Mission to China, December 1945–January 1947* (Lexington, VA, George C. Marshall Foundation, 1998), p. 513.
18. Odd Arne Westad, *Cold War and Revolution: Soviet–American Rivalry and the Origins of the Chinese Civil War* (New York, Columbia University Press, 1993), p. 81.
19. Steven I. Levine, *Anvil of Victory, The Communist Revolution in Manchuria, 1945–1948* (New York, Columbia University Press, 1987), p. 31.

208

20. Westad, *Cold War and Revolution*, p. 36.

21. Dick Wilson, *China's Revolutionary War* (London, Weidenfeld & Nicolson, 1991), p. 142.

22. Andrei M. Ledovsky, 'Marshall's Mission in the Context of U.S.S.R.–China–U.S. Relations', in Bland, *Marshall's Mediation*, p. 426.

23. For details of these missions, see Chonghal Petey Shaw, *The Role of the United States in Chinese Civil Conflicts, 1944–1949* (Salt Lake City, Charles Schlacks, Jr, 1991), esp. pp. 65–213.

24. Department of State, *United States Relations with China*, p. 606.

25. Bianco, *Origins*, p. 170.

26. Stuart R. Schram (ed.), *Chairman Mao Talks to the People: Talks and Letters, 1956–1971* (New York, Pantheon, 1974), p. 191.

27. Westad, *Cold War and Revolution*, pp. 93 and 170–1.

28. Ibid., p. 41.

29. Larry N. Shyu, 'In Search of Peace in Postwar China: The Domestic Agenda', in Bland, *Marshall's Mediation*, esp. p. 286.

30. Levine, *Anvil of Victory*, pp. 10 and 61; Westad, *Cold War and Revolution*, pp. 147–8.

31. Department of State, *United States Relations with China*, p. 138.

32. For the former view, see Westad, *Cold War and Revolution*, p. 150ff.; for the latter view, see Shaw, *Role of the United States*, p. 170.

33. Suzanne Pepper in Eastman, *Nationalist Era*, p. 299.

34. US Senate, Committee on Armed Services and Foreign Relations, *Hearings on the Military Situation in the Far East*, 1951, p. 2837.

35. For a discussion of the actual (i.e. domestic) roots of nationalist China's defeat see Lloyd E. Eastman, *Seeds of Destruction: Nationalist China in War and Revolution, 1937–1949* (Stanford, Stanford University Press, 1984), pp. 158–71.

36. Hallett Abend coined the term 'Cockpit of Asia'; see Melby, *Mandate of Heaven*, p. 83. The 'Anvil' designation comes from the title of Steven Levine's book, *Anvil of Victory*.

37. Levine, *Anvil of Victory*, p. 47.

38. Pepper in Eastman, *Nationalist Era*, p. 292.

39. Westad, *Cold War and Revolution*, p. 79.

40. Levine, *Anvil of Victory*, p. 104.

41. Westad, *Cold War and Revolution*, p. 87.

42. Ibid., p. 89.

43. Levine, *Anvil of Victory*, p. 30.

44. Liu, *Military History*, pp. 227–8.

45. George F. Botjer, *A Short History of Nationalist China, 1919–1949* (New York, G.P. Putnam, 1979), p. 248.

46. Levine, *Anvil of Victory*, p. 97.

47. Marc S. Gallicchio, *The Cold War begins in Asia: American East Asian Policy and the Fall of the Japanese Empire* (New York, Columbia University Press,

1988), pp. 59ff.

48. Joint Chiefs of Staff to General Albert C. Wedemeyer, 10 August 1945. Quoted in *FRUS*, 7, p. 528.

49. General Albert C. Wedemeyer to General George C. Marshall, 14 November 1945. Ibid., pp. 627–8.

50. General Albert C. Wedemeyer to General Dwight D. Eisenhower, 20 November 1945. Ibid., p. 653.

51. Levine, *Anvil of Victory*, p. 101.

52. Liu, *Military History*, p. 255.

53. Pepper in Eastman, *Nationalist Era*, p. 296.

Seven

1. John Merrill, *Korea: The Peninsular Origins of the War* (London and Toronto, Associated University Press, 1989); Bruce Cumings, *The Origins of the Korean War. Volume 1. Liberation and the Emergence of Separate Regimes* (Princeton, NJ, Princeton University Press, 1981) and Cumings, *The Origins of the Korean War. Volume 2. The Roaring of the Cataract* (Princeton, NJ, Princeton University Press, 1990). See also Gregory Henderson, *Korea: Politics of the Vortex* (Cambridge, MA, Harvard University Press, 1968) and Robert Scalapino and Chong-sik Lee, *Communism in Korea, Part 1: The Movement* (Berkeley and Los Angeles, University of California Press, 1972). The internal dimension to the war is also discussed in James Mills, review of Peter Lowe, *The Korean War* (Basingstoke, Macmillan, 2000), in *IHR Reviews in History* (December 2000) at www.history.ac.uk/reviews/ paper/millsjames.html. Allan R. Millett disputes this 'civil' as opposed to 'international' distinction to the war, arguing that the two are intertwined: Millett, 'The Korean War: A 50-Year Critical Historiography, *Journal of Strategic Studies*, 24/1 (March 2001), 193.

2. William Stueck, *The Korean War: An International History* (Princeton, NJ, Princeton University Press, 1995), p. 14.

3. Dae-Sook Suh, *The Korean Communist Movement, 1918–48* (Princeton, NJ, Princeton University Press, 1967), p. 297.

4. Joungwon Alexander Kim, *Divided Korea: The Politics of Development, 1945–1972* (Cambridge, MA, Harvard University Press, 1975), pp. 47–8.

5. Stueck, *Korean War*, p. 19.

6. Ibid., p. 20. In their attempt to promote democracy, the Americans encouraged the 'chaotic profusion' of more than fifty different political parties who all vied for power: Ki-baik Lee, *A New History of Korea* (Seoul, Ilchokak, 1984) (trans. Edward W. Wagner), p. 375.

7. Peter Lowe, 'The Cold War Hots Up', *BBC History Magazine*, 1/7 (November 2000), 41.

8. Robert J. Donovan, *Tumultuous Years: the Presidency of Harry S. Truman* (New York and London, Norton, 1982), p. 89.

9. Stueck, *Korean War*, p. 20.
10. Max Hastings, *The Korean War* (London, Papermac, 1993), p. 17.
11. Joyce and Gabriel Kolko, *The Limits of Power: The World and United States Foreign Policy, 1945–1954* (New York, Harper & Row, 1972), p. 279.
12. Hastings, *Korean War*, p. 21.
13. Quoted in Kolkos, *Limits of Power*, p. 280.
14. Donovan, *Tumultuous Years*, p. 90. There is some debate over whether Hodge ever actually made this remark about Koreans but it was reported that he had made such a comment: James Irving Matray, *The Reluctant Crusade: American Foreign Policy in Korea, 1941–1950* (Honolulu, HI, University of Hawaii Press, 1985), p. 53.
15. Michael Hickey, *The Korean War: The West Confronts Communism* (London, John Murray, 1999), pp. 10–12.
16. Hastings, *Korean War*, p. 19.
17. Ibid., p. 18.
18. Quoted in ibid., p. 19.
19. 'Korea: Annual Review for 1949' by Captain (Vyvyan) Holt in Seoul to Mr (Ernest) Bevin, received 30 January 1950. Public Records Office (PRO), Kew, London (hereafter PRO), FO371/84053, p. 3.
20. Hastings, *Korean War*, p. 29.
21. Quoted in Callum A. MacDonald, *Korea: The War before Vietnam* (London, Macmillan, 1986), p. 11.
22. General of the Army Douglas MacArthur (Tokyo) to the Chief of Staff (Eisenhower), 28 October 1946. From General Hodge in Department of State, *Foreign Relations of the United States. 1946. Volume 8. The Far East* (Washington, DC, US Government Printing Office, 1971), p. 751.
23. Kolkos, *Limits of Power*, pp. 289–92.
24. Cumings, *The Origins of the Korean War. Vol. 1*, p. 356.
25. 'Korea: Annual Review for 1949' by Captain (Vyvyan) Holt in Seoul to Mr (Ernest) Bevin, received 30 January 1950. PRO, FO371/84053, p. 2.
26. Cumings, *The Origins of the Korean War, Vol. 1*, p. 357.
27. 'Korea: Annual Review for 1949' by Captain (Vyvyan) Holt in Seoul to Mr (Ernest) Bevin, received 30 January 1950. PRO, FO371/84053, p. 2; Hastings, *Korean War*, pp. 31–2.
28. Kolkos, *Limits of Power*, p. 287–8.
29. Quoted in Hastings, *Korean War*, p. 31.
30. Kolkos, *Limits of Power*, p. 287.
31. Quoted in Bruce Cumings, *Korea's Place in the Sun: A Modern History* (New York and London, Norton, 1997), pp. 244–5.
32. Cumings, *The Origins of the Korean War, Vol. 1*, p. 384. The changes effected by the communists built on policies by the Japanese who had developed industry in the North, leaving the South with a more traditional society.
33. John Merrill, 'Internal Warfare in Korea, 1948–1950: The Local Setting of the Korean War', in Bruce Cumings (ed.), *Child of Conflict: The Korean–American*

Relationship, 1949–53 (Seattle and London, University of Washington Press, 1983), p. 136.

34. Cumings, *Origins of the Korean War. Vol. 2*, p. 597.
35. Peter Lowe, *The Origins of the Korean War* (London and New York, Longman, 1995 [1986]), p. 145.
36. See the discussion in Michael Schaller, *The American Occupation of Japan: The Origins of the Cold War in Asia* (New York and London, OUP, 1985), p. 279.
37. Merrill, *Peninsular*, p. 181.
38. Donovan, *Tumultuous Years*, p. 96.
39. George F. Kennan says that US policy in Japan also sent out an equivocal message that led to the Soviet decision to support a North Korean attack: Kennan, *Memoirs, 1925–1950* (London, Hutchinson, 1968), p. 395.
40. Peter Lowe, *The Korean War* (London, Macmillan, 2000), p. 14.
41. Minute by R.H. Scott, 25 June 1950. PRO, FO371/84059.
42. Robert M. Blum, *Drawing the Line: The Origin of the American Containment Policy in East Asia* (New York and London, Norton, 1982), p. 219.
43. Stueck, *Korean War*, p. 30.
44. Dennis D. Wainstock, *Truman, MacArthur, and the Korean War* (Westport, CT and London, Greenwood Press, 1999), p. 13.
45. Cumings, *The Origins of the Korean War. Vol. 2*, p. 423.
46. Sergei N. Goncharov, John W. Lewis and Xue Litai, *Uncertain Partners: Stalin, Mao and the Korean War* (Stanford, CA, Stanford University Press, 1993), p. 142.
47. Stueck, *Korean War*, p. 20.
48. Goncharov, Lewis and Litai, *Uncertain Partners*, p. 133.
49. Stephen Pelz, 'US Decisions on Korean Policy, 1943–50: Some Hypotheses', in Cumings (ed.), *Child of Conflict*, p. 118.
50. Jon Halliday and Bruce Cumings, *Korea: The Unknown War* (London, Viking, 1988), pp. 60–1.
51. Tokyo (Sir A. Gascoigne) to Foreign Office, 3 July 1950. PRO, FO371/84059.
52. Chen Jian, *China's Road to the Korean War: The Making of the Sino-Soviet Confrontation* (New York, Columbia University Press, 1994), p. 110.
53. Chen Jian and Yang Kuisong, 'Chinese Politics and the Collapse of the Sino-Soviet Alliance', in Odd Arne Westad (ed.), *Brothers in Arms: The Rise and Fall of the Sino-Soviet Alliance, 1945–1963* (Washington, DC and Stanford, CA, Woodrow Wilson Center Press and Stanford University Press, 1998), p. 251.
54. Cumings, *Korea's Place in the Sun*, p. 236.
55. Shu Guang Zhang, *Mao's Military Romanticism: China and the Korean War, 1950–53* (Lawrence, KA, Kansas University Press, 1995), p. 54.
56. Goncharov, Lewis and Litai, *Uncertain Partners*, pp. 131–2.
57. Dae-Sook Suh, *Kim Il Sung: The North Korean Leader* (New York, Columbia University Press, 1988), pp. 112–13.

58. Chen Jian and Yang Kuisong, 'Chinese Politics and the Collapse of the Sino-Soviet Alliance', in Westad (ed.), *Brothers in Arms*, pp. 250–1.

59. Robert R. Simmons, *The Strained Alliance: Peking, Pyongyang, Moscow and the Politics of the Korean Civil War* (London and New York, Free Press, 1975), p. 103.

60. John Lewis Gaddis, *Strategies of Containment: A Critical Appraisal of Postwar American National Security Policy* (New York and Oxford, OUP, 1982), p. 109.

61. Gye-Dong Kim, 'Who Initiated the Korean War', in James Cotton and Ian Neary (eds), *The Korean War in History* (Manchester, Manchester University Press, 1989), p. 37.

62. Kim, it has been argued, made a previous trip to Moscow in 1947 or 1948: see Millett, 'Korean War', 200.

63. Goncharov, Lewis and Litai, *Uncertain Partners*, p. 130.

64. Ibid., p. 135.

65. Kathryn Weathersby, 'Stalin, Mao and the End of the Korean War', in Westad (ed.), *Brothers in Arms*, pp. 91–2. For arms acquisition see Mark A. O'Neill, 'The Other Side of the Yalu: Soviet Pilots in the Korea War, Phase One, 1 November 1950–12 April 1951' (doctoral thesis, Florida State University, 1996); also TV programme *Korea: Russia's Secret War* (London, BBC *Timewatch*, 21 January 1996).

66. Chen Jian and Yang Kuisong, 'Chinese Politics and the Collapse of the Sino-Soviet Alliance', in Westad (ed.), *Brothers in Arms*, p. 251.

67. Yoo Sung Chul quoted in Goncharov, Lewis and Xue Litai, *Uncertain Partners*, p. 144.

68. Westad (ed.), introduction, *Brothers in Arms*, p. 14.

69. Ibid., p. 13.

70. Jian, *China's Road*, p. 106.

71. Ibid., p. 112.

72. For a more recent reworking of the Stone thesis see Michael J. Hogan, *Cross of Iron: Harry S. Truman and the Origins of the National Security State* (New York, CUP, 1998).

73. From Merrill, *Peninsular*, p. 35.

74. Karunakar Gupta, 'How did the Korean War Begin?', *China Quarterly*, 52 (October–December 1972), 700.

75. Merrill, *Peninsular*, p. 41.

76. Gupta, 'How did the Korean War Begin?', 700.

77. Cumings, *Korea's Place in the Sun*, p. 252.

78. Cumings, *Origins of the Korean War. Vol. 2*, p. 581.

79. Ibid., p. 618.

80. Quoted in Cumings, *Korea's Place in the Sun*, p. 254.

81. Cumings, *Origins of the Korean War. Vol. 2*, p. 617.

82. Stanley Sandler, 'The first casualty . . . Germ warfare, brainwashing and other myths about the Korean War', *Times Literary Supplement* (16 June 2000),

14–15.

83. Gye-Dong Kim, 'Who Initiated the Korean War', in Cotton and Neary (eds), *Korean War in History*, pp. 38–9.

84. Ibid., p. 39.

85. Quoted in Cumings, *Korea's Place in the Sun*, p. 250.

86. Merrill, *Peninsular*, p. 41.

87. Simmons, *Strained Alliance*, pp. 108 and 129.

88. Gye-Dong Kim, 'Who Initiated the Korean War?', in Cotton and Neary (eds), *Korean War in History*, pp. 44–5.

Eight

1. Spencer Tucker, *Vietnam* (Lexington, KY, University Press of Kentucky, 1999), p. 75 gives 16,544 as garrison total. Some authors give the total as 15,000: Bernard Fall, 'Dienbienphu: A Battle to Remember', in Marvin E. Gettleman (ed.), *Vietnam: History, Documents, and Opinions on a Major World Crisis* (New York, Fawcett, 1965), p. 106. Others have a total of 18,000: Tom Hartman and John Mitchell, *A World Atlas of Military History* (London, Leo Cooper, 1984), p. 76. The garrison included one woman – the French nurse Genevieve de Galard – whom the Vietminh left to look after the wounded when they overran the garrison. While French-led, the garrison included large numbers of North African, Foreign Legion and Vietnamese troops fighting for France.

2. Fall, 'Dienbienphu: A Battle to Remember', in Gettleman (ed.), *Vietnam: History, Documents, and Opinions*, p. 105.

3. The Geneva Conference followed on from the Berlin Conference and met to resolve issues on Korea (26 April–15 June 1954) and Indochina (8 May–21 July 1954).

4. From the title of Michael Maclear's *Vietnam: The 10,000 Day War* (London, Thames/Methuen, 1981).

5. R.E.M. Irving, *The First Indochina War: French and American Policy, 1945–54* (London, Croom Helm, 1975), p. 130.

6. Anthony James Joes, *The War for South Viet Nam, 1954–1975* (New York, Westport and London, Praeger, 1990), p. 28; Robert R. Randle, *Geneva 1954: The Settlement of the Indochinese War* (Princeton, NJ, Princeton University Press, 1969), pp. 359–60.

7. Edgar O'Ballance, *The Indo-China War 1945–1954: A Case Study in Guerrilla Warfare* (London, Faber & Faber, 1964), p. 241.

8. Quoted in King C. Chen, *Vietnam and China, 1938–1954* (Princeton, NJ, Princeton University Press, 1969), p. 305.

9. Anthony Short, *The Origins of the Vietnam War* (London and New York, Longman, 1989), p. 154; Chester L. Cooper, *The Lost Crusade: The Full Story of US Involvement in Vietnam from Roosevelt to Nixon* (London, MacGibbon & Kee, 1971), p. 79.

10. Philippe Devillers and Jean Lacoutre, *End of a War: Indochina, 1954* (New York, Praeger, 1969), p. 301.

11. William Conrad Gibbons, *The US Government and the Vietnam War: Executive and Legislative Roles and Relationships. Part 1: 1945–1960* (Princeton, NJ, Princeton University Press, 1986), p. 256.

12. U. Alexis Johnson to Congressional Research Service, 14 December 1982, quoted in Gibbons, *US Government*, pp. 256–7.

13. Gary H. Hess, 'Redefining the American Position in Southeast Asia: The United States and the Geneva and Manilla Conferences', in Lawrence S. Kaplan et al. (eds), *Dien Bien Phu and the Crisis of Franco-American Relations, 1954–55* (Wilmington, DE, Scholarly Books, 1990), p. 140.

14. Irving, *The First Indochina War*, p. 120.

15. Charles Fenn, *Ho Chi Minh: a biographical introduction* (London, Studio Vista, 1973), p. 111.

16. U. Alexis Johnson to Congressional Research Service, 14 December 1982, quoted in Gibbons, *US Government*, pp. 256–7.

17. Cooper, *The Lost Crusade*, pp. 90–1; Donald Lancaster, 'Power Politics at the Geneva Conference 1954', in Gettleman (ed.), *Vietnam: History, Documents, and Opinions*, pp. 136–7.

18. Mitchell Hall, *The Vietnam War* (London, Longman, 2000), p. 7.

19. Nguyen Khac Vien, *Vietnam: A Long History* (Hanoi, Gioi, 1999), pp. 285–6.

20. Qiang Zhai, *China and the Vietnam Wars, 1950–1975* (Chapel Hill, NC and London, University of North Carolina Press, 2000), p. 61.

21. Vien, *Vietnam*, p. 286; Tucker, *Vietnam*, p. 78.

22. Gabriel Kolko, *Vietnam: Anatomy of a War 1940–1975* (London, Unwin, 1987), p. 64.

23. Truong Nhu Tang, *Journal of a Vietcong* (London, Jonathan Cape, 1986), pp. 31–2.

24. Melvin Gurtov, *The First Vietnam Crisis: Chinese Communist Strategy and United States Involvement, 1953–54* (New York and London, Columbia University Press, 1967), p. 155.

25. Quoted in Gurtov, *First Vietnam Crisis*, p. 129.

26. Bernard B. Fall, *Viet-Nam Witness, 1953–66* (London, Pall Mall Press, 1966), p. 105.

27. R.B. Smith, *An International History of the Vietnam War. Volume 1. Revolution versus Containment 1955–61* (London, Macmillan, 1987 [1983]), p. 24.

28. Fenn, *Ho Chi Minh*, p. 113.

29. Randle, *Geneva 1954*, p. 360.

30. 'Declaration of the Government of the Democratic Republic of Viet-Nam on Readiness to Re-establish Normal Relations between Northern and Southern Vietnam, 4 February 1955', in Allan W. Cameron (ed.), *Viet-nam Crisis: A Documentary History. Volume I: 1940–1956* (London and Ithaca, NY,

Cornell University Press, 1971), p. 359.

31. Bui Tin, *Following Ho Chi Minh: The Memoirs of a North Vietnamese Colonel* (trans. Judy Stowe and Do Van) (London, Hurst, 1995), p. 23.

32. O'Ballance, *The Indo-China War*, map p. 248; Vien, *Vietnam*, p. 286.

33. Joes, *War for South Viet Nam*, p. 29.

34. James Cable, *The Geneva Conference of 1954 on Indochina* (London, Macmillan, 1986), p. 142.

35. Premier Ngo Dinh Diem: Statement Regarding the Geneva Agreement, 22 July 1954, in Cameron (ed.), *Viet-nam Crisis*, p. 355.

36. Jacques Dalloz, *The War in Indo-China, 1945–1954* (Dublin, Gill & Macmillan, 1990), p. 180.

37. Devillers and Lacoutre, *End of a War*, p. 390.

38. Irving, *First Indochina War*, p. 129.

39. Devillers and Lacoutre, *End of a War*, p. 307.

40. William Appleman Williams et al., *America in Vietnam: A Documentary History* (London and New York, Norton, 1989 [1985]), p. 142.

41. Cooper, *The Lost Crusade*, p. 75.

42. Ibid., n. p. 67.

43. Quoted in ibid., p. 64.

44. Fox Butterfield, 'The Truman and Eisenhower Years, 1945–60', in *New York Times, Pentagon Papers* (London, Routledge & Kegan Paul, 1971), p. 11.

45. Cooper, *The Lost Crusade*, p. 64.

46. Cooper, *The Lost Crusade*, p. 72; Fenn, *Ho Chi Minh*, p. 111; Donald Lancaster, *The Emancipation of French Indochina* (New York, Octagon, 1974), p. 300.

47. Irving, *First Indochina War*, p. 121.

48. Quoted in Scott Lucas, *Freedom's War: The US Crusade against the Soviet Union, 1945–56* (Manchester, Manchester University Press, 1999), p. 221.

49. 'First Plenary Session on Indochina, Geneva, 8 May 1954: The United States Delegation to the Department of State in Department of State', in Allen H. Kitchens and Neal H. Petersen (eds), *Foreign Relations of the United States, 1952–54, Vol. 16, The Geneva Conference* (Washington, DC, US Government Printing Office, 1981), pp. 736–7 (hereafter *FRUS*). Because some delegations refused to recognize other delegations, the layout of the meeting room at Geneva was subject to a laborious bargaining process before discussions could even start: Dalloz, *The War in Indo-China*, p. 175.

50. Eisenhower's Instruction to US Envoy at Geneva Talks, 12 May 1954 in *New York Times, Pentagon Papers*, p. 44.

51. Lancaster, *Emancipation*, p. 316; Williams et al., *America in Vietnam*, p. 139.

52. Gibbons, *US Government*, p. 240.

53. Randle, *Geneva 1954*, p. 353.

54. Irving, *First Indochina War*, p. 129.

55. Devillers and Lacoutre, *End of a War*, pp. 111–12.

56. Gibbons, *US Government*, p. 240.

57. Cable, *Geneva Conference*, p. 139.
58. Eighth Plenary Session on Indochina, Geneva, 21 July 1954. US Delegation to the Department of State, in Kitchens and Petersen (eds), *FRUS*, p. 1501.
59. The President's News Conference, 21 July 1954, in *Public Papers of the President of the United States. Dwight D. Eisenhower. 1954* (Washington, DC, US Government Printing Office, 1960), p. 642.
60. Stanley Karnow, *Vietnam: A History* (London, Pimlico, 1994 [1983]), pp. 220–1.
61. Devillers and Lacoutre, *End of a War*, p. 112. Senator Knowland labelled the Conference a 'Far Eastern Munich': Cooper, *The Lost Crusade*, p. 70.
62. Eighth Plenary Session on Indochina, Geneva, 21 July 1954. US Delegation to the Department of State, in Kitchens and Petersen (eds), *FRUS*, p. 1503.
63. Dulles: Statement at a News Conference, 23 July 1954, in Cameron (ed.), *Viet-Nam Crisis*, p. 326; Williams et al., *America in Vietnam*, p. 140.
64. Randle, *Geneva 1954*, p. 524.
65. Ibid., pp. x and 568.
66. Ibid., p. 560.
67. Ibid., p. 568.
68. Short, *Origins*, pp. 328–9.
69. Smith, *International History*, p. 19.
70. Dulles to C. Douglas Dillon (US ambassador in Paris), 7 July 1954, in Gareth Porter (ed.), *Vietnam: The Definitive Documentation of Human Decisions. Volume 1* (London, Heyden, 1979), p. 625.
71. Hall, *Vietnam War*, p. 8; introduction to ch. 12 of Cameron (ed.), *Viet-nam Crisis*, p. 334; Joes, *War for South Viet Nam*, p. 43.
72. U.A. Johnson to Congressional Research Service, 14 December 1982, quoted in Gibbons, *US Government*, pp. 256–7.
73. Robert S. McNamara, *In Retrospect: The Tragedy and Lessons of Vietnam* (New York, Random House, 1995), p. 33.

Conclusion

1   For a discussion of this, see David A. Welch, *Justice and the Genesis of War* (Cambridge: CUP, 1993), esp. ch.7.
2   Fritz Fischer, *Germany's Aims in the First World War* (New York: Norton, 1967); Norman J.W. Goda, *Tomorrow the World: Hitler, Northwest Africa and the Path toward America* (College Station, TX: A & M UP, 1998).
3   For a discussion of this conflict, see Charles *Tripp, A History of Iraq* (Cambridge: CUP, 2000), pp.248-79.
4   See M. Hughes, *'Collusion Across the Litani?'*, in E. Rogan and A. Shlaim (eds), *The War for Palestine* (Cambridge, CUP, 2007).

Bibliography

PRIMARY SOURCES

Unpublished State Papers

THE NATIONAL ARCHIVES (PUBLIC RECORD OFFICE), LONDON
Foreign Office Political Correspondence (FO371)

Private Papers

BRITISH LIBRARY, LONDON
A.J. Balfour
Lord Curzon

LIDDELL HART CENTRE FOR MILITARY ARCHIVES, KING'S COLLEGE LONDON
General G.F. Milne

HOUGHTON LIBRARY, HARVARD UNIVERSITY, CAMBRIDGE MA
Ellis Loring Dresel
Walter Hines Page

HOUSE OF LORDS RECORD OFFICE, LONDON
David Lloyd George

IMPERIAL WAR MUSEUM, LONDON
Field Marshal Henry Wilson

Printed

Bunyan, James and Fisher, H.H. (eds), *The Bolshevik Revolution, 1917–1918: Documents and Materials* (Stanford, CA, Stanford University Press, 1934)
Butler, Rohan and Bury, J.P.Y. (eds), *Documents on British Foreign Policy* (London, HMSO, 1958), Series I, Vol. 8

Butler, Rohan and Pelly, M.E. (eds), *Documents on British Policy Overseas* (London, HMSO, 1984), Series I, Vol. 1

Cameron, Allan W., *Viet-Nam Crisis: A Documentary History. Volume 1: 1940–1956* (London and Ithaca, NY, Cornell University Press, 1971)

Department of State, *United States Relations with China with Special Reference to the Period 1944–1949* (Washington, DC, US Government Printing Office, 1949)

——, *Foreign Relations of the United States: Diplomatic Papers 1945. Volume 7. The Far East* (Washington, DC, US Government Printing Office, 1969)

——, *Foreign Relations of the United States, 1946. Volume 6* (Washington, DC, US Government Printing Office, 1969)

——, *Foreign Relations of the United States 1946. Volume 8. The Far East* (Washington, DC, US Government Printing Office, 1971)

——, *Foreign Relations of the United States 1949. Volume 6. The Near East, South Asia, and Africa* (Washington, DC, US Government Printing Office, 1977)

——, *Foreign Relations of the United States, 1952–54. Volume 16. The Geneva Conference* (eds Allen H. Kitchens and Neal H. Petersen) (Washington, DC, US Government Printing Office, 1981)

Freundlich, Yehoshua (ed.), *Documents on the Foreign Policy of Israel. Volume 2, October 1948–April 1949. Companion Volume* (Jerusalem, Israel State Archives, 1984)

Gettleman, Marvin E. (ed.), *Vietnam: History, Documents, and Opinions on a Major World Crisis* (New York, Fawcett, 1965)

Gooch, G.P. and Temperley, H. (eds), *British Documents on the Origins of the War, 1888–1914* (London, HMSO, 1926–38)

Link, Arthur S. (ed.), *The Deliberations of the Council of Four (March 24–June 28, 1919). Notes of the Official Interpreter Paul Mantoux* (Princeton, NJ, Princeton University Press, 1992)

Matthew, H.C.G. (ed.), *The Gladstone Diaries: Volume 7, January 1869–June 1871* (Oxford, Clarendon Press, 1982)

Medzini, Meron (ed.), *Israel's Foreign Relations. Selected Documents, 1947–74. Volume 1* (Jerusalem, Ministry for Foreign Affairs, 1976)

Pelly, M.E. and Yasamee, H.J. (eds), *Documents on British Policy Overseas* (London, HMSO, 1990), Series I, Vol. 5

Pentagon Papers, New York Times (London, Routledge & Kegan Paul, 1971)

Porter, Gareth (ed.), *Vietnam: The Definitive Documentation of Human Decisions. Volume 1* (London, Heyden, 1979)

Public Papers of the Presidents of the United States. Dwight D. Eisenhower, 1954 (Washington, DC, US Government Printing Office, 1960)

Rosenthal, Yemina (ed.), *Documents on the Foreign Policy of Israel. Volume 3. Armistice Negotiations with the Arab States, December 1948–July 1949* (Jerusalem, Israel State Archives, 1983)

——, *Documents on the Foreign Policy of Israel. Volume 3. Armistice Negotiations with the Arab States, December 1948–July 1949. Companion Volume* (Jerusalem, Israel State Archives, 1983)

Schram, Stuart R. (ed.), *Chairman Mao Talks to the People: Talks and Letters, 1956–1971* (New York, Pantheon, 1974)

Seymour, Charles (ed.), *The Intimate Papers of Colonel House* (Boston, Houghton Mifflin, 1928)

Taylor, A.J.P. (ed.), *Lloyd George: A Diary by Frances Stevenson* (London, Hutchinson, 1971)

US Senate, Committee on Armed Services and Foreign Relations, *Hearings on the Military Situation in the Far East*, 1951

Williams, William Appleman et al. (eds), *America in Vietnam: A Documentary History* (New York and London, Norton, 1989 [1985])

Memoirs

Azcárate, Pablo de, *Mission in Palestine, 1948–52* (Washington, DC, The Middle East Institute, 1966)

Copeland, Miles, *The Game of Nations: The Amorality of Power Politics* (London, Weidenfeld & Nicolson, 1969)

Eisenhower, Dwight D., *The White House Years: Mandate for Change, 1953–1956* (New York, Doubleday, 1963)

Glubb, John Bagot, *A Soldier with the Arabs* (London, Hodder & Stoughton, 1957)

Grew, Joseph C., *Turbulent Era: A Diplomatic Record of Forty Years* (London, Hammond, 1953)

Lloyd George, David, *Memoirs of the Peace Conference* (New York, Howard Fertig, 1972), reprint of *Truth about the Peace Treaties* (1938)

McGhee, George, *Envoy to the Middle World: Adventures in Diplomacy* (New York, Harper & Row, 1983)

McNamara, Robert S., *In Retrospect: The Tragedy and Lessons of Vietnam* (New York, Random House, 1995)

Melby, John F., *The Mandate of Heaven: Record of a Civil War, China 1945–49* (Toronto, University of Toronto Press, 1968)

Phillips, William, *Ventures in Diplomacy* (Boston, The Beacon Press, 1952)

Tang, Truong Nhu, *Journal of a Vietcong* (London, Jonathan Cape, 1986)

Tin, Bui, *Following Ho Chi Minh: The Memoirs of a North Vietnamese Colonel* (trans. Judy Stowe and Do Van) (London, Hurst, 1995)

SECONDARY SOURCES

Bibliography

Books

Aitken, William Maxwell (Lord Beaverbrook), *The Decline and Fall of Lloyd George* (London, Collins, 1963)

Andrew, Christopher, *Théophile Delcassé and the Making of the Entente Cordiale: A Reappraisal of French Foreign Policy, 1898–1905* (London, Macmillan, 1968)

Bar-Joseph, Uri, *The Best of Enemies: Israel and Transjordan in the War of 1948* (London, Frank Cass, 1987)

Barak, Oren, *The Lebanese Army: A National Institution in a Divided Society* (New York, UP, 2009)

Bark, Dennis L. and Gress, David R., *A History of West Germany, Volume 1. From Shadow to Substance, 1945–1963* (Oxford, Blackwell, 1993)

Barnes, Harry Elmer, *The Genesis of the World War: An Introduction to the Problem of War Guilt* (New York, Alfred A. Knopf, 1927)

Becker, Jean-Jacques, *1914: Comment les Français sont entrés dans la guerre. Contribution à l'étude de l'opinion publique printemps–été 1914* (Paris, Presses de la Fondation Nationale des Sciences Politiques, 1977)

Bianco, Lucien, *Origins of the Chinese Revolution, 1915–1949* (Stanford, CA, Stanford University Press, 1971)

Black, Jeremy, *Why Wars Happen* (London, Reaktion Books, 1998)

Blum, Robert M., *Drawing the Line: The Origins of the American Containment Policy in East Asia* (New York and London, Norton, 1982)

Bond, Brian, *The Pursuit of Victory: From Napoleon to Saddam Hussein* (Oxford, OUP, 1996)

Botjer, George F., *A Short History of Nationalist China, 1919–1949* (New York, G.P. Putnam, 1979)

Bregman, Ahron and El-Tahri, Jihan, *The Fifty Years War: Israel and the Arabs* (London, Penguin, 1998)

Bretton, Henry L., *Stresemann and the Revision of Versailles: A Fight for Reason* (Stanford, CA, Stanford University Press, 1953)

Bullock, Alan, *Hitler and Stalin: Parallel Lives* (London, HarperCollins, 1991)

Butow, Robert J.C., *Japan's Decision to Surrender* (Stanford, CA, Stanford University Press, 1954)

Cable, James, *The Geneva Conference of 1954 on Indochina* (London, Macmillan, 1986)

Caplan, Neil, *The Lausanne Conference, 1949: A Case Study in Middle East Peacemaking* (Tel Aviv University, Moshe Dayan Center for Middle Eastern and African Studies, 1993)

Carroll, E. Malcolm, *French Public Opinion and Foreign Affairs, 1870–1914* (Hamden, CT, Archon Books, 1964)

Cecil, Lady Gwendolen, *Life of Robert Marquis of Salisbury* (London, Hodder & Stoughton, 1921)

Chen, King C., *Vietnam and China, 1938–1954* (Princeton, NJ, Princeton University Press, 1969)

Churchill, Winston S., *The Second World War, Volume 1: The Gathering Storm* (London, Cassell & Co., 1948)

Clausewitz, Carl von, *On War* (London, Penguin, 1968)

Clogg, Richard, *A Concise History of Greece* (Cambridge, CUP, 1992)

Cohen, Stephen F., *Bukharin and the Bolshevik Revolution: A Political Biography, 1888–1938* (London, Wildwood House, 1974)

Cooper, Chester L., *The Lost Crusade: The Full Story of US Involvement in Vietnam from Roosevelt to Nixon* (London, MacGibbon & Kee, 1971)

Cotton, James and Neary, Ian (eds), *The Korean War in History* (Manchester, Manchester University Press, 1989)

Craig, Gordon A., *Germany 1866–1945* (Oxford, OUP, 1981)

Crowe, Sibyl and Corp, Edward, *Our Ablest Public Servant: Sir Eyre Crowe, 1864–1925* (Braunton, Merlin Books, 1993)

Cumings, Bruce, *The Origins of the Korean War: Vol. 1. Liberation and the Emergence of Separate Regimes* (Princeton, NJ, Princeton University Press, 1981)

Cumings, Bruce (ed.), *Child of Conflict: The Korean–American Relationship, 1949–53* (Seattle and London, University of Washington Press, 1983)

——, *The Origins of the Korean War. Vol. 2. The Roaring of the Cataract* (Princeton, NJ, Princeton University Press, 1990)

——, *Korea's Place in the Sun: A Modern History* (New York and London, Norton, 1997)

Dakin, Douglas, *The Unification of Greece, 1770–1923* (London, Ernest Benn, 1972)

Dalloz, Jacques, *The War in Indo-China, 1945–1954* (Dublin, Gill & Macmillan, 1990)

Deighton, Anne, *The Impossible Peace: Britain, the Division of Germany and the Origins of the Cold War* (Oxford, Clarendon Press, 1990)

Deutscher, Isaac, *Stalin: A Political Biography* (Harmondsworth, Penguin, 1966)

Devillers, Philippe and Lacoutre, Jean, *End of a War: Indochina, 1954* (New York, Praeger, 1969 [1960 in French])

Dickinson, G. Lowes, *The International Anarchy, 1904–1914* (London, George Allen & Unwin, 1937)

Dobkin, Marjorie Housepian, *Smyrna, 1922: The Destruction of a City* (Kent, OH and London, Kent State University Press, 1988)

Dockrill, Michael L. and Douglas Goold, J., *Peace Without Promise: Britain and the Peace Conferences, 1919–23* (London, Batsford, 1981)

Donovan, Robert J., *Tumultuous Years: The Presidency of Harry S. Truman* (New York and London, Norton, 1984)

Eastman, Lloyd E., *Seeds of Destruction: Nationalist China in War and Revolution, 1937–1949* (Stanford, CA, Stanford University Press, 1984)

Eastman, Lloyd E. et al., *The Nationalist Era in China, 1927–1949* (Cambridge, CUP, 1991)

Ebenstein, William, *The German Record: Political Portrait* (New York, Farrar & Rinehart, 1945)

Eichengreen, Barry, *Gold Fetters: The Gold Standard and the Great Depression, 1919–1939* (Oxford, OUP, 1992)

Eksteins, Modris, *Rites of Spring: The Great War and the Birth of the Modern Era* (Boston and New York, Houghton Mifflin, 1989)

Evans, Laurence, *United States Policy and the Partition of Turkey, 1914–24* (Baltimore, MD, Johns Hopkins Press, 1965)

Ewart, John S., *The Roots and Causes of the Wars (1914–1918)* (New York, George H. Doran, 1925)

Eytan, Walter, *The First Ten Years: A Diplomatic History of Israel* (London, Weidenfeld & Nicolson, 1958)

Fairbank, John King, *The Great Chinese Revolution, 1800–1985* (New York, Harper & Row, 1986)

Fall, Bernard B., *Viet-Nam Witness, 1953–66* (London, Pall Mall Press, 1966)

Fay, Sidney Bradshaw, *The Origins of the World War* (New York, Macmillan, 1929)

Feis, Herbert, *Between War and Peace: The Potsdam Conference* (Princeton, NJ, Princeton University Press, 1960)

Fenn, Charles, *Ho Chi Minh: a Biographical Introduction* (London, Studio Vista, 1973)

Ferguson, Niall, *The Pity of War* (London, Allen Lane, 1998)

Ferro, Marc, *The Great War 1914–1918* (London, Routledge, 1973)

Figes, Orlando, *A People's Tragedy: The Russian Revolution, 1891–1924* (London, Pimlico, 1997)

Fischer, Fritz, *Germany's Aims in the First World War* (New York, Norton, 1967)

Fisher, H.A.L., *A History of Europe* (London, Edward Arnold, 1936)

Flapan, Simha, *The Birth of Israel: Myths and Realities* (New York, Pantheon, 1984)

Forster, Edward S., *A Short History of Modern Greece, 1821–1956* (London, Methuen, 1958)

Fromkin, David, *A Peace To End All Peace: Creating the Modern Middle East, 1914–22* (London, Penguin, 1991)

Fuller, J.F.C., *The Conduct of War, 1789–1961* (London, Methuen & Co., 1972)

Gabbay, Rony, *A Political Study of the Arab–Jewish Conflict* (Paris, Minard, 1959)

Gaddis, John Lewis, *Strategies of Containment: A Critical Appraisal of Postwar American National Security Policy* (New York and Oxford, OUP, 1982)

Gallicchio, Marc S., *The Cold War Begins in Asia: American East Asian Policy and the Fall of the Japanese Empire* (New York, Columbia University Press, 1988)

Geiss, Imanuel, *The Question of German Unification, 1806–1996* (London and New York, Routledge, 1997)

Bibliography

Gibbons, William Conrad, *The US Government and the Vietnam War: Executive and Legislative Roles and Relationships. Part 1: 1945–1960* (Princeton, NJ, Princeton University Press, 1986 [1984])

Gilbert, Martin, *Sir Horace Rumbold: Portrait of a Diplomat, 1869–1941* (London, Heinemann, 1973)

Goda, Norman J.W., *Tomorrow the World: Hitler, Northwest Africa and the Path toward America* (College Station, TX, A & M University Press, 1998)

Goldstein, Erik, *Wars and Peace Treaties, 1816–1991* (London and New York, Routledge, 1992)

Goncharov, Sergei N., Lewis, John W. and Litai, Xue, *Uncertain Partners: Stalin, Mao, and the Korean War* (Stanford, CA, Stanford University Press, 1993)

Gooch, G.P., *Franco-German Relations, 1871–1914* (London, Longman, Green & Co., 1922)

Gurtov, Melvin, *The First Vietnam Crisis: Chinese Communist Strategy and United States Involvement, 1953–1954* (New York and London, Columbia University Press, 1967)

Hall, Mitchell, *The Vietnam War* (London, Longman, 2000)

Halliday, Jon and Cumings, Bruce, *Korea: The Unknown War* (London, Viking, 1988)

Hancock, W.K., *Smuts: The Sanguine Years, 1870–1919* (Cambridge, CUP, 1962)

Hankey, Maurice (Lord Hankey), *The Supreme Control: At the Paris Peace Conference* (London, George Allen & Unwin, 1963)

Harington, Charles, *Tim Harington Looks Back* (London, John Murray, 1940)

Hastings, Max, *The Korean War* (London, Papermac, 1993)

Hayne, M.B., *The French Foreign Office and the Origins of the First World War, 1898–1914* (Oxford, Clarendon Press, 1993)

Heller, Joseph, *The Birth of Israel, 1945–1949: Ben-Gurion and His Critics* (Gainesville, FL, University Press of Florida, 2000)

Helmreich, Paul C., *From Paris to Sèvres: The Partition of the Ottoman Empire at the Peace Conference of 1919–20* (Columbus, OH, Ohio State University Press, 1974)

Henderson, Gregory, *Korea: Politics of the Vortex* (Cambridge, MA, Harvard University Press, 1968)

Herrmann, David G., *The Arming of Europe and the Making of the First World War* (Princeton, NJ, Princeton University Press, 1996)

Hickey, Michael, *The Korean War: The West Confronts Communism* (London, John Murray, 1999)

Horne, Alistair, *The Fall of Paris: The Siege and the Commune, 1870–1* (London, The Reprint Society, 1967)

Howard, Harry N., *The Partition of Turkey: A Diplomatic History, 1913–1923* (Norman, OK, University of Oklahoma Press, 1931)

Howard, Michael, *Studies in War and Peace* (London, Temple Smith, 1959)

——, *The Franco-Prussian War: The German Invasion of France, 1870–1871*

(London, Rupert Hart-Davis, 1961)

——, *War in European History* (Oxford, OUP, 1976)

——, *The Causes of Wars and Other Essays* (London, Temple Smith, 1983)

Hsu, Kai-yu, *Chou En-lai: China's Grey Eminence* (Garden City, NJ, Doubleday, 1968)

Hudson, G.F., *The Hard and Bitter Peace: World Politics since 1945* (London, Pall Mall Press, 1966)

Hughes, Matthew and Seligmann, Matthew S. (eds), *Leadership in Conflict, 1914–18* (Barnsley, Leo Cooper, 2000)

Hurd, Douglas, *The Search for Peace: A Century of Peace Diplomacy* (London, Warner Books, 1997)

Iriye, Akira, *The Cold War in Asia: A Historical Introduction* (Englewood Cliffs, NJ, Prentice-Hall, 1974)

Irving, R.E.M., *The First Indochina War: French and American Policy, 1945–54* (London, Croom Helm, 1975)

Jeffery, Keith, *The British Army and the Crisis of Empire 1918–22* (Manchester, Manchester University Press, 1984)

Jian, Chen, *China's Road to the Korean War: The Making of the Sino-American Confrontation* (New York, Columbia University Press, 1994)

Joes, Anthony James, *The War for South Viet Nam, 1954–1975* (New York, Praeger, 1990)

Jordan, David Starr, *Alsace-Lorraine. A Study in Conquest: 1913* (Indianapolis, IN, The Bobbs-Merrill Company, 1916)

Kagan, Donald, *On the Origins of War* (London, Pimlico, 1997 [1995])

Kaplan, Lawrence S. et al. (eds), *Dien Bien Phu and the Crisis of Franco-American Relations, 1954–55* (Wilmington, DE, Scholarly Books, 1990)

Karnow, Stanley, *Vietnam: A History* (London, Pimlico, 1994 [1983])

Karsh, Efraim, *Fabricating Israeli History: The 'New Historians'* (London, Frank Cass, 2000 [1997])

Keiger, John F.V., *France and the Origins of the First World War* (Basingstoke, Macmillan, 1983)

——, *Raymond Poincaré* (Cambridge, CUP, 1997)

Kennan, George F., *Memoirs, 1925–1950* (London, Hutchinson, 1968)

——, *The Fateful Alliance: France, Russia, and the Coming of the First World War* (Manchester, Manchester University Press, 1984)

Kennedy, Paul M., *The Rise and Fall of the Great Powers: Economic Change and Military Conflict from 1500 to 2000* (New York, Random House, 1987)

Keylor, William R., *The Twentieth-Century World: An International History* (Oxford, OUP, 2nd edn, 1992)

Keynes, John Maynard, *The Economic Consequences of the Peace* (London, Macmillan, 1919)

Kim, Joungwon Alexander, *Divided Korea: The Politics of Development, 1945–1972* (Cambridge, MA, Harvard University Press, 1975)

Bibliography

Kinross, Patrick Balfour (Lord Kinross), *Atatürk: The Rebirth of a Nation* (London, Weidenfeld & Nicolson, 1964)

Kissinger, Henry, *A World Restored: Metternich, Castlereagh and the Problems of Peace, 1812–1822* (Boston, Houghton Mifflin, 1979)

——, *Diplomacy* (New York and London, Simon & Schuster, 1994)

Kolko, Joyce and Gabriel, *The Limits of Power: The World and United States Foreign Policy, 1945–1954* (New York, Harper & Row, 1972)

Lancaster, Donald, *The Emancipation of French Indochina* (London, OUP, 1961)

Lee, Ki-baik, *A New History of Korea* (trans. Edward W. Wagner) (Seoul, Ilchokak, 1984)

Lee, Steven Hugh, *Outposts of Empire: Korea, Vietnam and the Origins of the Cold War in Asia, 1949–1954* (Liverpool, Liverpool University Press, 1995)

Lentin, Anthony, *Guilt at Versailles: Lloyd George and the Pre-History of Appeasement* (London, Methuen, 1985)

Levine, Steven I., *Anvil of Victory: The Communist Revolution in Manchuria, 1945–1948* (New York, Columbia University Press, 1987)

Link, Arthur S., *Woodrow Wilson: Revolution, War, and Peace* (Arlington Heights, IL, Harland Davidson, 1979)

Liu, F.F., *A Military History of Modern China, 1924–1949* (Princeton, NJ, Princeton University Press, 1956)

Louis, Wm. Roger, *The British Empire in the Middle East: Arab Nationalism, the United States, and Postwar Imperialism* (Oxford, Clarendon Press, 1985)

Lowe, Peter, *The Origins of the Korean War* (London and New York, Longman, 1995 [1986])

——, *The Korean War* (Basingstoke and London, Macmillan, 2000)

Lucas, Scott, *Freedom's War: The US Crusade against the Soviet Union, 1945–56* (Manchester, Manchester University Press, 1999)

McCullough, Edward E., *How the First World War Began: The Triple Entente and the Coming of the Great War of 1914–1918* (Montreal, Black Rose Books, 1999)

MacDonald, Callum A., *Korea: The War before Vietnam* (London, Macmillan, 1986)

McEvedy, Colin, *Penguin Atlas of Recent History: Europe since 1815* (Harmondsworth, Penguin, 1982)

Macfie, A.L., *Atatürk* (London and New York, Longman, 1994)

Maclear, Michael, *Vietnam: The 10,000 Day War* (London, Thames/Methuen, 1981)

MacMillan, Margaret, *Peacemakers: The Paris Conference of 1919 and its Attempt to End War* (London, John Murray, 2001)

Mango, Andrew, *Atatürk* (London, John Murray, 1999)

Ma'oz, Moshe, *Syria and Israel: From War to Peacemaking* (Oxford, Clarendon Press, 1995)

Marks, Sally, *The Illusion of Peace: International Relations in Europe, 1918–1933* (London, Macmillan, 1976)

Matray, James Irving, *The Reluctant Crusade: American Foreign Policy in Korea, 1941–50* (Honolulu, HI, University of Hawaii Press, 1985)

Maurer, John H., *The Outbreak of the First World War: Strategic Planning, Crisis Decision Making, and Deterrence Failure* (Westport, CT, Praeger, 1995)

Mayer, Arno J., *Politics and the Diplomacy of Peacemaking: Containment and Counterrevolution at Versailles, 1918–1919* (New York, Alfred A. Knopf, 1967)

Merrill, John, *Korea: The Peninsular Origins of the War* (London and Toronto, Associated University Press, 1989)

Miscamble, Wilson D., *George F. Kennan and the Making of American Foreign Policy, 1947–1950* (Princeton, NJ, Princeton University Press, 1992)

Montgelas, Count Max, *The Case for the Central Powers: An Impeachment of the Versailles Verdict* (New York, Alfred A. Knopf, 1925)

Morris, Benny, *The Birth of the Palestinian Refugee Problem, 1947–1949* (Cambridge, CUP, 1987)

——, *1948 and After: Israel and the Palestinians* (Oxford, Clarendon Press, 1994 [1990])

——, *Israel's Border Wars, 1949–56: Arab Infiltration, Israeli Retaliation, and the Countdown to the Suez War* (Oxford, Clarendon Press, 1993)

——, *Righteous Victims: A History of the Zionist–Arab Conflict, 1881–1999* (London, John Murray, 2000)

——, *1948: A History of the First Arab-Israeli War* (New Haven, CT, Yale UP, 2008)

Nicolson, Harold, *Peacemaking 1919* (London, Constable, 1933)

O'Balance, Edgar, *The Indo-China War 1945–1954: A Study in Guerrilla Warfare* (London, Faber & Faber, 1964)

Oren, Michael B., *Origins of the Second Arab–Israel War: Egypt, Israel and the Great Powers, 1952–56* (London, Frank Cass, 1992)

Ovendale, Ritchie, *The Origins of the Arab–Israeli Wars* (Harlow, Longman, 1992)

Pappé, Ilan, *The Making of the Arab–Israeli Conflict, 1947–51* (London and New York, IB Tauris, 1992)

Parker, W.H., *Mackinder: Geography as an Aid to Statecraft* (Oxford, Clarendon Press, 1982)

Pinson, Koppel S., *Modern Germany: Its History and Civilization* (New York, The Macmillan Co., 1955)

Pipes, Richard, *The Russian Revolution, 1899–1919* (London, Collins Harvill, 1990)

Rabinovich, Itamar, *The Road Not Taken: Early Arab–Israeli Negotiations* (London and New York, OUP, 1991)

Randle, Robert R., *Geneva 1954: The Settlement of the Indochina War* (Princeton, NJ, Princeton University Press, 1969)

Rathmell, Andrew, *Secret War in the Middle East: The Covert Struggle for Syria, 1949–1961* (London and New York, IB Tauris, 1995)

228

Rawlinson, A., *Adventures in the Near East, 1918–1922* (London, Jonathan Cape, 1934 [1923])

Rock, Stephen R., *Why Peace Breaks Out: Great Power Rapprochement in Historical Perspective* (Chapel Hill, NC, University of North Carolina Press, 1989)

Rogan, Eugene L. and Shlaim, Avi (eds), *The War for Palestine: Rewriting the History of 1948* (Cambridge, CUP, 2001, revised edition, 2007)

Sainsbury, Keith, *The Turning Point: Roosevelt, Stalin and Chiang Kai-Shek, 1943: The Moscow, Cairo and Teheran Conferences* (Oxford, OUP, 1985).

Sandler, Stanley, *The Korean War: No Victors, No Vanquished* (London, Routledge, 1999)

Scalapino, Robert and Lee, Chong-sik, *Communism in Korea, Part 1: The Movement* (Berkeley and Los Angeles, University of California Press, 1972)

Schaller, Michael, *The American Occupation of Japan: the Origins of the Cold War in Asia* (New York and Oxford, OUP, 1985)

Schapiro, Leonard, *The Origins of the Communist Autocracy: Political Opposition in the Soviet State. First Phase, 1917–1922* (London, G. Bell & Sons, 1955)

Schmidt, Royal J., *Versailles and the Ruhr: Seedbed of World War II* (The Hague, Martinus Nijhoff, 1968)

Schmitt, Bernadotte E. and Vedeler, Harold C., *The World in the Crucible, 1914–1919* (New York, Harper & Row, 1984)

Schuker, Stephen A., *American 'Reparations' to Germany, 1919–33: Implications for the Third-World Debt Crisis* (Princeton, NJ, Princeton University Press, 1988)

Schwabe, Klaus, *Woodrow Wilson, Revolutionary Germany and Peacemaking 1918–1919: Missionary Diplomacy and the Realities of Power* (Chapel Hill, NC, University of North Carolina Press, 1985)

Seale, Patrick, *The Struggle for Syria: A Study of Post-War Arab Politics, 1945–1958* (New Haven, CT and London, Yale University Press, 1987 [1965])

——, *Asad of Syria: The Struggle for the Middle East* (London, IB Tauris, 1988)

Seligmann, Matthew S., *Rivalry in Southern Africa, 1893–99: The Transformation of German Colonial Policy* (Basingstoke, Macmillan, 1998)

Shalev, Aryeh, *The Israel–Syria Armistice Regime, 1949–1955* (Boulder, CO and Jerusalem, Westview & Jerusalem Post, 1993)

Shaw, Chonghal Petey, *The Role of the United States in Chinese Civil Conflicts, 1944–1949* (Salt Lake City, UT, Charles Schlacks, Jr, 1991)

Shlaim, Avi, *Collusion Across the Jordan: King Abdullah, the Zionist Movement and the Partition of Palestine* (Oxford, Clarendon Press, 1988)

——, *The Iron Wall: Israel and the Arab World* (London, Allen Lane, 2000)

——, *The Lion of Jordan: The Life of King Hussein in War and Peace* (New York, Knopf, 2007)

Short, Anthony, *The Origins of the Vietnam War* (London and New York, Longman, 1989)

Silverman, Dan P., *Reluctant Union: Alsace-Lorraine and Imperial Germany, 1871–1918* (University Park, PA, Pennsylvania State University Press, 1972)

Simmons, Robert R., *The Strained Alliance: Peking, Pyongyang, Moscow and the Politics of the Korean Civil War* (London and New York, Free Press, 1975)

Smith, Michael Llewellyn, *Ionian Vision: Greece in Asia Minor, 1919–1922* (London, Allen Lane, 1973)

Smith, R.B., *An International History of the Vietnam War. Volume 1. Revolution versus Containment, 1955–61* (London, Macmillan, 1987 [1983])

Sonyel, S.R., *Turkish Diplomacy: Mustafa Kemal and the Turkish Nationalist Movement* (London and Beverly Hills, CA, Sage, 1975)

——, *The Turco-Greek Conflict* (Ankara, Cyprus-Turkish Cultural Association, 1985)

Stern, Fritz, *Dreams and Delusions: The Drama of German History* (London, Weidenfeld & Nicolson, 1987)

Stevenson, David, *Armaments and the Coming of War: Europe 1904–1914* (Oxford, OUP, 1996)

Stone, I.F., *The Hidden History of the Korean War* (London, Turnstile Press, 1952)

Stueck, William, *The Korean War: An International History* (Princeton, NJ, Princeton University Press, 1995)

Suh, Dae-Sook, *The Korean Communist Movement, 1918–48* (Princeton, NJ, Princeton University Press, 1967)

——, *Kim Il Sung: The North Korean Leader* (New York, Columbia University Press, 1988)

Taylor, A.J.P., *The Trouble Makers: Dissent over Foreign Policy, 1792–1939* (Bloomington, IN, Indiana University Press, 1958)

——, *The Origins of the Second World War* (Harmondsworth, Penguin, 1964)

——, *How Wars Begin* (London, Futura, 1980)

Temperley, H.W.V. (ed.), *A History of the Peace Conference of Paris, Vol. 6* (London, Henry Frowde/Hodder & Stoughton, 1924)

Tocqueville, Alexis de, *Democracy in America* (New York, Alfred A. Knopf, 1976)

Tolstoy, Leo, *War and Peace* (London, Macmillan, 1943)

Trachtenberg, Marc, *A Constructed Peace: The Making of the European Settlement, 1945–1963* (Princeton, NJ, Princeton University Press, 1999)

Tripp, Charles, *A History of Iraq* (Cambridge, CUP, 2000)

Tsou, Tang, *America's Failure in China, 1941–50* (Chicago, University of Chicago Press, 1963)

Tucker, Spencer C., *Vietnam* (Lexington, KY, University Press of Kentucky, 1999)

Turner, L.C.F., *Origins of the First World War* (New York and London, Norton, 1970)

Ulam, Adam B., *Lenin and the Bolsheviks, The Intellectual and Political History of the Triumph of Communism in Russia* (London, Fontana, 1969)

——, *Stalin: The Man and His Era* (London, IB Tauris, 1989)

Urbach, Karina, *Bismarck's Favourite Englishman, Lord Odo Russell's Mission to Berlin* (London, IB Tauris, 1999)

Vien, Nguyen Khac, *Vietnam: A Long History* (Hanoi, Gioi, 1999)

Volkogonov, Dmitri, *The Rise and Fall of the Soviet Empire* (London, HarperCollins, 1998)

Wainstock, Dennis D., *Truman, MacArthur, and the Korean War* (Westport, CT and London, Greenwood Press, 1999)

Walder, David, *The Chanak Affair* (London, Hutchinson, 1969)

Walzer, Michael, *Just and Unjust Wars: A Moral Argument with Historical Illustrations* (London, Basic Books, 1992 [1977])

Welch, David A., *Justice and the Genesis of War* (Cambridge, CUP, 1993)

Westad, Odd Arne, *Cold War and Revolution: Soviet–American Rivalry and the Origins of the Chinese Civil War* (New York, Columbia University Press, 1993)

Westad, Odd Arne (ed.), *Brothers in Arms: The Rise and Fall of the Sino-Soviet Alliance, 1945–1963* (Washington, DC and Stanford, CA, Woodrow Wilson Center Press and Stanford University Press, 1998)

Wheeler-Bennett, John W., *The Forgotten Peace: Brest-Litovsk, March 1918* (New York, William Morrow & Co., 1939)

Whitson, William W. (with Huang, Chen-Hsia), *The Chinese High Command: A History of Communist Military Policies, 1927–71* (London, Macmillan, 1973)

Willis, James F., *Prologue to Nuremberg: The Politics and Diplomacy of Punishing War Criminals of the First World War* (Westport, CT, Greenwood Press, 1982)

Wilson, Dick, *China's Revolutionary War* (London, Weidenfeld & Nicolson, 1991)

Windrow, Martin, *The Last Valley: Dien Bien Phu and the French Defeat in Vietnam* (London: Weidenfeld & Nicolson, 2004)

Winter, Jay and Baggett, Blaine, *1914–18: The Great War and the Shaping of the 20th Century* (London, BBC Books, 1996)

Wu, Tien-wei, *The Sian Incident: A Pivotal Point in Modern Chinese History* (Ann Arbor, MI, University of Michigan Press, 1976)

Yergin, Daniel, *Shattered Peace: The Origins of the Cold War and the National Security State* (Boston, Houghton Mifflin, 1977)

Zhai, Qiang, *China and the Vietnam Wars, 1950–1975* (Chapel Hill, NC and London, University of North Carolina Press, 2000)

Zhang, Shu Guang, *Mao's Military Romanticism: China and the Korean War, 1950–53* (Lawrence, KA, Kansas University Press, 1995)

Zürcher, Erik J., *Turkey: A Modern History* (London and New York, IB Tauris, 1997)

Bibliography

Journal Articles

Caplan, Neil, review article, 'Zionism and the Arabs: Another Look at the "New" Historiography', *Journal of Contemporary History*, 36/2 (2001), 345–60

Finkelstein, Norman, 'Myths, Old and New', *Journal of Palestine Studies*, 21/1 (1991), 66–89

Förster, Stig, 'Der deutsche Generalstab und die Illusion des kurzen Krieges, 1871–1914. Metakritik eines Mythos', *Militärgeschichtliche Mitteilungen*, 54 (1995), 61–95

Glubb, John Bagot, 'Violence on the Jordan–Israel Border: A Jordanian View', *Foreign Affairs*, 4 (1954), 552–62

Gupta, Karunakar, 'How did the Korean War Begin?', *China Quarterly*, 52 (1972), 699–716

Hewitson, Mark, 'Germany and France before the First World War: A Reassessment of Wilhelmine Foreign Policy', *English Historical Review*, 115 (2000), 570–606

Khouri, Fred J., 'Friction and Conflict on the Israeli–Syrian Front', *Middle East Journal*, 17 (1963), 14–34

Lowe, Peter, 'The Cold War Hots Up', *BBC History Magazine*, 1/7 (2000), 40–2

McDougall, Walter A., 'Political Economy versus National Sovereignty: French Structures for German Economic Integration after Versailles', *Journal of Modern History*, 51 (1979), 4–23

Marks, Sally, 'The Myths of Reparations', *Central European History*, 17 (1978), 231–55

Masalha, Nur, 'A Critique of Benny Morris', *Journal of Palestine Studies*, 21/1 (1991), 90–7

Millett, Allan R., 'The Korean War: A 50-Year Critical Historiography', *Journal of Strategic Studies*, 24/1 (March 2001), 188–224.

Morris, Benny, 'The Crystallization of Israeli Policy Against a Return of Arab Refugees, April–December 1948', *Studies in Zionism*, 6/1 (1985), 85–118

——, 'Response to Finkelstein and Masalha', *Journal of Palestine Studies*, 21/1 (1991), 98–114

——, review of Efraim Karsh, *Fabricating Israeli History*, entitled 'Refabricating 1948', *Journal of Palestine Studies*, 27/2 (1998), 81–95

Oren, Michael, 'The Diplomatic Struggle for the Negev, 1946–56', *Studies in Zionism*, 10/2 (1989), 197–215

Perla, Shlomo, 'Israel and the Palestine Conciliation Committee', *Middle Eastern Studies*, 26/1 (1990), 113–18

Sandler, Stanley, 'The first casualty . . . Germ warfare, brainwashing and other myths about the Korean War', *Times Literary Supplement* (16 June 2000), 14–15

Seligmann, Matthew S., 'Germany and the Origins of the First World War in the Eyes of the American Diplomatic Establishment', *German History*, 15 (1997), 307–32

Shlaim, Avi, 'Husni Za'im and the Plan to Resettle Palestinian Refugees in Syria', *Journal of Palestine Studies*, 15/4 (1986), 68–80

——, 'The Debate about 1948', *International Journal of Middle East Studies*, 27 (1995), 287–304

Trachtenberg, Marc, 'Reparations at the Paris Peace Conference', *Journal of Modern History*, 51 (1979), 24–44

Wasserstein, Bernard, 'Old historians and new', *Jerusalem Post* (27 December 1999)

Chapters in Books

Benton, Gregor, 'Communist Guerrilla Bases in Southeast China after the Start of the Long March', in Kathleen Hartford and Steven M. Goldstein (eds), *Single Sparks: China's Rural Revolutions* (Armonk, NY, ME Sharpe, 1989)

Clogg, Richard, 'King's College, London and Greece, 1915–22', in *Greece and Great Britain during World War 1* (Thessalonika, Institute for Balkan Studies, 1985)

Davison, Roderic H., 'Turkish Diplomacy from Mudros to Lausanne', in Gordon A. Craig and Felix Gilbert (eds), *The Diplomats, 1919–1939* (Princeton, NJ, Princeton University Press, 1953)

Jian, Chen and Kuisong, Yang, 'Chinese Politics and the Collapse of the Sino-Soviet Alliance', in Odd Arne Westad (ed.), *Brothers in Arms: The Rise and Fall of the Sino-Soviet Alliance, 1945–1963* (Washington, DC and Stanford, CA, Woodrow Wilson Center Press and Stanford University Press, 1998)

Kim, Gye-Dong, 'Who Initiated the Korean War?', in James Cotton and Ian Neary (eds), *The Korean War in History* (Manchester, Manchester University Press, 1989)

Kim, Hak-Joon, 'China's Non-Involvement in the Origins of the Korean War: A Critical Reassessment of the Traditionalist and Revisionist Literature', in James Cotton and Ian Neary (eds), *The Korean War in History* (Manchester, Manchester University Press, 1989)

Ledovsky, Andrei M., 'Marshall's Mission in the Context of U.S.S.R.–China–U.S. Relations', in Larry I. Bland (ed.), *George C. Marshall's Mediation Mission to China, December 1945–January 1947* (Lexington, VA, George C. Marshall Foundation, 1998)

Marks, Sally, '1918 and After: The Postwar Era', in Gordon Martel (ed.), *The Origins of the Second World War Reconsidered: The A.J.P. Taylor Debate after Twenty-Five Years* (London, Unwin Hyman, 1986)

Masalha, Nur, 'A Critique of Benny Morris', in Ilan Pappé (ed.), *The Israel/Palestine Question* (London and New York, Routledge, 1999)

Matray, James I., 'Korea: Test Case of Containment in Asia', in Bruce Cumings (ed.), *Child of Conflict: The Korean–American Relationship, 1949–53* (Seattle and London, University of Washington Press, 1983)

Bibliography

Merrill, John, 'Internal Warfare in Korea, 1948–1950: The Local Setting of the Korean War', in Bruce Cumings (ed.), *Child of Conflict: The Korean–American Relationship, 1949–53* (Seattle and London, University of Washington Press, 1983)

Mombauer, Annika, 'Helmuth von Moltke: A General in Crisis?', in Matthew Hughes and Matthew S. Seligmann (eds), *Leadership in Conflict, 1914–1918* (Barnsley, Leo Cooper, 2000)

Pappé, Ilan, 'British Rule in Jordan, 1943–55', in Michael J. Cohen and Martin Kolinsky (eds), *Demise of the British Empire in the Middle East: Britain's Responses to Nationalist Movements, 1943–55* (London, Frank Cass, 1998)

Pelz, Stephen, 'US Decisions on Korean Policy, 1943–50: Some Hypotheses', in Bruce Cumings (ed.), *Child of Conflict: The Korean–American Relationship, 1949–53* (Seattle and London, University of Washington Press, 1983)

Reynolds, David, 'The European Dimension of the Cold War', in Melvyn P. Leffler and David S. Painter (eds), *Origins of the Cold War: An International History* (London and New York, Routledge, 1994)

Rosenberg, William G., 'Russian Labor and Bolshevik Power: Social Dimensions of Protest in Petrograd after October', in Daniel H. Kaiser (ed.), *The Workers' Revolution in Russia, 1917: the View from Below* (Cambridge, CUP, 1987)

Schlesinger, Jr, Arthur M., 'Origins of the Cold War', in Robert A. Divine (ed.), *Causes and Consequences of World War II* (Chicago, Quadrangle Books, 1969)

Shyu, Larry N., 'In Search of Peace in Postwar China: The Domestic Agenda', in Larry I. Bland (ed.), *George C. Marshall's Mediation Mission to China, December 1945–January 1947* (Lexington, VA, George C. Marshall Foundation, 1998)

Taithe, B., 'Reliving the Revolution: War and Political Identity during the Franco-Prussian War', in Bertrand Taithe and Tim Thornton (eds), *War: Identities in Conflict, 1300–2000* (Stroud, Sutton Publishing, 1998)

Weathersby, Kathryn, 'Stalin, Mao and the End of the Korean War', in Odd Arne Westad (ed.), *Brothers in Arms: The Rise and Fall of the Sino-Soviet Alliance, 1945–1963* (Washington, DC and Stanford, CA, Woodrow Wilson Center Press and Stanford University Press, 1998)

Westad, Odd Arne, 'Could the Chinese Civil War have been Avoided? An Exercise in Alternatives', in Larry I. Bland (ed.), *George C. Marshall's Mediation Mission to China, December 1945–January 1947* (Lexington, VA, George C. Marshall Foundation, 1998)

Woodward, David, '"Black Jack" Pershing: The American Proconsul in Europe', in Matthew Hughes and Matthew S. Seligmann (eds), *Leadership in Conflict, 1914–1918* (Barnsley, Leo Cooper, 2000)

Doctoral Theses

Adelson, Roger Dean, 'The Formation of British Policy Towards the Middle East, 1914–1918' (doctoral thesis, Washington University, 1972)

Bibliography

O'Neill, Mark, 'The Other Side of the Yalu: Soviet Pilots in the Korea War Phase One, 1 November 1950–12 April 1951' (doctoral thesis, Florida State University, 1996)

Films

Cold War: Comrades, 1917–45 (London, BBC, 19 September 1998)
Korea: Russia's Secret War (London, BBC *Timewatch*, 21 January 1996)
The 50 Years War: Israel and the Arabs (London, Brook Lapping, 1998)
1914–1918: Total War and *1914–1918: The Crucible* (London, BBC, 1997)

Websites

Mills, James, review of Peter Lowe, *The Korean War* (Basingstoke, Macmillan, 2000), in *IHR Reviews in History* at www.history.ac.uk/reviews/paper/shlaimavi.html (accessed 30 May 2009)

Shlaim, Avi, response to review of *The Iron Wall: Israel and the Arab World* (London, Allen Lane/Penguin, 2000), in *IHR Reviews in History* at www.history.ac.uk/reviews/paper/millsjames.html (accessed 30 May 2009)

Index

Index

Index

242